MAPPING THE SECOND WORLD WAR

MAPPING THE SECOND WORLD WAR

THE KEY BATTLES OF THE EUROPEAN THEATRE FROM ABOVE

MICHAEL SWIFT AND **MICHAEL SHARPE**

CONWAY

ACKNOWLEDGEMENTS

The National Archives were the source of all the maps used in this book. Crown Copyright material in the National Archives is reproduced by permission of the Controller of Her Majesty's Stationery Office. Images are reproduced by courtesy of National Archives.

This edition first published in the United Kingdom in 2014 by
Conway, an imprint of Pavilion Books Company Ltd
1 Gower Street
London WC1E 6HD
www.conwaypublishing.com
Twitter: @conwaybooks

© PRC Publishing 2002

Distributed in the US and Canada by Sterling Publishing Co. Ltd
387 Park Avenue South, New York, NY 100016-8810

British Library Cataloguing in Publication Data: A catalogue record for this book is available from the British Library.

ISBN 9781844862498
Printed by Toppan Leefung Printing Ltd, China

To receive regular email updates on forthcoming Conway titles, email info@conwaypublishing.com with Conway Update in the subject field.

CONTENTS

Introduction 6

The Clouds of War —

      Europe 1918–1939 6

The Second World War 10

Battle of the Atlantic 15

War in the Air 16

The Covert War 18

The Final Solution 19

The War Outside Europe 20

Note on the Maps 21

The Maps

Blitzkrieg in the West —

      April–May 1940 22

      14–15 May 1940 24

Dunkirk, May–June 1940 25

Operation 'Seelöwe', July 1940 26

Battle of Britain fighter defences, 1940 27

U-Boat War, August 1940 28

U-Boat War, September 1940 29

U-Boat War, August–September 1940 . 30

Action against *Bismarck,* 27 May 1941 32

Bulgaria, February 1941 33

Tobruk: Operation 'Crusader',

      December 1941 34

St. Nazaire, 27–28 March 1942 36

Brest, August 1941 37

'Channel Dash', 12 February 1942 . . . 37

Alam Halfa, 16 July 1942 38

Dieppe: Operation 'Jubilee',

      19 August 1942 39

Russia: Kalach,

      24 July–10 August 1942 40

Southwest Russia and the Caucasus,

14 August 1942–10 October 1942 42

Convoy PQ18, 2 September 1942 44

El Alamein, 24–25 October 1942 45

Deception prior to El Alamein,

      21–23 October 1942 48

German night air defences,

      December 1942 50

Crimea, 1942 52

Southwest Russia and the Caucasus,

19 November 1942–7 February 1943 . 53

Malta, air defences 1943 54

Tunisia, February 1943 55

Tunisia, 18 February–15 March 1943 . 57

Möhne Dam, May 1943 58

Marlag POW camp, Lübeck,

      January 1944 59

Russia, 1 June 1943 60

Sicily: Operation 'Husky',

      10 June 1943 61

Italy: Operation 'Avalanche', Salerno,

      9 September 1943 66

USAAF Eighth Air Force,

      5 August 1943 68

Italy: Monte Cassino, 11 May 1944 . . . 69

Italy: Operation 'Shingle', Anzio,

      January 1944 70

Yugoslavia, 1 November 1943 72

Agents in the Balkans, 1944 73

Guerrilla movements within Yugoslavia,

      April 1944 74

Athens, November 1943 76

Belgrade, February 1944 77

Sofia, January 1944 78

Tirana, November 1943 79

Ljubljana, 1944 79

Berlin, RAF target map, 1944 80

Peenemünde, 1944 82

D-Day: German coastal batteries,

      6 June 1944 84

D-Day: German positions in France,

      1944 85

D-Day: Allied air operations,

      6 June 1944 86

D-Day: U.S. Navy bombardment plan,

      6 June 1944 87

D-Day: 'Omaha' Beach

      6 June 1944 88

D-Day: Operation 'Neptune',

      6 June 1944 88

D-Day: 'Gold' and 'Juno' Beach defences,

      6 June 1944 90

D-Day: 'Sword' Beach, 1944 92

D-Day: German defences on 'Omaha'

      Beach, 6 June 1944 94

D-Day: German defences on 'Utah'

      Beach, 6 June 1944 96

D-Day: Mulberry Harbours,

      6 June 1944 98

French Resistance, 1944 100

SOE arms' drops to Maquis, 1944 . . . 101

Normandy: U.S. First Army St. Lô before

      breakout, 1944 102

Normandy: Operation 'Goodwood',

      18 July 1944 104

Normandy: Operation 'Spring',

      31 July 1944 107

Normandy: Operation 'Totalise',

      August 1944 108

Normandy: Falaise Pocket,

      7 August 1944 109

Boulogne defences,

      12 September 1944 112

Calais defences, 12 September 1944 113

Gestapo HQ Paris, 1944 114

Operation 'Market',

      17 September 1944 115

Operation 'Market Garden',

      September 1944 116

U.S. 82nd Airborne Division, Nijmegen,

      September 1944 118

Operation 'Market Garden',

      17 September 1944 120

Stalag Luft III POW camp, 1944 124

RAF escape map, 1944 125

Battle of the Bulge, December

      1944–February 1945 126

Operation 'Veritable',

      8 February 1945 128

River Roer, 10 January 1945 130

Operation 'Varsity', March 1945 131

Allied zones of occupation,

      Northwest Europe, 1945 132

Hannover bombing damage assessment,

      1945 134

Operation 'Plunder', Crossing the Rhine,

      March 1945 136

River Rhine, March 1945 138

North Germany,

      February–March 1945 140

Eastern Front: German collapse,

      1–8 May 1945 141

British–Russian Zone Boundaries,

      1945 142

War Crimes: Treblinka, ... 143

Index of Maps 144

INTRODUCTION

World War II represented a watershed in world history. At the start of the war, Britain — and its Empire — represented the strongest of the world's superpowers. Although its economic domination was no longer as great as it had been in the 19th century, and other emerging powers — particularly the United States — had acquired status as economic superpowers, nevertheless Britain, either directly or indirectly, ruled almost a third of the globe. The British Empire had even expanded after World War I, and in the interwar period administered many of the former German colonies and had mandates for administration of much of the Middle East. While there were increasing strains within the Empire, Britain was still the dominant force. The Royal Navy — even though many of its ships were old, outdated and ill-equipped — gave the country a presence throughout the globe and helped to maintain the country's influence.

It was a country, however, that had seen much of its power reduced by a debilitating war — the 'war to end all wars' that had killed off a generation of young men all over Europe from the Dardanelles to Russia. In the immediate post-World War I years, many politicians reflected the will of a populace sickened by such loss and were prepared to make any sacrifice to stop another conflict. Today we call them 'appeasers'. In Britain this policy of appeasement had a less obvious, more pragmatic political reason: a further war would represent a real threat to the British Empire, a threat that was not worth the risk. After the fall of France in 1940, such threats were again raised, and it seems clear that one weapon in Hitler's political arsenal was to guarantee the British Empire — which he believed helped the world's power balance — had Britain capitulated. Churchill defeated the appeasers and, by defying Nazi Germany, set the Empire against Hitler.

It is important to recall, when examining these maps, that most of Britain's military and political leaders believed strongly in the Empire and in its defence. Much of the strategic planning — particularly in the Far East where much of the Empire was situated — was devoted to ensuring the Empire's survival. Even in Europe and North Africa, these concerns were evident. These can be best seen, perhaps, in the destruction of the French fleet immediately after the French surrender in 1940, and the defence of Egypt and the Suez Canal. Control of the canal was an essential part of Britain's supply route to and from the Empire.

Despite tentative rearmament in the immediate prewar years, Britain was singularly ill-equipped to go to war. Moreover, as many of these maps will show, a number of the early war military actions undertaken were both ill-thought through and unsuccessful. Names like Narvik, Dunkirk and Crete are all evidence of British failure. Despite these failures, Britain stood alone, undefeated against both the might of the Third Reich and its allies and those critics who felt that defeat was imminent, for almost two years.

In the end, however, the appeasers were proved correct. World War II did sound the death-knell for the British Empire as self-determination and independence came first to the Indian sub-continent and later to Africa and the other colonies. Britain had, for the second time in a generation, been forced to mortgage its future to ensure its present and the freedom of Europe from German domination. Its spirit had never been broken, and those who celebrated both VE-Day in May 1945 and VJ-Day three months later had every justification for so doing. But in helping to defeat the fascist states of Europe and the Japanese Empire, Britain paid the ultimate price and lost its position of domination: the world powerhouses of the postwar years would be the United States and Russia, both late entrants into the war.

In the end, however, the political realities of postwar politics were not the major issue. The battles of World War II were fought with a common aim: to rid the world of two evil regimes and in doing so the Western Allies had made, arguably, the most important contribution to civilisation in the 20th century.

The Clouds of War — Europe 1918–1939

Following the Armistice on the Western Front in November 1918, there were demands that the conquered powers, in particular Germany and the Hapsburg Empire, should be made to pay for their defeat, although there were politicians who warned that the imposition of too harsh a settlement would lead only to resentment and the likelihood of further conflict. These siren voices were ignored in the general rush for retribution. The result was the Treaty of Versailles, signed on 28 June 1919 (although only reluctantly by Germany).

Perceived in Germany as unfair, particularly as it labelled the country guilty of causing the war, the treaty was a major factor in the ultimate rise of Adolf Hitler. The treaty saw certain parts of the former German state transferred. Denmark received, after a plebiscite, the area of North Schleswig; France regained Alsace-Lorraine; Upper Silesia, part of East Prussia, passed to Poland; the port of Danzig was to be administered by the League of Nations, and both Belgium and the newly created

Czechoslovakia also received territory. In addition, France was allowed to occupy the Saarland for 15 years, and the Rhineland was to be demilitarised. The end result was that Germany was split in two, with the remains of East Prussia separated from the rest of the country by a Polish corridor. It also resulted in sizeable German minorities in many surrounding countries. Finally, Germany was stripped of its overseas colonies, forced to pay significant financial reparations and was restricted in the scope of military equipment that the postwar armed forces could operate.

The other major casualty of the war was the Austrian Empire. The Treaties of St. Germain and Trianon in 1919 and 1920 effectively brought the end of the empire and the creation of new independent states, such as Hungary and Czechoslovakia. To the south, the various Slav states (Serbia, Montenegro, Croatia, Slovenia and Bosnia) were united to form the new Kingdom of Yugoslavia. Romania was also to gain a considerable amount of land (despite having been virtually defeated and only re-entering the war on 9 November 1918). Romania gained Transylvania and Bessarabia along with much of the Hungarian Plain. This resulted in the country acquiring a sizeable Hungarian minority.

One further consequence of World War I was the creation of the League of Nations. Established in 1920, the league was designed to encourage peace by the settlement of disputes through arbitration. It was based in Geneva and had the backing of a number of highly influential politicians, among whom was President Wilson of the United States. However, as a result of the country's refusal to ratify the Treaty of Versailles, and the resultant move towards isolationism, the United States never became a member. This fatally weakened the League of Nations, particularly when, after 1930, fascists states such as Italy and Germany increasingly ignored it. Germany resigned its membership in 1933 (having joined only in 1926) and Italy did likewise in 1937. In the build-up to World War II, the league was powerless to intervene as the world's great powers acted without reference to it. The league, however, was not to be formally dissolved until 1946 when the new United Nations was established.

German defeat in 1918 had one further consequence. Kaiser Wilhelm II was forced to abdicate and, thereafter, went into exile. The monarchy was replaced by a new democracy. The German Federal Republic between 1918 and 1933 was known as the Weimar Republic since the National Constituent Assembly was held at Weimar in February 1919. The new republic was beset with problems from the start. Faced by huge economic problems, the new state was plunged into hyper-inflation at a time when internal conflict — between extremists of both left and right — was rife. It was against this background that the National Socialist German Workers' Party (the NSDAP — the nascent Nazi party) grew up. This party was soon to have a charismatic leader in Adolf Hitler, who first came to national prominence in 1923 when the party attempted a putsch in Munich. Arrested and gaoled, Hitler took the opportunity of his brief imprisonment to compile his political testament *Mein Kampf* (My Struggle).

To the east, following the Bolshevik Revolution of October 1917, there was a period of civil war in Russia. Britain and others supplied support — albeit in a fairly half-hearted form — to the opponents of Lenin while World War I was still progressing. However, with peace in the west, the imperative to keep the eastern front alive disappeared, and between 1918 and 1921 resistance to the new regime was eliminated. The leader of the October Revolution, Lenin (Vladimir Ilyich Ulyanov) was, however, to remain in power only until his death on 21 January 1924. Lenin was ultimately to be replaced by Stalin as Soviet leader, but not until internal conflict within the Communist Party was concluded. Leon Trotsky, Stalin's great rival, was forced into exile (and ultimately murdered). During the 1930s Stalin's power was further increased by his systematic purges of the party and the military. There is little doubt that one factor in the German army's initial successes in 1941 was Stalin's elimination of most of the higher echelons of the Soviet military.

Back in Germany, the mid-1920s saw a gradual move toward increased prosperity. While there was still resentment over the hated Treaty of Versailles, this was latent as the economy grew. The period was not one of great success for Hitler, but his time was to come. German prosperity was based on insecure footings and, with the Wall Street Crash of 1929 and the Great Depression that followed it, the economy collapsed. Economic failure and political instability led, on 30 January 1933, to Adolf Hitler being appointed chancellor by the then president, Hindenburg. A non-Nazi, Franz von Papen, was appointed Vice-Chancellor in the belief that he would be able to keep Hitler's excesses under control. However, the Reichstag Fire — of 27 February 1933 — was the pretext upon which Hitler was able to launch a programme of measures that would ultimately stifle opposition and allow the Nazi party to achieve total power.

The rise of fascism was one of the most common threads through much of interwar Europe. The threat of Bolshevism was widely perceived to be real and the old order, in countries like Spain, Portugal and Italy, was in terminal decline. It was to be in Italy where fascism was first to achieve power.

Although Italy had been one of the beneficiaries of the treaties that concluded World War I, the immediate postwar years were marked by increasing social tension. By early 1921, the country was in a state of virtual civil war, with riots in many major cities (such as Milan and Florence). Faced by a real threat of a communist revolution, the Italian King, Victor Emmanuel III, appointed Benito Mussolini as Prime Minister in October 1922. During the month, fascists had taken control of a number of Italian cities and, at the suggestion of Mussolini, numbers of supporters were to march on Rome. Although characterised in fascist mythology as a dramatic usurpation of power, the 'March on Rome' was in many ways no more than a parade; Mussolini himself travelled to the city by express train.

Following his appointment as prime minister, Mussolini adopted dictatorial powers during November. Parliamentary opposition was, however, allowed until the murder of the socialist Deputy Giacomo Matteotti by a fascist gang on 10 June 1924. Later, from 1928 onward, a full dictatorship with a single party state was established. Domestically, Mussolini established a programme of public works that reduced unemployment and also restored good relations with the Vatican (through the Lateran Treaty of 1929). Abroad, Italy adopted an aggressive foreign policy that was to lead to the invasion of Abyssinia (Ethiopia — the only state of Africa that had escaped European colonisation by that date) in 1935. This invasion was a watershed in the gradual elimination of the League of Nations as a force for international mediation.

Portugal was another country to succumb to Fascist dictatorship. Here the monarchy had been overthrown on 5 October 1910 when, after a three-day rebellion in Lisbon, King Manuel II had been forced to flee to Britain. Historically, England had been Portugal's oldest ally, and thus an obvious location for the monarch to go into exile. Initially, the new democratic republican government undertook a number of popular reforms, particularly in terms of reducing the power of the church. However, by the early 1920s, the government was causing considerable resentment as a result of increased corruption; this was exacerbated by the country's poverty and, in 1926, the democratic government was overthrown by a military dictatorship. One of the leaders of the new military government was Antonio de Oliviera Salazar, who was appointed Minister of Finance in 1928. He was to become leader in 1932. The following year Portugal adopted a fascist constitution. Despite this, however, Portugal was to play no role in World War II — Lisbon becoming a synonym for intrigue between the competing forces — and the dictatorship was to survive for 30 years after the war. It was only on 25 April 1974 that Salazar's successor — Caetan (who had succeeded in 1968) — was overthrown in a military coup.

Prior to World War II, it was to be in Spain that war was again to tarnish Europe. As with its neighbour on the Iberian Peninsula, Spain's transition to fascism occurred after the establishment of a republic. In April 1931 the then King of Spain, Alfonso XIII, was forced to abdicate. The new republican government was formed of assorted left-wing political parties. However, Spain's formidable armed forces resented the increasing trend of the government, led by President Azana, towards anti-clericalism and socialism. The first rebellions occurred amongst the forces that were stationed in two Spanish enclaves in Morocco — Ceuta and Melilla — in July 1936 and this spread quickly to forces on the mainland. The insurgents were initially led by General Sanjurjo, but following his death in September 1936, leadership was assumed by General Francisco Franco Bahamonde, formerly the governor of the Canary Islands. Franco was declared Chief of the Spanish State in October 1936, although the Republicans retained control of a number of major population centres, such as Madrid, Bilbao, Barcelona and Valencia. Other districts came out in support of the so-called Nationalists; these areas included Seville and Cadiz. The scene was set for a bloody civil war in which more than a million people were killed and which provided a precursor for the more destructive war that was to come later in the decade.

The Spanish Civil War, fought between 1936 and 1939, is often seen as a trial for the future war. This it certainly wasn't, although it is true that the Germans and, to a lesser extent, the Italians supplied the Nationalists with men and equipment — the Kondor Legion — while the Russians provided advisers for the Republicans. The Spanish Civil War was widely seen as an ideological struggle, inspiring many to fight, particularly on the Republican side. The International Brigade, made up of idealistic volunteers (including George Orwell the author) from many countries, fought on the Republican side. The destruction of the war, particularly resulting from the indiscriminate bombing of cities, was to inspire one of the greatest of all 20th century works of art — Picasso's 'Guernica'.

The Spanish Civil War was won by the Nationalists; the force of arms provided by Germany and Italy — breaching the policy of non-intervention advocated by Britain and France — helped sway the balance. Toward the end of the war, the Republican side was increasingly riven by ideological disputes and the final surrender of Madrid came on 28 March 1939.

Despite Hitler's support for Franco, Spain was also to remain neutral during World War II and, like Portugal, was to remain a dictatorship well after the war. In the case of Spain, Franco nominated Juan Carlos, grandson of Alfonso XIII, to succeed him. Franco died on 20 November 1975 and, two days later, Juan Carlos acceded to the throne. Despite early opposition and several near coups, Spain has now firmly established itself as a constitutional monarchy.

In Germany, the new Nazi regime moved quickly after the Reichstag fire to remove internal opposition. Externally, Hitler commenced the policy of territorial aggrandisement that was to lead inexorably to the onset of World War II. To a certain extent, Hitler's ambitions were facilitated by the fact that the previous regime had largely ignored the Versailles restrictions on the scale and nature of the German armed forces. After 1933, Hitler was to increase dramatically the expenditure on the armed forces while at the same time undertaking a massive programme of civil works that had the effect both of reducing domestic unemployment and increasing the efficiency of the economy. It was under Hitler that many of the great motorways — *Autobahnen* — were constructed; it was purely coincidental, of course, that it was along these same roads the invasion forces were to move.

The first stage in the reintegration of the German state into Europe came in early 1935 when, following a plebiscite held by the League of Nations, the Saarland — occupied by France since 1920 — voted to return to German control. This was followed in March 1936 by German troops marching into the previously demilitarised Ruhr. This was a flagrant breach of the terms of the Treaty of Versailles. Hitler at the time was concerned about the French and British reaction; he need not have been concerned as the prevailing view was that the Ruhr was part of Germany's back yard.

The undoubted success that reacquiring the Ruhr represented emboldened Hitler. Also in 1936, Hitler and Mussolini formed an alliance — the Axis — that was central to the strategic background to World War II. In November 1937 Hitler secretly instructed his generals to prepare for expansion abroad. The first phase of this came with the integration of Austria — his homeland — in 1938. Anschluss, as German-Austrian unification was known, had been a demand of both Germans and Austrians in 1918. However, it had been expressly forbidden by the Treaty of Versailles; France, in particular, being concerned by the rise of a new powerful German-speaking nation. In 1931 a proposed customs union between Germany and Austria had been abandoned because France believed that it was a first step

towards *Anschluss*. Three years later, in July 1934, an attempted Nazi coup in Austria failed, although the Austrian chancellor (Dolfuss) was assassinated. A new Austrian chancellor, Schuschnigg, attempted to prevent a German take-over through holding a plebiscite on Austrian independence. However, he was forced to resign on 11 March 1938 and the new Austrian chancellor, Seyss-Inquart, was pro-Nazi. On the following day, Seyss-Inquart invited German troops to invade and on 13 March 1938 *Anschluss* was proclaimed. A month later, on 10 April, a vote in Austria came out with a 99.75% vote in favour of *Anschluss*.

For the western powers, most notably Britain and France, this was the era of appeasement. While there were dissenting voices — such as that of Winston Churchill — in both countries warning of the inevitability of war if Hitler were not stopped, there was no great appetite in either country for confrontation with Germany. Both Britain and France had lost nearly a complete generation in the trenches of World War I and there was a reluctance to see a similar carnage 20 years later. Moreover, French strategic thinking — based upon its perceived shortage of men of fighting age — was to concentrate upon defence while Britain was increasingly concerned with the maintenance of its global empire.

The signal that peace was unlikely to be preserved in the long term came later in 1938. As part of the post-World War I settlement (through the Treaty of St. Germain), the new nation of Czechoslovakia had been granted the Sudetenland. This area was populated largely by Germans who were resentful of their rule from Prague. It was the question of the Sudetenland that was to bring Europe to the brink of war in the autumn of 1938. The Sudetenland formed the natural border between Germany and Czechoslovakia and could also lay claim both to rich mineral resources and, at Pilsen, the largest munitions factory in Central Europe. In 1935 a new political party, financed by the Nazis and led by Konrad Henlein, appeared. The Sudetendeutsche Partei had considerable success in local elections and campaigned for reunion with Germany. This demand was taken up by Hitler and, during much of the summer of 1938, it appeared that both Britain and France, which had given guarantees of Czech sovereignty, would be prepared to go to war over the Sudetenland. However, following Mussolini's intervention and the visit of the then British Prime Minister, Neville Chamberlain, to Munich in September 1938, the Munich Agreement, signed on 29 September, saw the Sudetenland ceded to Germany. In exchange, Britain, France, Germany and Italy guaranteed the independence of the rest of the Czech state. Chamberlain returned to London and a hero's welcome; his promise of 'peace in our time' reflected the popular desire to avoid war at almost any price.

The loss of the Sudetenland fatally weakened Czechoslovakia, since its anti-German defences were concentrated in the area ceded to Germany, and also undermined anti-German sentiment in Russia. The inability of the west to defend the Czechs deeply affected the Russian world view, particularly as it was both an ally of the Czechs and also uninvited to the Munich talks. The belief that the west would happily see Hitler as a countermeasure to Bolshevism was undoubtedly a factor in the signing of the Russian-German 'Pact of Steel'. Sections of Czechoslovakia were also ceded to Hungary and Poland; in all, Czechoslovakia lost 16,000 square miles of territory in 1938, of which 10,000 passed to Germany. In March 1939 Germany occupied Bohemia and Moravia when the Czech government requested German military protection.

While at Munich, Hitler had promised that the Sudetenland represented his last territorial claim in Europe, but there remained one major issue outstanding — the Polish corridor. After Versailles, the new state of Poland was granted much of eastern Silesia along with a corridor to the coast that separated East Prussia from the rest of Germany. In addition, the port city of Danzig (Gdansk) had been declared a free port under the jurisdiction of the League of Nations (with the Poles handling foreign affairs and other matters), although the city's senate had been controlled by a pro-Nazi grouping after 1933. Contrary to his earlier protestations, Hitler stepped up his campaign against the Poles, engineering a number of border incidents; the road to war was clear.

World War II

On 1 September 1939, following the successful conclusion of negotiations with Russia (the infamous Ribbentrop-Molotov Pact), Germany launched its Blitzkrieg ('Lightning War') attack on western Poland. As guarantors of Polish independence, Britain and France demanded an immediate German withdrawal. When no assurances were received from Germany that hostilities would cease and that German forces would withdraw to their original borders, Britain and France declared war on 3 September 1939.

Neither Britain nor France, however, were in a position to assist the Poles,

whose ill-equipped forces put up a strong defence of their country, particularly when the Soviet Union invaded Poland from the east. However, in spite of the bravery of its armed forces, Poland was quickly defeated, with the country divided between Germany and Russia. The German victory in Poland was to herald a period known as the 'Phoney War' in the west. Although both Britain and France continued their preparations for war, neither took aggressive action. This was partly the result of French strategy, which saw its border Maginot Line as a strong defensive line which would not easily be breached. Britain's military strength lay primarily with the Royal Navy and it was only gradually that the Royal Air Force and army were strengthened. A British force was sent to France in anticipation of a possible invasion, but during this period the war was, from a British standpoint, fought at sea and in the air. German submarines, the infamous U-boats, launched a campaign — the Battle of the Atlantic — against transatlantic convoys and also achieved considerable success when sinking the battleship HMS *Royal Oak* in the naval base at Scapa Flow in the Orkneys. This German success was countered when the *Admiral Graf Spee* was scuttled on 17 December 1939 after the Battle of the River Plate.

The period of peace on the western front was soon shattered. In April 1940 German forces invaded first Denmark and then Norway. Such was the rapidity of the German invasion of the former that the citizens of Copenhagen initially thought that a film was being made when German soldiers were first spotted in the streets. While Denmark was quickly subjugated, Norway was to prove more difficult for the Germans and, in an effort to bolster Norwegian resistance, British forces were despatched to the northern port of Narvik. Part of the British strategy at this point was to route forces through Norway (and neutral Sweden) on to Finland, where assistance would have been offered to the Finns — embroiled from autumn 1939 in an often overlooked campaign against Russia over the disputed territory to the north of Leningrad. In the event, the British involvement at Narvik was to prove disastrous and the more ambitious elements of the strategy were not pursued. Eventually the Germans achieved victory in Norway in June 1940, but not before the Norwegian King, Haakon VII, escaped to Britain and set up a government in exile.

Even while the Germans were trying to defeat Norway, the next phase of the war was launched. On 10 May 1940, German forces invaded the Netherlands and Belgium; the former was defeated in four days and the latter within three weeks. Bypassing the Maginot Line, Germany also invaded France and, despite the efforts of the small British expeditionary force and the French army, quickly forced the Allied

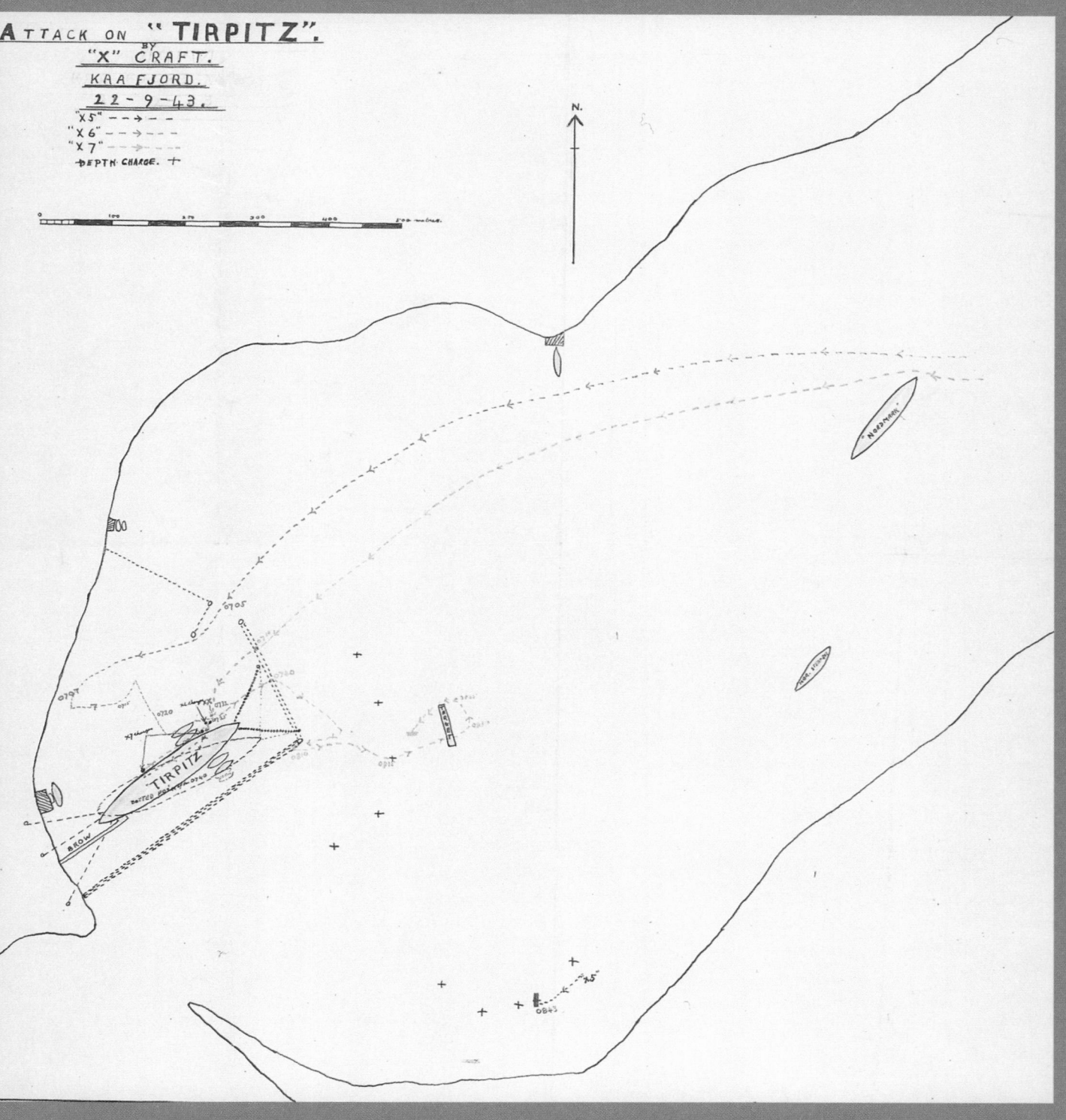

ATTACK ON "TIRPITZ".
BY "X" CRAFT.
KAA FJORD.
22-9-43.

X-craft attack on the *Tirpitz* 22 September 1943

LEFT: Rough sketch of the attack by British X-craft on the German battleship *Tirpitz* at her mooring in Kaafjord Ford, Norway, on 22 September 1943. X-craft were midget submarines, 48ft long and with a maximum diameter of just 5ft 6in — barely enough room for the crew of four. Detachable mines or explosives were fitted to the outside of the hull. Two of the vessels, *X-6* and *X-7*, traversed 1,000 miles of open sea to attack the *Tirpitz*, crippling her to the extent that she was unfit for sea until April 1944. For this action the commanders of both *X-6* and *X-7* (Lt D. Cameron, RNR and Lt B.C.G. Place respectively) were awarded the Victoria Cross. MR 1015

army to retreat. British forces retreated towards the Channel where, helplessly disorganised and without their heavy weapons, they awaited the coup de grâce from the German Panzers. However Hitler, for reasons never fully explained (although they included Goering's promise to destroy Britain by air and the concerns of the army commanders that their men and machines were coming to the end of their tether), held back his troops for long enough for the bulk of British forces to be rescued by sea from Dunkirk.

By the end of June, the Battle of France was over, and the French government surrendered. France was initially to be divided, the north and west of the country was formally occupied by the Germans; the rest of the country was left under the control of the Vichy government, led by Marshal Pétain.

With the French defeat, Britain was left alone to defend democracy in Europe. Although there were a number of influential figures who advocated coming to an accommodation with Germany, Churchill's position was resolute. His position was certainly bolstered by his faith in help from the United States, whose sympathies were gradually to swing towards Britain, although initially many significant voices within the U.S. establishment — most notably the ambassador in London Joseph Kennedy — believed that it was only a matter of time before Britain would be forced to capitulate.

The next phase of the German offensive was to launch an aerial attack upon the Royal Air Force. German commanders realised that, without control of the air over the English Channel, any possible invasion of the British Isles would be a failure. While preparations were made for Operation 'Sealöwe', as the proposed invasion was codenamed, through the transfer of barges to the Channel ports, Hermann Goering, head of the Luftwaffe, sent his bombers and fighters against the Royal Air Force. The late summer of 1940 was to witness the Battle of Britain, when 'The Few', in their Hurricanes and Spitfires, took on the might of the Luftwaffe. Initially, German tactics — to attack the air fields and other air defences — were successful in undermining the limited strength that the RAF possessed. However, following a raid by the RAF on Berlin, German tactics altered; in place of the attacks on the airfields, the Blitz was launched against Britain's towns and cities. Destructive while these raids were, none the less they relieved the immediate pressure from the stretched Fighter Command and, gradually, the RAF was able to prevent the Germans achieving the air superiority they needed. For the remainder of the war, Britain was to undergo continuous aerial attack — either from aircraft or from the

infamous V-1 and V-2 rockets — but victory in the Battle of Britain ensured that invasion was never a realistic proposition after the summer of 1940. Indeed, by the autumn Hitler had already turned his eyes to the east and was planning the invasion of Russia.

Elsewhere, however, the war in Europe did not progress well for Britain. Italy joined on Germany's side on 10 June 1940, while Britain had been forced to take pre-emptive action against the French fleet. French ships in British ports were seized on 3 July 1940 and those elsewhere — in particular in the ports of Dakar and Mers-el-Kébir — were attacked. These attacks resulted in the sinking of many of the vessels and numerous French casualties. These actions were undertaken in order to prevent the Vichy government allowing the ships to be used by the German navy and thus altering the balance of power on the high seas in favour of the Third Reich.

While preparations for Operation 'Barbarossa' — the German invasion of Russia — proceeded, in April 1941 Hitler was forced to divert his troops toward Yugoslavia and Greece following an unsuccessful Italian attempt at invasion. Already heavily committed to the defence of Egypt and the Suez Canal against the threat from Italian forces marching eastwards from Libya, Britain determined to support Greece in its defence against the Germans as it had provided a guarantee to Greece in April 1939. Some 62,000 British soldiers were landed in Greece in order to bolster the defence of the country, on Churchill's orders, but the strategy failed and some 50,000 were quickly withdrawn, leaving much of their equipment behind. Defeat in Greece meant total Axis control of the Balkans. For the British, worse was to follow, with the successful German invasion of the island of Crete; British forces were forced to withdraw, following the landing of German paratroops, at the end of May 1941.

Crete had been occupied by the British in October 1940 as it dominated the eastern Mediterranean and was within flying range of North Africa. It was perceived as a base for possible operations in Greece and the Balkans. Following the British defeat on the mainland, the island's defences were further strengthened by the transfer of exhausted soldiers from Greece, taking the garrison to some 28,000 under General Freyberg. However, lacking strong air support and decent anti-aircraft defences, the island was vulnerable to airborne attack. The German invasion — codenamed Operation 'Mercury' — was commanded by General Löhr and envisaged some 13,000 paratroopers and 9,000 mountain troops landing. The invasion started on 20 May 1941 and the Germans secured control of most of the island after a week of heavy fighting. For four nights from 28 May the Royal Navy evacuated much of the British garrison, but suffered heavy losses in the process with three cruisers and six destroyers being sunk. British losses totalled some 4,000 killed and wounded with some 12,000 captured. Crete was to be the last occasion when the Germans used a mass paratroop drop; although there were plans for further airborne invasions, particularly around the Suez Canal, and the British feared an attack on the pivotal island of Malta, these came to nothing. Hitler had much more grandiose plans afoot.

The abortive campaigns in Greece and on Crete significantly weakened British forces in North Africa. The earlier incursions by the weak Italian forces had been repulsed and the British army was marching westward. Fearful for the consequences of any Italian defeat in Africa, Hitler had despatched Rommel with the newly established Afrika Korps in order to bolster Italian defences. The North African campaign was, for the next 12 months, to shift dramatically towards German success. The threat to the Suez Canal and British influence in the Middle East was real and, if Rommel had been better supplied, would no doubt have proved decisive.

However, Hitler's attention was to turn from the potential triumph of North Africa to a much greater prize — Soviet Russia. Despite the non-aggression pact, Hitler's forces and those of his allies — Finland, Hungary and Romania — launched Operation 'Barbarossa' on 22 June 1941 over a 2,000-mile front line. The ensuing campaign, which was to prove the most significant of the war in Europe, was to last five years and cost the lives of many millions, both combatants and civilians. Initially, Axis success was unprecedented; vast swathes of territory were conquered as the ill-prepared and ill-equipped Red Army was forced to retreat. In areas such as the Ukraine, formerly under Soviet domination, the arriving Axis forces were welcomed as liberators. However, the atrocities committed by both sides ensured that the initial enthusiasm for liberation was soon converted into resentment and, ultimately, into a violent guerrilla and partisan war that lasted until Germany's ultimate defeat. Although the initial German advance was held back by the harsh winter of 1941–42 and by Russian counter-attacks in early 1942, a second push during mid-1942 saw the German forces reach the outskirts of Moscow and Stalingrad.

Strategically, mid-1942 marked the peak of German power. With the Japanese attack on Pearl Harbor in December 1941 and Hitler's rash declaration of war against the United States, the industrial might of the U.S. was brought into the conflict. Tacit support for Britain was suddenly converted into the overt supply of vast quantities of men and equipment. In North Africa, the struggling British army, with its

back to the canal, received a major boost through the appointment of Bernard Montgomery to head the Eighth Army. This charismatic leader, aided by an influx of American-supplied equipment, saw the tide in North Africa turned following a spectacular victory at El Alamein at the end of October 1942. Defeated and dispirited, the Afrika Korps was soon on the retreat.

In Russia, a change of tactics and improved equipment saw the Red Army initially hold the German advance of 1942 and then, through judicious use of the pincer movement, first encircle and then annihilate the German Sixth Army in Stalingrad under von Paulus. The surrender of von Paulus and his staff in January 1943 represented a major disaster for Hitler and, from that point, the Eastern Front gradually retreated as Russian forces exploited the increasing weakness of the German and Axis forces.

The first Anglo-American invasion in the west came with the attack on North Africa on 8 November 1942 — Operation 'Torch'. The immediate result of this was that Hitler took total control of the previously unoccupied area of France, while the remaining French fleet was scuttled at Toulon in order to prevent it falling into German hands. Faced by war on two fronts in North Africa, Hitler sent reinforcements to Rommel, who prepared a strong defensive line — the Mareth Line — in Tunisia in order to prevent the British Eighth Army's westward advance. However, co-ordinated attacks on both the western and eastern fronts in Africa led to a massive German and Italian defeat, with some 250,000 taken prisoner in April 1943.

The next phase in the attack on Nazi Europe in the west came with the Anglo-American invasion of Sicily. Parallel with preparations for invasion, both the Royal Air Force and the Americans increased dramatically their aerial bombardment of Germany and Nazi-occupied Europe, striking at industrial, military and urban targets. May 1943, for example, saw the RAF launch its first 1,000-bomber raid on Cologne. The invasion of Europe began on 9 July 1943 with the attack on Sicily. Italian forces largely surrendered with little resistance, although the German garrison put up a strong fight. In Rome, however, a palace coup on 25 July 1943 saw Mussolini deposed from power; faced by the increasing weakness of his southern ally, Hitler increased the number of German troops in Italy. However, these were powerless to prevent a further Allied landing, this time on the Italian mainland, on 3 September 1943. The new Italian administration — led by Marshal Badalgio — had already started secret talks with the Allies over surrender and, by mid-September 1943, the Italians were effectively at war with Germany. In the face of Italian treachery and Allied pressure, the German forces retreated northward to a defensive line to the south of Rome. Gradually, however, the German strongpoints, such as Monte Cassino, fell to intense Allied pressure. Rome fell in June 1944 and Florence in August.

Although the Italian Front occupied a considerable number of German men and much equipment, it was not the full Western Front demanded by the Russians; this could only be achieved through the invasion of France. To this end the Allies gathered a huge arsenal of men and equipment to launch the biggest seaborne invasion in military history. The risks in such an endeavour were enormous and, in order to minimise these, a policy of disinformation was launched. This implied that the actual invasion would be around Calais and resulted in the Germans stationing the bulk of their defensive forces in that region; it was only when the actual invasion occurred — on 6 June 1944 — in the area to the west of Caen, that this deception became clear.

Operation 'Overlord', as the invasion of France was codenamed, was masterminded by future U.S. President Dwight D. Eisenhower, with the actual invasion troops commanded by the British commander, Bernard Montgomery, the victor of El Alamein. Landing on five beaches (codenamed 'Gold', 'Sword', 'Juno', 'Omaha' and 'Utah'), a strong beach-head was established before the mislocated German reserves were able to get into action. The scale of the actual invasion force was staggering: some 5,000 ships along with 13,000 aircraft from the USAAF alone were involved, as was the construction of two temporary harbours — codenamed 'Mulberries' — for use until normal facilities were captured. The initial phase of the D-Day landings saw some 150,000 Allied troops land by the evening of the first day. Although there had been stiff resistance in certain areas — most notably on the American beaches 'Omaha' and 'Utah' — the Allied landing, which had been supported by numerous airborne assaults with paratroopers and glider-borne troops, had been safely accomplished.

From the beach-head, Allied forces gradually fanned out eastward and northeastward, although there was much dissent within the higher levels of the Allied command structure at Montgomery's apparent reluctance to break out of the beach-head earlier. Within a month of the D-Day landings, one million Allied troops had landed in France through Normandy and the German army was forced to retreat towards the Seine. Some 100,000 Germans surrendered in the Falaise pocket and Hitler's defensive position weakened further when, on 15 August, a further Allied

invasion, led by General Patch, took place in southern France. Patch's army quickly marched up the Rhône Valley. In the north, Paris was liberated in late August 1944 and the Allied advance continued towards the Netherlands and the Rhine Valley. There were occasional Allied setbacks, such as at Arnhem (when an over-ambitious scheme failed to capture the bridges) and by the German counter attack in the Ardennes, the Battle of the Bulge, but the failure of the latter meant that Hitler's last chance in the west had disappeared.

By early 1945, with the Russians advancing apace in the east and with the Allied forces heading eastward, the Nazi state was close to collapse. Hitler committed suicide in his Berlin bunker on 30 April 1945, two days after Russian and American forces had met on the Elbe, and on 7 May 1945 Germany surrendered unconditionally. World War II in Europe was over; it would not be until 14 August 1945 that the war in the Far East ended, with the Japanese surrendering after atomic bombs dropped on Hiroshima and Nagasaki.

Battle of the Atlantic

The tactic of trying to prevent supplies reaching Britain by sea was not new; it had been tried by Napoleon at the start of the 19th century and by the German navy during World War I. Britain, as a country, lacked the raw materials to sustain its population and military effort. Without vast quantities of imported raw materials and food, the country would have found it impractical to remain in the war. Historically, Britain's Industrial Revolution had been based upon the importation of raw materials and the export of manufactured goods at considerable profit. At a time of war, such an economic base fundamentally weakened the country.

Realising this weakness, the Germans deployed surface warships and submarines right from the start of the war. At the outbreak of war, the German navy, the *Kriegsmarine*, had 46 operational U-boats; these were tasked both with attacking the Royal Navy and with sinking merchant vessels. The surface vessels, such as the *Admiral Graf Spee*, were of limited importance, although they did achieve some success and did offer a 'nuisance value' in that they tied up British forces in their discovery and destruction. Up until the end of 1939, U-boats had sunk a total of 114 vessels — but more than 5,500 had successfully reached their destination.

The strategic balance in the Battle of the Atlantic was to change with the German successes of 1940. Following the fall of Norway, the Low Countries and France, the Kriegsmarine was able to launch attacks from the newly acquired Atlantic and North Sea bases. In addition, the Kriegsmarine was also strengthened by additional surface vessels and by long-range aircraft from the Luftwaffe. The British were stretched, even after the acquisition of 50 elderly vessels from the U.S. Navy, and during 1940 the level of losses increased dramatically. In the six months to the end of 1940, some three million tons of merchant vessels — with the materials they carried — were sent to the bottom of the Atlantic. Large numbers of new U-boats added to the German strength, enabling them to operate as coordinated teams — the Wolfpacks.

However, the British did have some successes. In May 1941 the German battleship *Bismarck* was sunk and other German surface vessels rarely posed a major threat thereafter. Improved British tactics also saw the Admiralty given operational control of the RAF's Coastal Command while other technical advances, such as improved radar, aided the anti-submarine campaign. Despite this, however, Allied merchant vessels continued to be lost in great numbers.

The British position was further enhanced in March 1941 when the U.S. Lend-Lease Act became law. This enabled Britain to order ships for construction in U.S. boatyards and obtain other military equipment. Gradually the U.S. took over a certain amount of escort duty in the western Atlantic. A critical event occurred in May 1941 when the British captured an intact 'Enigma' coding machine from U-110. This enabled the British code-breakers at Bletchley Park to gain an advantage in the intelligence war and also provide information about the operational plans of active U-boats.

The balance of the Battle of the Atlantic swung from Axis to Allied forces and then back towards the Germans in 1942. Much of the strength of Coastal Command was transferred to Bomber Command to assist with the strategic bombing campaign and, after Pearl Harbor, much of the U.S. Navy strength was transferred to the Pacific in order to bolster the campaign against the Japanese. In addition, new and larger U-boats were able to operate in areas well away from the Allied air cover and in areas well away from the traditional sea lanes followed by Allied convoys. In 1942 a total of 1,160 ships was sunk by U-boats, and by the start of 1943 Britain was suffering severe shortages of many raw materials. In early 1943 the situation again worsened for the Allies as German codes were changed and the intelligence hitherto available through Bletchley Park dried up.

However, by mid-1943 the balance again shifted towards the Allies. New and faster escort vessels along with long-range aircraft became available, as did improved technological support. The hunters had become the hunted. In April 1943 15 U-boats were sunk, followed by 30 in May; a further 74 were destroyed between June and August during which time only 58 Allied merchant ships were sunk.

While by mid-1943 the German ambition to eliminate Britain from the war through cutting off its vital lines of supply were no longer practical, the U-boat arm continued to play an important role right through until the end of the war. There were further technical developments that improved U-boat performance after mid-1943, but these were never sufficient to bring victory. However, the threat remained until the end; in May 1945 159 U-boats surrendered while a further 203 were scuttled by their crews.

War in the Air

Although aircraft had featured in the First World War, it was to be during the Second World War that air power became a major factor in the strategic balance. During the interwar years there was an increasing belief that air power alone could win wars. The theory was that nations could be driven to surrender in the face of heavy bombing. Experience during the Spanish Civil War, where the Luftwaffe had gained considerable knowledge, had tended to confirm this belief. Moreover, air superiority was increasingly important during the course of the war; one factor in the ultimate German defeat was that the Luftwaffe had largely ceased to be an effective fighting force by the later years of the war.

Brief mention has already been made of the role that aircraft played in the German 'Blitzkrieg' tactics and in the decision not to proceed with Operation 'Sealion' (the invasion of Britain). Once the immediate threat of invasion ceased, the British were able to take the war to the heart of Germany through the efforts of the Royal Air Force's Bomber Command. The tactics adopted by Bomber Command's C-in-C, Air Chief Marshal Sir Arthur Harris, have, since the end of the war, been criticised, but at the time there was a strong belief in the campaign. Bomber Command targeted military, industrial and civilian targets, with the intention of undermining civilian morale. Many German towns and cities were attacked, often places that lacked an obvious strategic importance. After one such raid, on the historically important city of Lübeck in early 1942, Hitler launched retaliatory raids against equally important English cities; known as the Baedeker Raids, as they targeted places prominently featured in the Baedeker travel guide to Britain, the cities of York, Canterbury, Norwich, Exeter and Bath suffered major damage.

The intensity of the Allied campaign against German targets increased with the arrival of United States' forces from 1942 onward. Bomber Command's successes increased with the creation of the Pathfinder Force, aircraft specially tasked with the highlighting of targets for the main bomber force, and by the introduction of larger and more capable aircraft, such as the Avro Lancaster. Of the raids undertaken by the RAF, few achieved such fame as the Dambusters Raid of 16 May 1943, when aircraft of No 617 Squadron, led by Wing Commander Guy Gibson, undertook precision raids against the dams across the Möhne and Eder dams in the Ruhr valley. Using specially designed bombs developed by Sir Barnes Wallis, the raid was to be a great propaganda success, albeit with significant losses — seven out of the 19 aircraft used failed to return.

By the end of the war, most German cities had suffered varying degrees of damage as a result of this aerial onslaught, although many of the more controversial raids — such as that against Dresden in February 1945 — occurred late in the war when, arguably, the need for such wholesale destruction was less obvious.

The Covert War

Espionage and covert operations have always been a significant part of the history of warfare. There have been, however, few wars where such activity was so important than in the Second World War. With much of Europe occupied by the forces of Germany and its allies, Britain initially and later the Allies, relied to a considerable extent upon both intelligence gathering in occupied countries and on the activity of the various resistance and partisan groups in fomenting trouble. The level of resistance varied from country to country; in Denmark, for example, which was treated by the Germans as almost a model for its control of the satellite states, resistance to German occupation was limited until later on in the war. In France, however, the resistance to the German occupation started almost from the moment of the French surrender in 1940 and was to grow dramatically as the war progressed. On the other hand, French resistance was divided between various factions. There were de

Gaulle's Free French forces, but many were reluctant to join this — initially believing it would fail if Britain collapsed or surrendered after the French surrender. There was also the communist-inspired National Liberation League, formed in 1941 after the German invasion of Russia when the previously quiescent pro-Soviet elements were encouraged to undertake acts of sabotage against the occupying German forces.

British support for the resistance in Europe came in a number of forms. First, there were regular drops of arms and supplies to resistance cells. These were undertaken by the RAF. During the course of the war, considerable quantities of arms and equipment were parachuted into occupied territory. A second part of these covert operations was the placement of agents into occupied Europe. These agents were tasked with both the organisation of local resistance cells and the transmission of information back to the United Kingdom. These agents were recruited and trained by the British Special Operations Executive (SOE; established in July 1940) which was joined by the U.S. Office of Strategic Services (OSS) in 1943. In Western Europe SOE operations were of varying success, and large numbers of both agents and resistance officers were captured and executed. Many of the resistance cells were penetrated by the Gestapo — the German secret police — resulting in large numbers of casualties. In the Netherlands, some 20,000 were killed as a result of German reprisals and there were numerous atrocities perpetrated on the civilian population of France.

It was to be in the Balkans — where SOE aided considerably the partisan activity in Yugoslavia and elsewhere — that the benefits of this covert activity were to be most significant. The terrain of these countries made it relatively easy to run a guerrilla war and, in partisan leaders like Tito (the future leader of communist Yugoslavia), there were local warlords capable of undertaking this activity. Partisan activity in the Balkans helped to tie down a significant section of the Axis forces at crucial times.

Once the Allied invasion of Europe was under development, the importance of the French resistance grew significantly and in the build-up to D-Day in June 1944, the resistance was responsible for a great deal of sabotage. This sabotage was of considerable importance in delaying the arrival of German forces to Normandy in those crucial first days after the beach-head had been established.

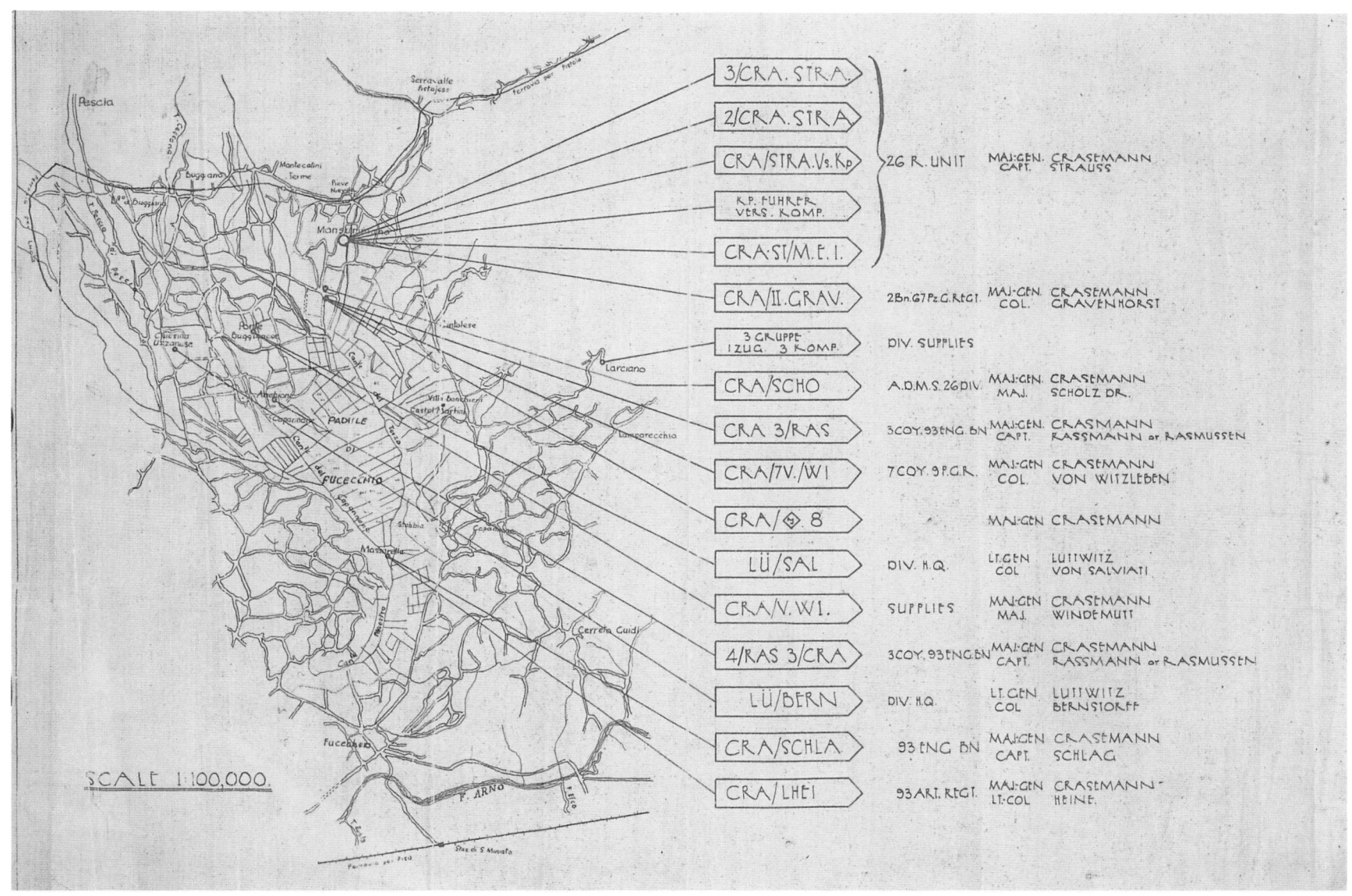

26 Panzergrenadier Division locations
August 1944

This is a detailed plan of the area around the Fucecchio Marshes showing the unit signs discovered there when the Allies took it. They belonged to 26th Panzergrenadier Division and were interpreted to indicate the names of officers in charge of various units: the name seen most often is that of Generalmajor Eduard Crasemann the divisional CO. WO 310/105

The Final Solution

In a war where barbarism was evinced in many of the theatres of operation, particularly on the Eastern Front and in the Balkans, there was no greater crime against humanity perpetrated than the mass elimination of Europe's Jewish population by the Nazis. Although other minority groups — such as gypsies and homosexuals — were also to be persecuted and murdered, it was the fate of Europe's Jews that was the greatest blight on 20th century history.

The overt anti-Semitism of the Nazi party was clear from the earliest writings of Adolf Hitler and, from the moment that the Nazis came to power in Germany in 1933, persecution became rife. Initially, the Nazi authorities allowed the Jewish population of Germany and, later, Austria to emigrate, although as the 1930s progressed, this became increasingly difficult as emigration to British-controlled Palestine was limited after 1936 and as there was a marked increase in the reluctance of other countries to take huge numbers of refugees.

With the onset of war, even the relatively limited exodus permitted by the Nazi authorities ceased and a new policy — the 'Final Solution' (*Endlösung*) — came into force. Whilst historians have argued since the end of the war as to the culpability of individual figures within the Nazi party over the elimination of millions of Jews, it is clear that genocide was the intention from the earliest days of the war. The use of phrases like 'resettlement' and 'the final solution' were covers for officials unable or unwilling to describe their activities in even more explicit terms.

It was with the opening of the Eastern Front following the Nazi invasion of Russia in June 1941 that the true horrors of the Nazi policy came to the fore. Behind the advancing army came squads — the *Einsatzgruppen* — made up men drawn from the SS and Gestapo as well as local anti-Semitic sympathisers whose task it was to eliminate the so-called '*Untermenschen*' — the Jews, gypsies and other groups who did not fulfil the criteria of the Aryan race.

Whilst forced labour camps had been established in the late 1930s, the decision to build additional camps for the purpose of murdering millions of these 'undesirables' was taken at a meeting held at the Reich Chief Security Office at Wannsee (a suburb of Berlin) in January 1942. This meeting was attended by 15 high-ranking SS officers and was chaired by Reinhard Heydrich. The minutes of the meeting do not make explicit the intention of making the 'final solution' a campaign of mass murder, but this was what was effectively the result. A network of camps — names of which live on in infamy (including Sobibor, Treblinka, Belsen and Auschwitz) — was established and the systematic transporting of Jews from Germany, from the ghettos established in places like Warsaw and from the other occupied territories commenced.

In the three years from 1942 until the final defeat of Nazi Germany in May 1945, it is believed that some five million of Europe's 11 million Jewish population died in these camps. There were examples where action by the local population ensured that the Jewish population could escape — as in the case of Denmark where the bulk of the small Jewish population was spirited across to Sweden before they could be seized — and there were odd individuals, such as the Swedish diplomat Raoul Wallenberg, who risked their own lives to enable small numbers to evade capture. But these escapees were the lucky ones; many others were to make the one-way journey to the gas chambers of the concentration camps.

The War Outside Europe

Although this book concentrates on maps covering the Second World War in Europe and North Africa, it is important to note that the war outside these theatres, particularly in the Far East, was to have a dramatic impact on the European conflict. It was the Japanese attack on Pearl Harbor and the subsequent declaration of war on the United States by Germany that ultimately led the U.S. out of its isolation and into the anti-fascist coalition in Europe.

The war in the Far East had its origins in the attempts by the Japanese to extend their sphere of influence throughout the region. The Japanese had gained a foothold on the Asian mainland following their annexation of Korea in 1910. The next stage in Japanese expansion occurred in September 1931 when, after using the Mukden Incident — an explosion allegedly inspired by the Chinese on the South Manchuria Railway — as a pretext, the Japanese seized the city of Mukden. Between then and early 1932 Japanese control was extended over much of Manchuria, starting a war with the Chinese that was to last until 1945. The Japanese named their puppet state in Manchuria Manchukuo, a state which was recognised only by Germany and Italy. Full scale war between Japan and China resumed on 7 July 1937, with Japanese forces overrunning the north and capturing Shanghai. Nanking fell in December 1937 and Canton and Hankow in the following October. British and U.S. military aid was supplied to the Kuomintang army under General Chiang Kai-shek while communist guerrillas under Mao Tse-tung were also active. The war in China was to occupy up to one million Japanese troops during World War II, which helped to reduce Japanese capabilities elsewhere.

World War II extended to the Far East when, on Sunday 7 December 1941, Japanese forces launched an attack on the U.S. Navy at Pearl Harbor in Hawaii. At the time there had been no declaration of war and diplomatic activity was still in hand, although in order to undertake the action Japanese forces had put to sea on 26 November 1941. During the two-hour aerial attack, the U.S. Navy lost 19 ships (including five battleships) and other losses included 120 aircraft and 2,400 men. The destruction wrought at Pearl Harbor gave the Japanese an immediate advantage, which they used to the full during the early phases of the war in Asia, as the country's forces rapidly expanded through the territories of the British, French and Dutch in the region.

Simultaneous with the attack on Pearl Harbor, Japanese forces invaded Malaya, quickly overrunning the British colony and capturing the strategically important island of Singapore — 'a day of ignominy' Winston Churchill called it — with its Royal Navy base and RAF airfield in February 1942. In December 1941 it attacked the British colony of Hong Kong, forcing it to surrender on Christmas Day. The Japanese advance was swift and by mid-1942 their power extended through Indo-China (aided by the pro-German Vichy government in France since Indo-China was a French colony), the Philippines, Indonesia and Burma. The threat to British-controlled India was great particularly as many native Indians saw the rise of the Japanese as a potential means for gaining independence. The Japanese even established an Indian National Army, under Subhas Chandra Bose, that recruited prisoners captured during the advance through Burma. Japanese forces had made incursions into the Indian Ocean, and had even bombed Australia.

However, once the United States had recovered from the trauma of Pearl Harbor and had reinforced its forces in the Far East, the Japanese military was heavily stretched, fighting the Chinese in China, the British in Burma and the Americans in the Pacific islands. On 3–6 June 1942 the Battle of Midway between U.S. and Japanese naval forces resulted in a heavy defeat for the Japanese under Admiral Yamamoto. Although the United States forces had defeated the Japanese earlier at Coral Sea, the Battle of Midway was crucial in that it thwarted continued Japanese expansion in New Guinea (with a very real threat to northern Australia) and resulted in the loss of four aircraft carriers — crucial vessels in the Pacific War — and numerous aircraft. The victory, under Admiral Nimitz, at Midway was a turning point; it was followed on 12 August 1942 by the U.S. invasion of Guadalcanal, the first offensive action undertaken by U.S. forces and the first real reverse that the Japanese had suffered.

From Midway onwards, the war in the east turned into a war of attrition. U.S. forces gradually regained much of the lost territory by a process of island hopping. Each invasion, however, resulted in significant casualties. On the Asian mainland, British and Empire forces held the Indian border and were gradually in a position both to defeat the attempted Japanese advances of early 1944 and then mount a counter-attack in the late summer of 1944. The whole of Burma had been recaptured when Rangoon, the country's capital, was entered by British forces on 6 May 1945.

As the war gradually turned against the Japanese, increasingly desperate measures were adopted by the nation's forces. Of these the most famous were the *Kamikaze* ('Divine Wind') pilots of the Japanese Air Force, trained by Admiral Onishi. These pilots, whose task it was to dive bomb U.S. naval ships with their aircraft, were first employed during the struggle for the Philippines in 1944. During the final stages of the war many thousand Kamikaze missions were carried out. During April 1945 alone, some 1,400 missions were undertaken, resulting in the loss of 26 Allied vessels with a further 160 damaged. However, the inevitable losses incurred and the problems of training reduced the efficacy of the Kamikaze pilots as the war progressed.

By 1945, there was a growing realisation in Allied minds that the only way that Japan would be defeated would be through an actual invasion of the Japanese island group. This, inevitably, would be costly both in terms of manpower and equipment. Moreover, until the supply routes were guaranteed free from potential Japanese disruption, any such invasion would be risky. Thus, whilst the Allied powers drew up plans for an invasion of Japan, an alternative strategy was to be employed.

Even before the outbreak of World War II in Europe scientists had been involved in projects to develop atomic energy. Both Britain and the United States were aided in their development work by refugees from Europe. Despite the loss of many scientists, Germany was also in the race to develop atomic weaponry, its research base in Norway being the target for both SOE and aerial attack. The German programme ultimately ceased in February 1944 when a boat carrying all the country's supplies of heavy water was sunk by the Norwegian resistance.

In 1942, the United States established the Manhattan Project under Brigadier-General Leslie Groves and the first nuclear reaction was shown in December 1942 at the University of Chicago. In August 1943 it was agreed between Winston Churchill and Franklin D. Roosevelt that the two countries' nuclear programmes should be united and a Combined Policy Committee was established in Washington for that purpose.

The primary location for research was at Los Alamos, in New Mexico, where the project was controlled by J. Robert Oppenheimer. On 16 July 1945 the first of three bombs was successfully exploded; the Allied powers now had their alternative to the manned invasion of Japan. The first atomic bomb — 'Little Boy' — was dropped on Hiroshima on 6 August 1945; this was followed on 9 August by the second — 'Fat Man' — on Nagasaki. Five days later, on 14 August, the Japanese capitulated.

Note on the Maps

All the maps illustrated in this book have been drawn from the large collection held by The National Archives (TNA) at Kew in west London. This is the major holding of all public documents in the United Kingdom. The maps are derived from a number of government departments and reflect the interests and concerns at the time they were compiled. The maps incorporated in this selection are drawn primarily from contemporary Second World War sources and many of them have been annotated by the commanders or operational staff who used them. This additional information adds greatly to their value as historical documents. The contemporary annotation by commanders or other operational staff reflects the concerns at the time and helps to provide a fascinating insight into the minds of the leading British military figures of the war. All the maps have their TNA reference number at the end of the caption to facilitate further research.

RIGHT: Map from Operation 'Husky', Sicily, 10 June 1943 **(see page 62)**.

DEFENCES OF
THE FARO OR MESSINA STRAIT

From Admiralty Chart No. 177.
Natural Scale 1 : 30,350.
Figures on the land express the heights in feet above the sea.
SOUNDINGS IN FATHOMS

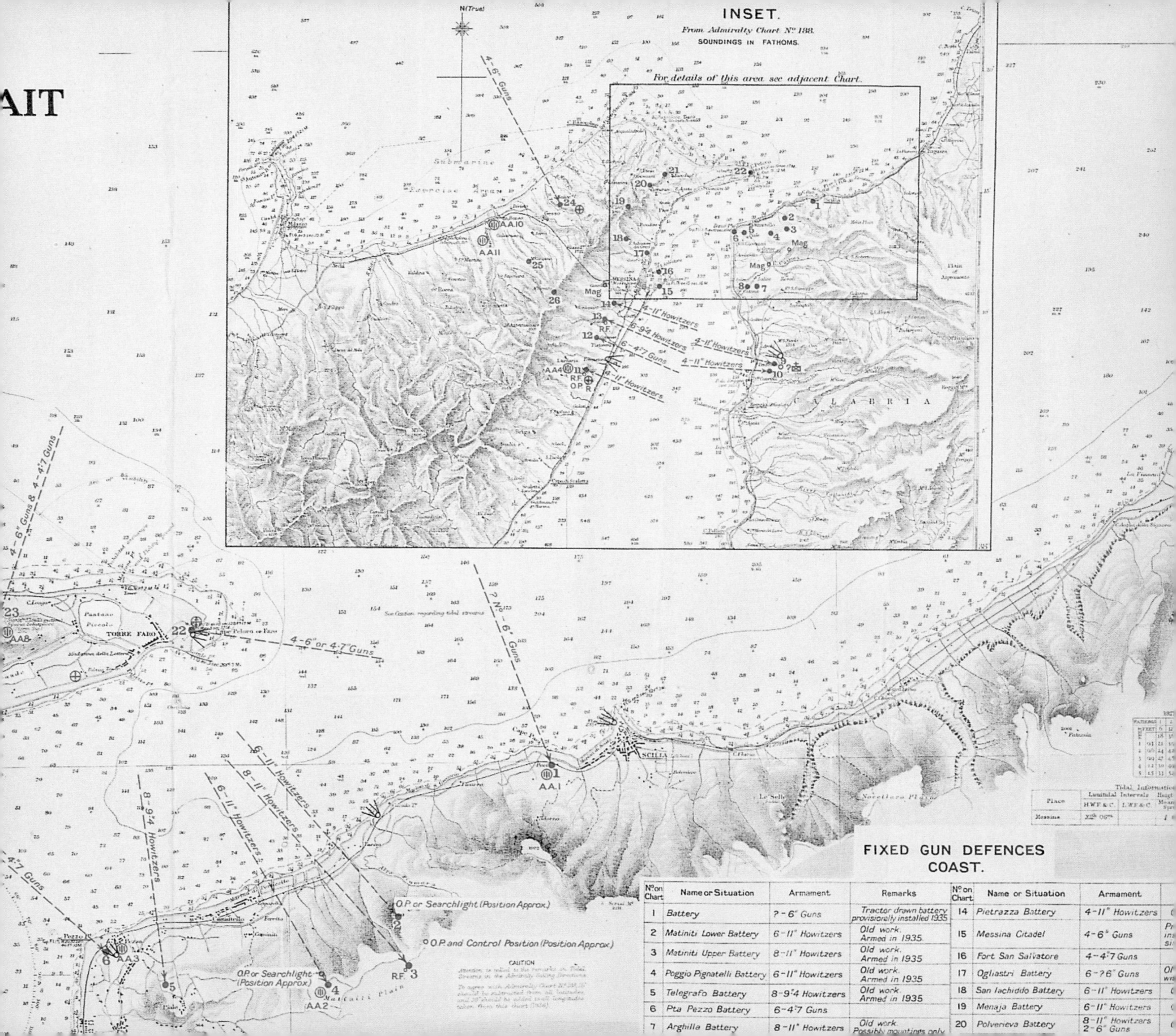

THE MAPS

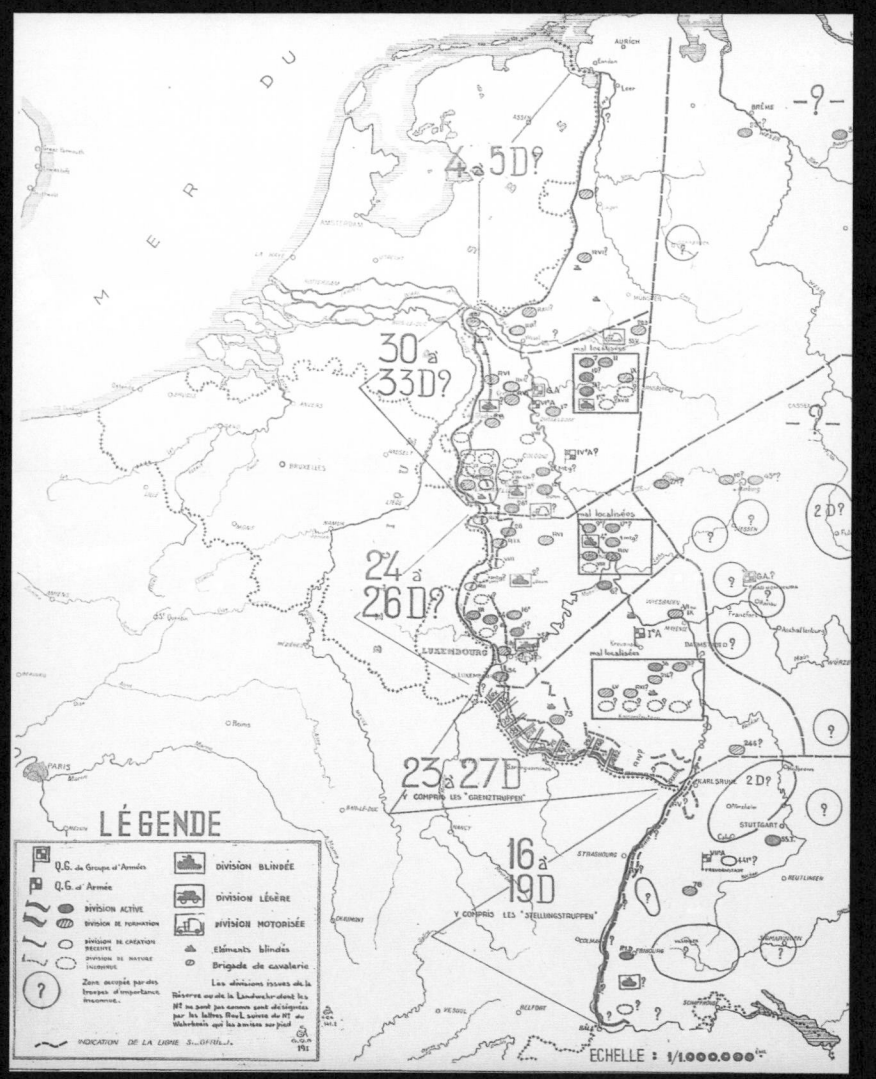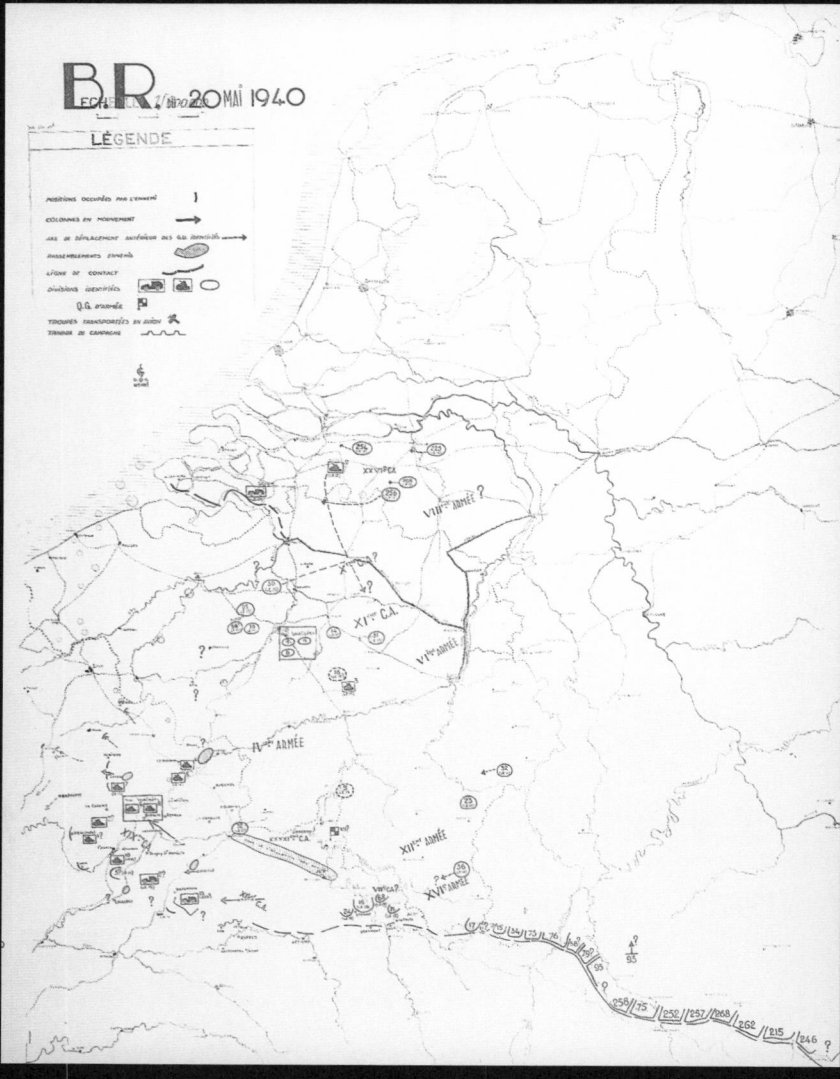

BLITZKRIEG IN THE WEST, APRIL–MAY 1940

ABOVE AND RIGHT: These French maps show troop dispositions in the weeks prior to and after the German assault in the West. From the first map it is possible to surmise that the French were in the dark about the strength and location of the German divisions threatening them. Unexpectedly, the attack came through the heavily wooded Ardennes region to the north of Luxembourg, only thinly defended because it had been deemed impassable to armour. The general confusion and lack of effective intelligence is again demonstrated by the map dated 20 May, by which stage the German forces had broken through the Allied line at Sedan and were rapidly encircling them. The final map, dated 28 May, shows the completed encirclement, with von Kleist's tanks effectively cutting off the Allied forces in the north. The evacuation from Dunkirk had already been underway for four days. WO 197/107 (1) (5) (10)

B.R. DU 28 MAI 1940

G.A. "B"

G.A. "A"

XVIIIᵉᵐᵉ ARMÉE

VIᵉᵐᵉ ARMÉE

IVᵉᵐᵉ ARMÉE

XIIᵉᵐᵉ ARMÉE

XVIᵉᵐᵉ ARMÉE

GRUPPE v. KLEIST

GRUPPE HOTH

LÉGENDE

- Q.G. DE GROUPE D'ARMÉE
- Q.G. D'ARMÉE
- Q.G. DE CORPS D'ARMÉE
- POSITIONS OCCUPÉES PAR L'ENNEMI
- COLONNES EN MOUVEMENT
- AXE DE DÉPLACEMENT ANTÉRIEUR DES G.U. IDENTIFIÉS
- LIGNE DE CONTACT

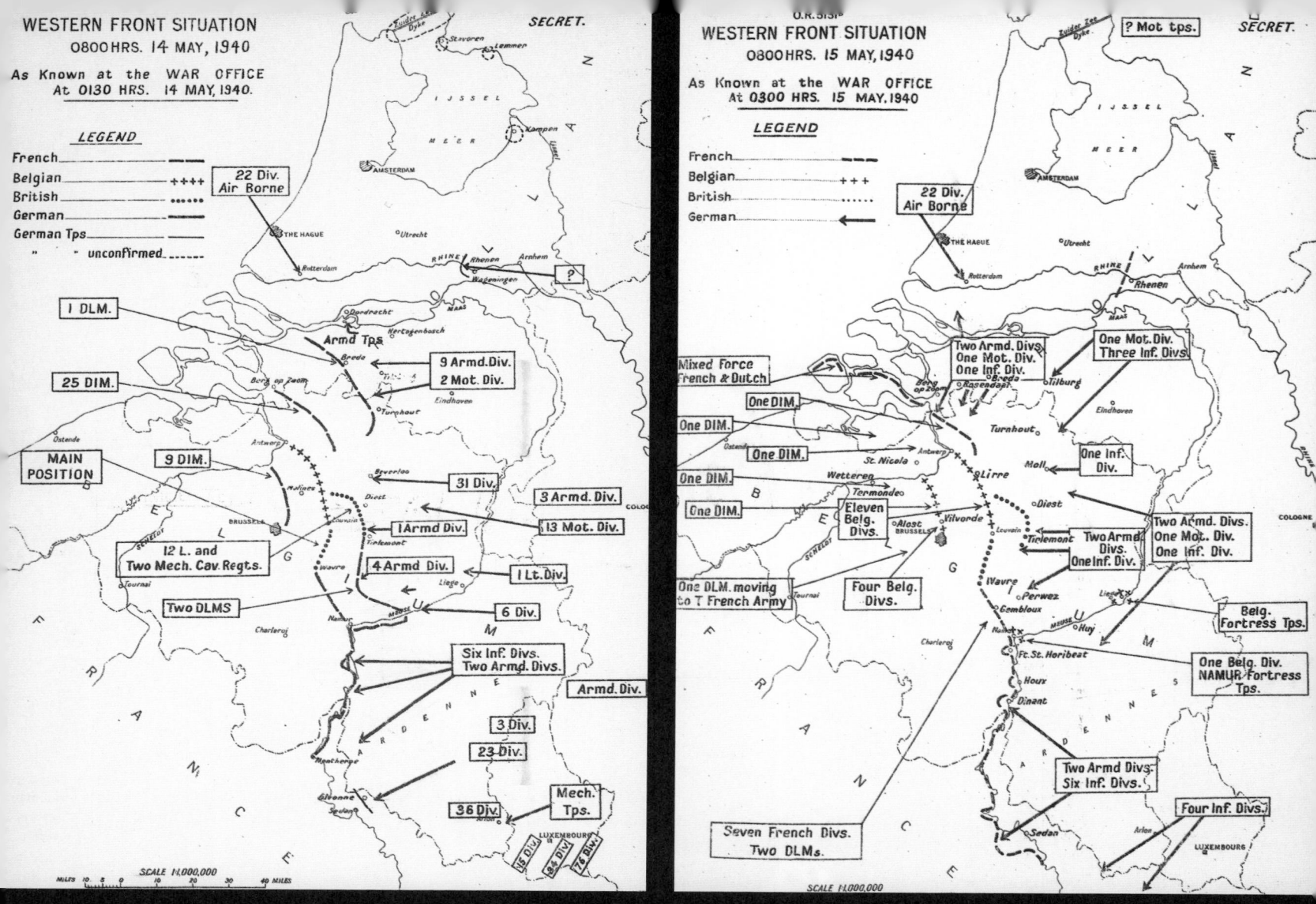

BLITZKRIEG IN THE WEST, 14–15 MAY 1940

ABOVE LEFT AND RIGHT: Maps showing the disposition of German forces on 14 and 15 May 1940, a few days after Blitzkrieg had been unleashed on the West. Within a week of the opening of the western offensive on 10 May the Allied armies of France, Britain, Belgium and Holland were in serious trouble. None of their commanders had predicted that the Germans would make an armoured thrust through the Ardennes Forest (at bottom right)

and correspondingly the bulk of their strength was concentrated in the northeast. Beginning on the 10th seven Panzer divisions under Rommel, Kleist and Reinhardt pushed through the Ardennes and across the River Meuse with almost no losses. The breakthrough came at Sedan on the 13th, when a 50-mile hole in the French line was ripped open. The Germans were then able to drive to the Channel almost unbindered. MEO 189 (15) (16

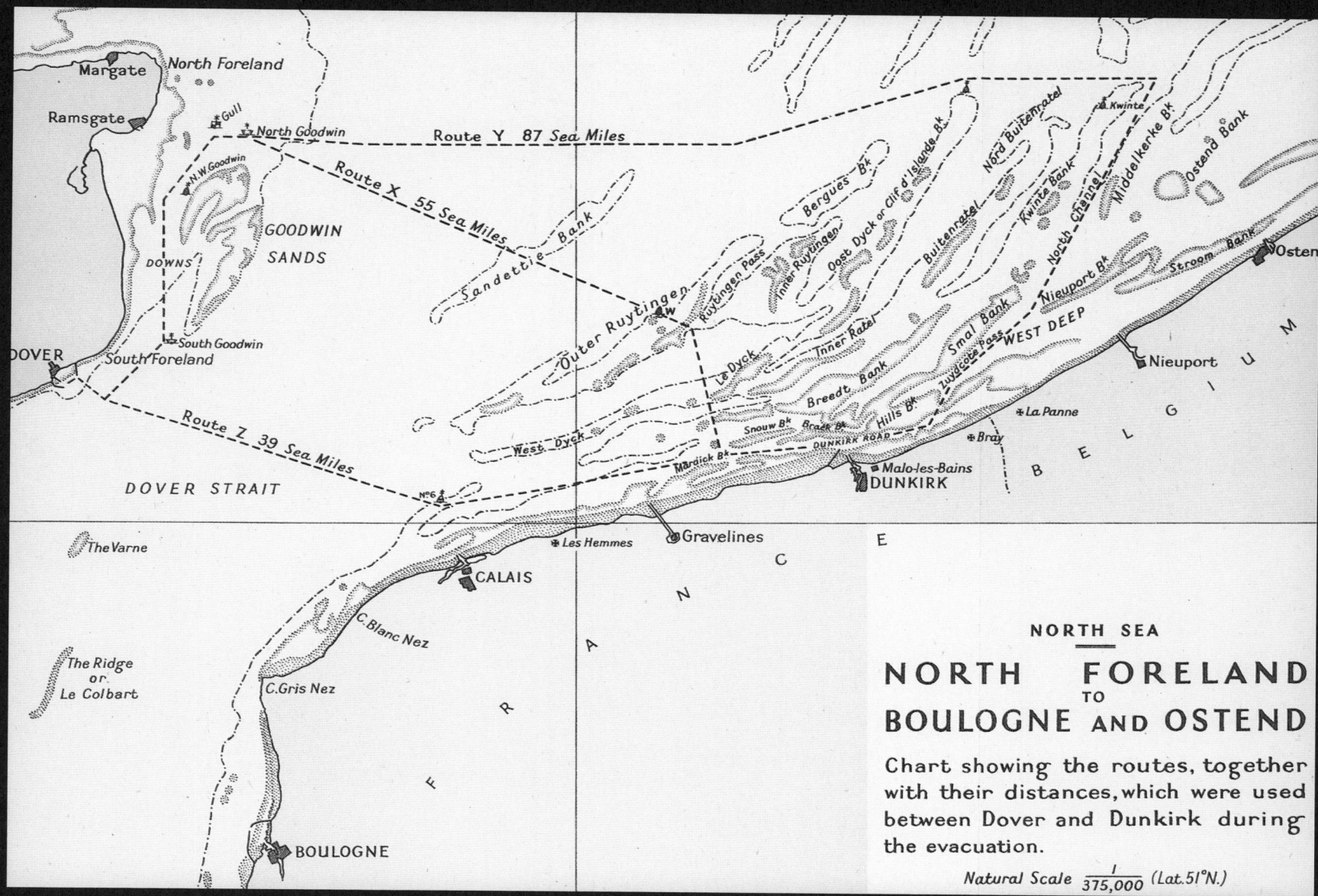

NORTH SEA

NORTH FORELAND
TO
BOULOGNE AND OSTEND

Chart showing the routes, together with their distances, which were used between Dover and Dunkirk during the evacuation.

Natural Scale $\frac{1}{375,000}$ (Lat. 51°N.)

DUNKIRK, MAY–JUNE 1940

ABOVE: Map of the French coast from Boulogne to Ostend, showing the three routes for British ships evacuating troops from the beaches. Operation 'Dynamo', as the evacuation was named, was completed between 26 May and 4 June 1940. In that period some 940 ships, 40 British, Dutch, French and Belgian naval vessels and the rest a rag-tag bag of privately owned vessels, ferried 338,226 mostly British troops to safety across the Channel. The question as to why Hitler stopped the advance of his army into the Dunkirk area thus allowing the evacuation at Dunkirk will remain a mystery. Influenced by Goering's view that the Luftwaffe would finish off the British, and aware of the extended lines of supply and tiredness of his troops, Hitler halted the advance and the boost to British morale was incalculable. ADM 1/19997

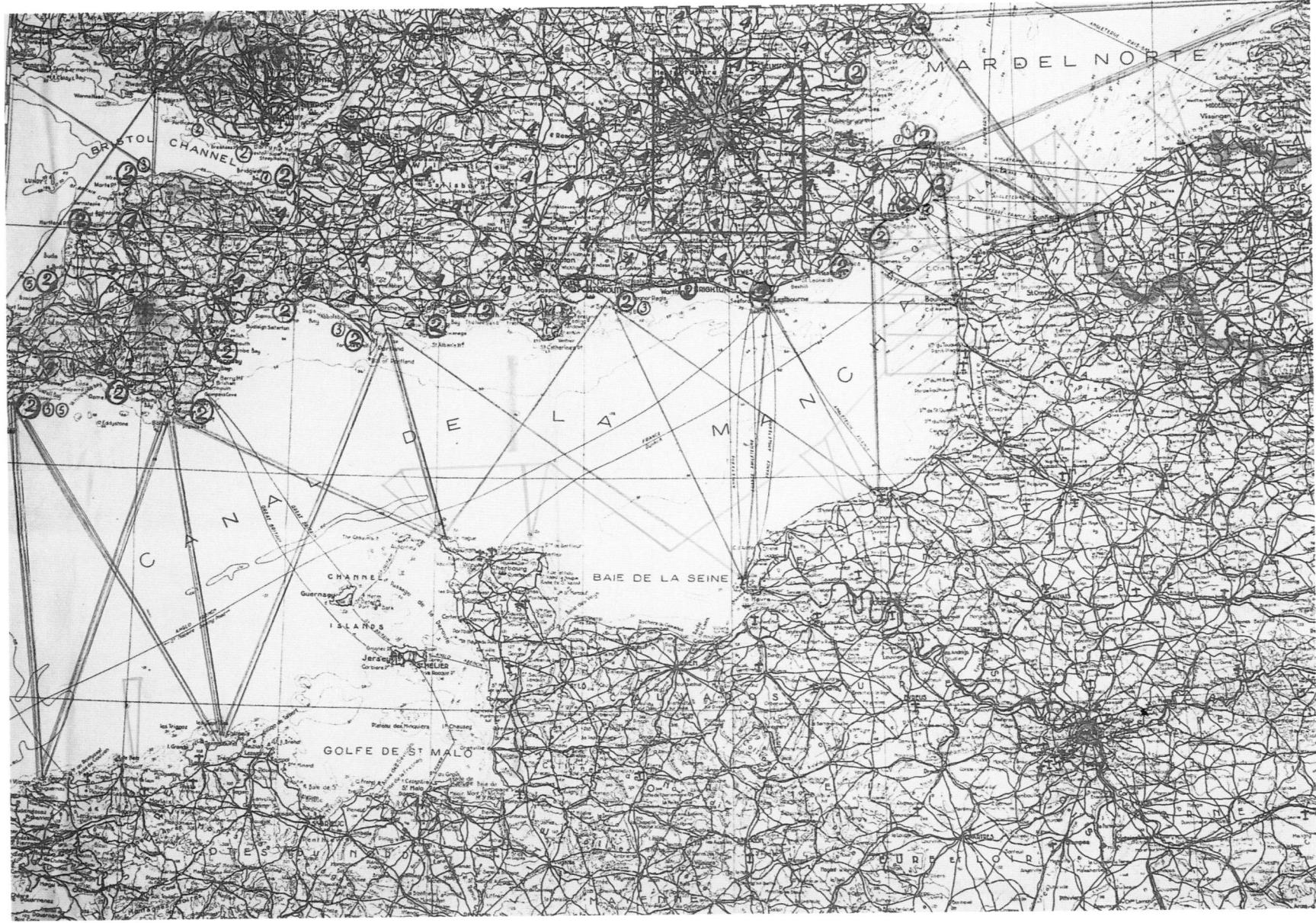

OPERATION 'SEELÖWE', JULY 1940

A captured map showing the proposed method of German invasion of England, with annotation by the British Air Ministry. When Goering failed to deliver the crushing defeat of the RAF that he had confidently predicted, Hitler was left with no option but to call off the invasion, codenamed "Seelöwe" (Sealion). MPI 593

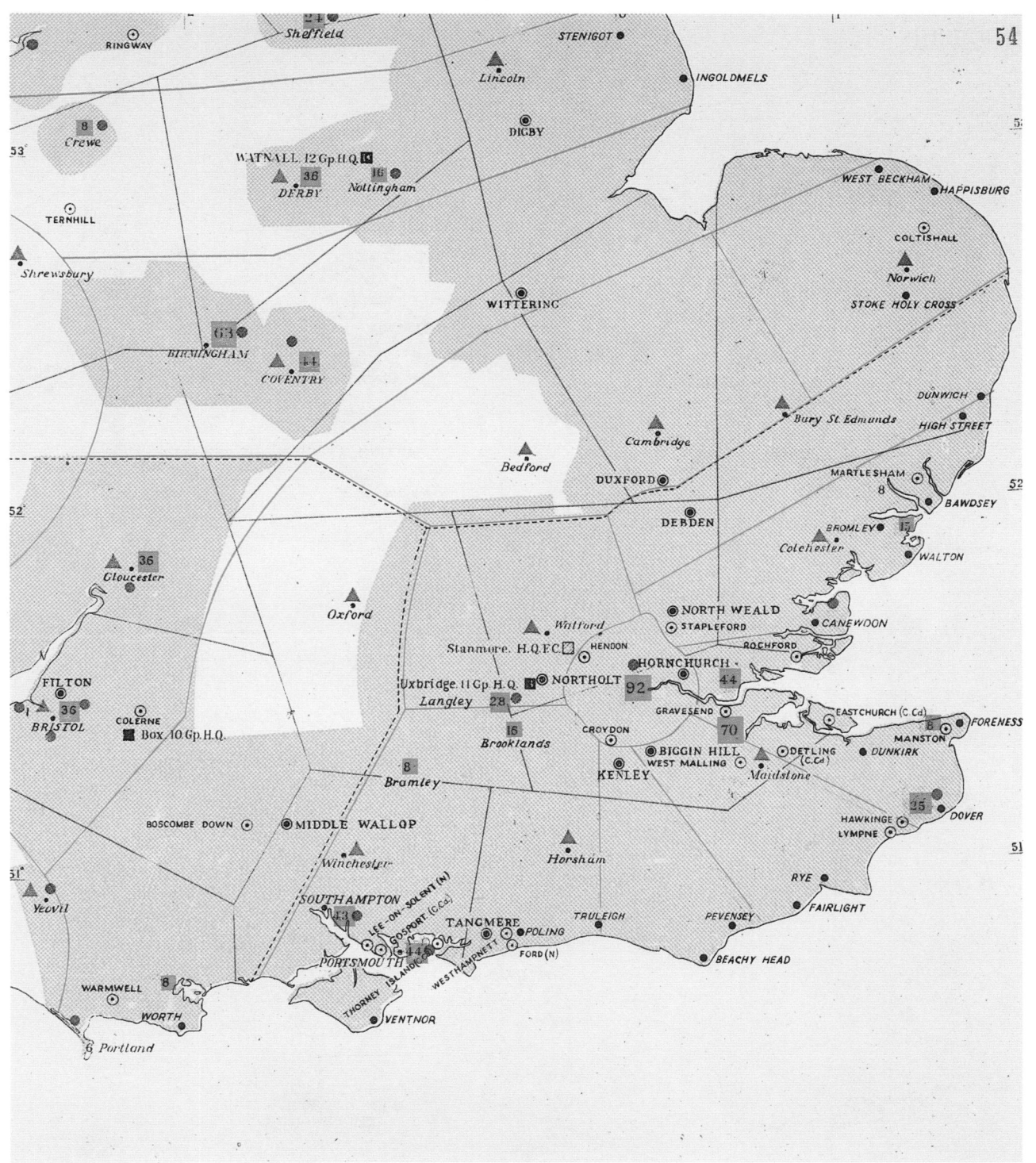

BATTLE OF BRITAIN FIGHTER DEFENCES, 1940

LEFT: Map showing the dispositions of RAF fighter airfields and control centres for the Battle of Britain. The dotted line marks the divisions between the fighter groups, No 11 in the southeast, No 12 in the eastern counties and No 10 in the south west. These are further divided into sectors, each with its own controlling station (in caps). The solid black dots shown the location of high and low level radar stations (Chain Home and Chain Low). AIR 41/16

U-BOAT WAR, AUGUST 1940

RIGHT: Chart of U-boat sightings for the month of August 1940, at which time the German submarines were wreaking terrible havoc among poorly defended and organised British shipping fleets. The map shows to good effect the Coastal Command tactic of employing lightly armed Avro Ansons on coastal patrol work, while long-range patrolling was undertaken by Short Sunderland and Lockheed Hudson squadrons. MFQ 583 (14)

U-BOAT WAR, SEPTEMBER 1940

FAR RIGHT: This chart illustrates the dramatic increase in the intensity of air traffic over the English Channel in September 1940, as fear of an imminent invasion grew. Coastal Command aircraft and personnel were redeployed to the south coast in anticipation of the invasion (and to make up for pilot losses in Fighter Command), and encounters with U-boats around the British coastline fell correspondingly. Note also how reconnaissance of the French, Dutch and German channel ports has been stepped up. MFQ 583 (19)

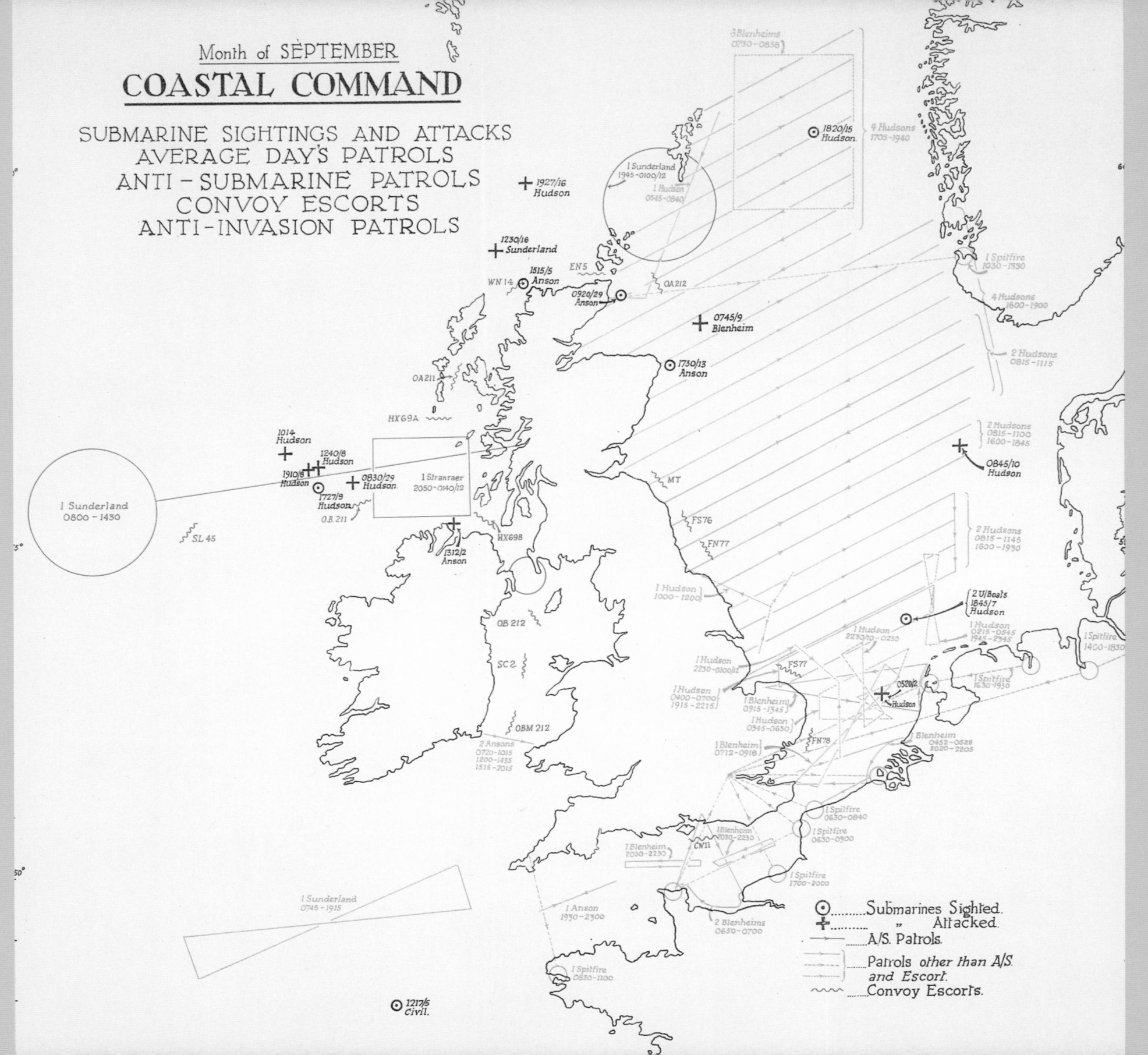

Month of SEPTEMBER
COASTAL COMMAND

SUBMARINE SIGHTINGS AND ATTACKS
AVERAGE DAY'S PATROLS
ANTI-SUBMARINE PATROLS
CONVOY ESCORTS
ANTI-INVASION PATROLS

3 Blenheims
0730-0858

1820/15
Hudson

4 Hudsons
1705-1940

1 Sunderland
1945-0100/12

1 Hudson
0545-0840

1927/16
Hudson

1 Spitfire
1030-1330

1230/16
Sunderland

4 Hudsons
1600-1900

EN 5

WN 14   1515/5
Anson

0920/29
Anson

OA 212

0745/9
Blenheim

2 Hudsons
0815-1115

1730/13
Anson

OA 211

2 Hudsons
0815-1100
1600-1845

HX 69A

1014
Hudson

1240/8
Hudson

0830/29
Hudson

1 Stranraer
2050-0140/12

MT

0845/10
Hudson

1910/8
Hudson

1727/9
Hudson

1 Sunderland
0800-1430

O.B.211

SL 45

HX 69B

FS 76

2 Hudsons
0815-1145
1600-1930

FN 77

1312/2
Anson

1 Hudson
1000-1200

2 U/Boats
1845/7
Hudson

OB 212

1 Hudson
2230/10-0230

1 Hudson
0215-0545
1945-2245

1 Spitfire
1400-1830

1 Hudson
2250-0300/11

SC 2

FS 77

0520/2
Hudson

1 Spitfire
1630-1930

1 Hudson
0400-0700
1915-2215

1 Blenheim
0915-1345

1 Hudson
0545-0650

OBM 212

1 Blenheim
0712-0918

FN 78

Blenheim
0452-0528
2020-2205

2 Ansons
0720-1015
1800-1455
1515-2015

1 Spitfire
0630-0840

1 Spitfire
0650-0900

1 Blenheim
2030-2250

CN 11

1 Spitfire
1700-2000

1 Sunderland
0745-1915

1 Anson
1930-2300

⊙........... Submarines Sighted.
☩...........   „   Attacked.
→........... A/S. Patrols.
.... Patrols *other than A/S.*
   and Escort.
~~~........ Convoy Escorts.

2 Blenheims
0650-0700

1 Spitfire
0630-1100

⊙ 1217/5
Civil.

WEEKLY DIAGRAM OF U-BOAT WARFARE.

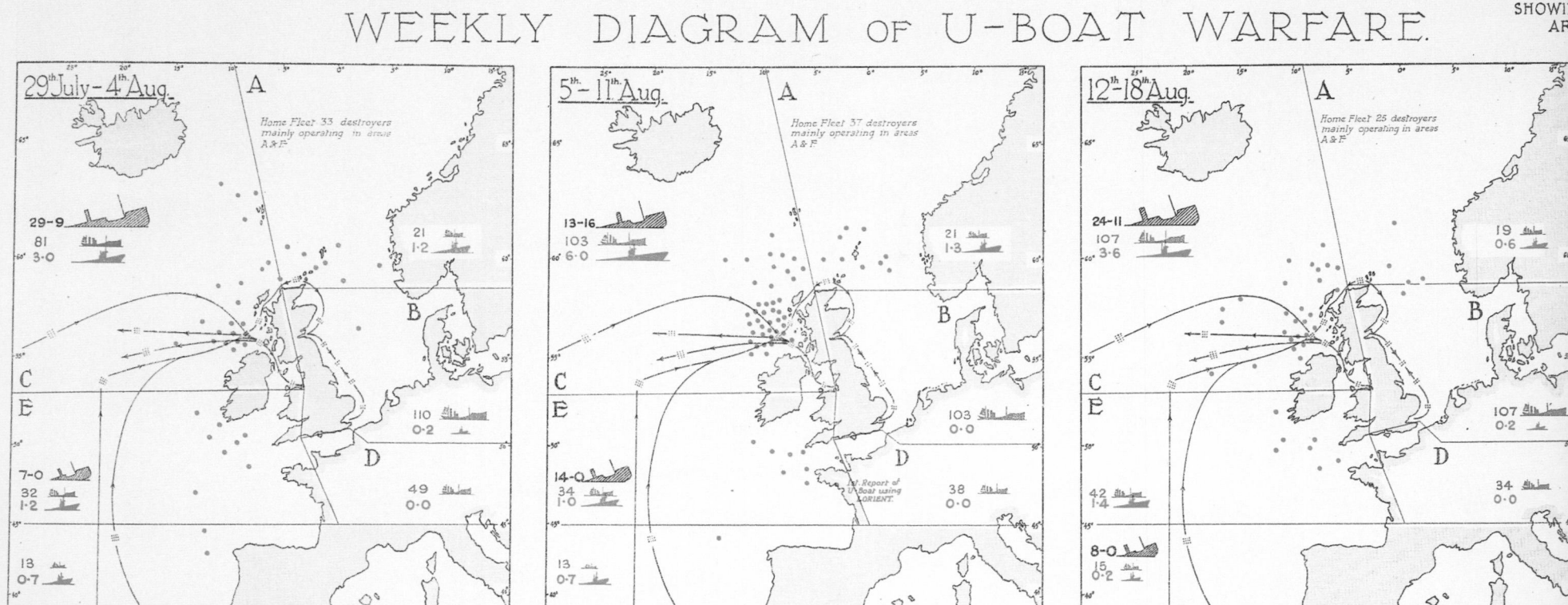

A/S. Warfare Division. Sept. 1940.

U-BOAT WAR, AUGUST–SEPTEMBER 1940

ABOVE AND RIGHT: The capitulation of France in June 1940 allowed Admiral Doenitz to relocate his U-boats to the French Atlantic ports of St. Nazaire, Brest and Lorient. From here they could range out far into the Atlantic, and began to take a heavy toll on British shipping. This British chart of U-boat movements covers the most intensive period of the Battle of Britain, and shows how the U-boats massed at the northern and southern ends of the Irish Sea attempted to blockade Liverpool and Bristol during those vital months. MFQ 583 (17)

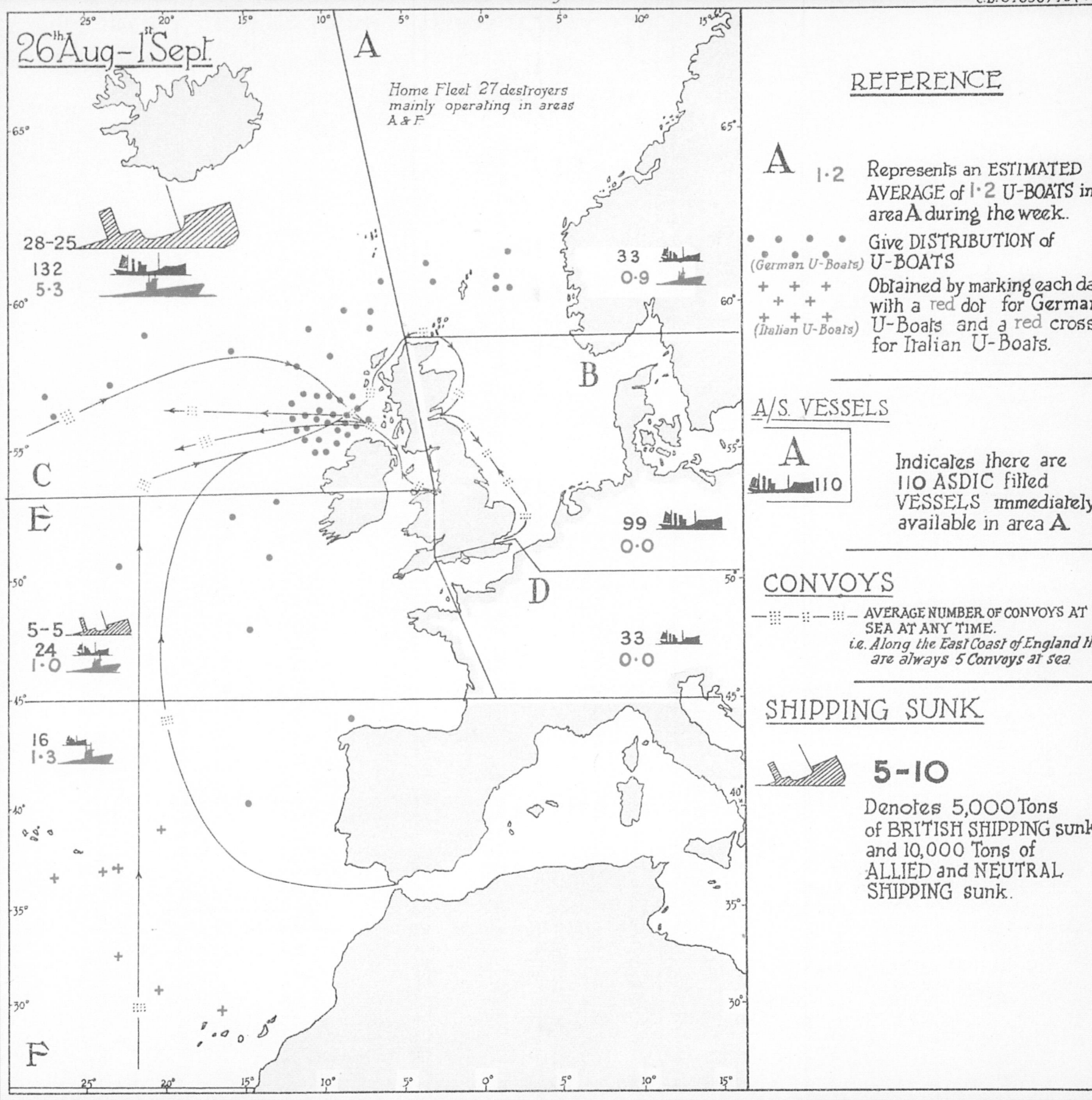

26th Aug – 1st Sept.

Home Fleet 27 destroyers mainly operating in areas A & F

A

B

C

D

E

F

28-25
132
5·3

33
0·9

99
0·0

33
0·0

5-5
24
1·0

16
1·3

REFERENCE

A 1·2 Represents an ESTIMATED AVERAGE of 1·2 U-BOATS in area A during the week.

(German U-Boats) • • • • Give DISTRIBUTION of U-BOATS

(Italian U-Boats) + + + Obtained by marking each day with a red dot for German U-Boats and a red cross for Italian U-Boats.

A/S. VESSELS

A ▮▮▮ 110 Indicates there are 110 ASDIC fitted VESSELS immediately available in area A.

CONVOYS

▦—▦—▦ AVERAGE NUMBER OF CONVOYS AT SEA AT ANY TIME.
i.e. Along the East Coast of England there are always 5 Convoys at sea.

SHIPPING SUNK

5-10 Denotes 5,000 Tons of BRITISH SHIPPING sunk and 10,000 Tons of ALLIED and NEUTRAL SHIPPING sunk.

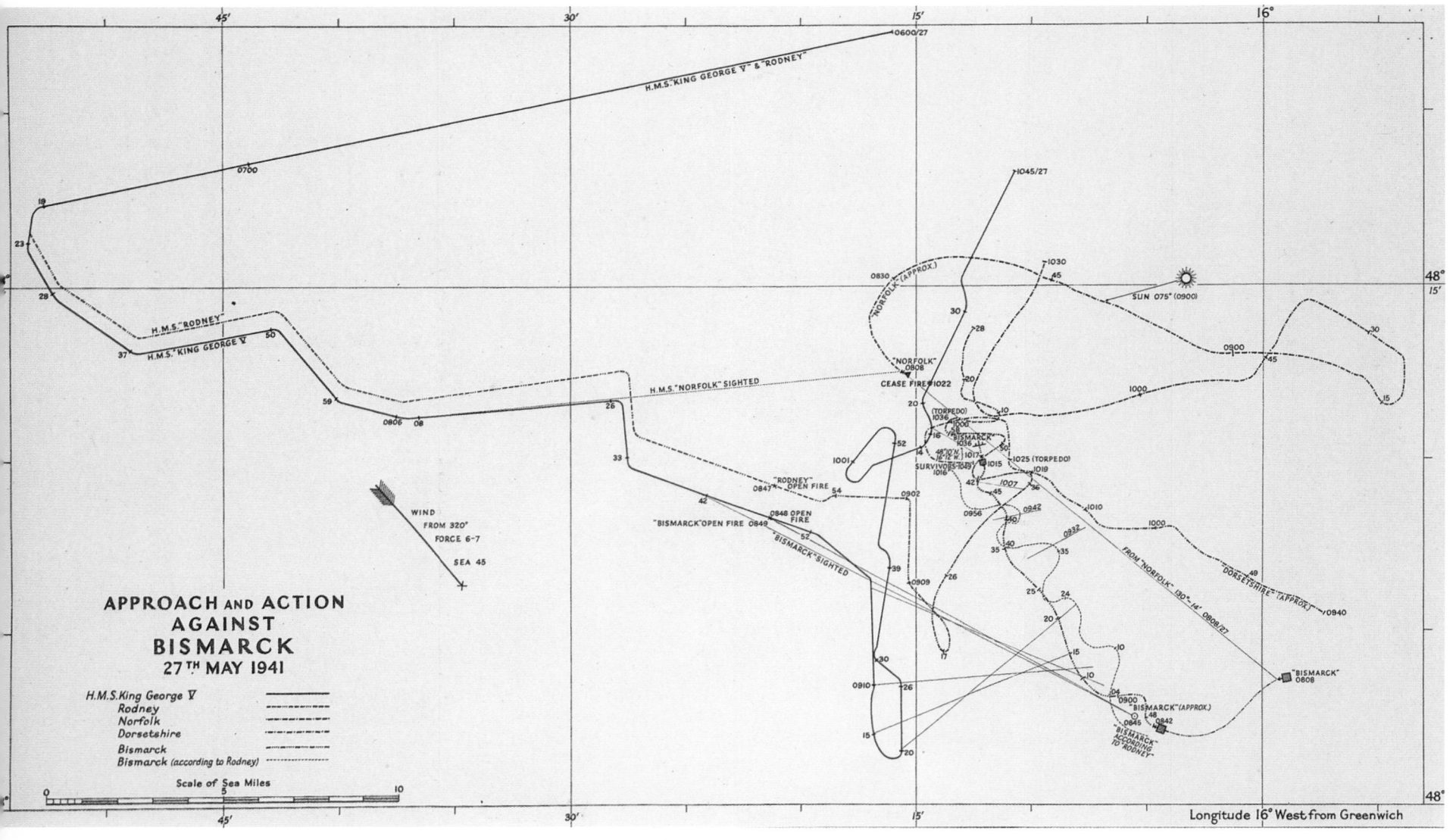

APPROACH AND ACTION
AGAINST
BISMARCK
27TH MAY 1941

H.M.S.King George V	
Rodney	
Norfolk	
Dorsetshire	
Bismarck	
Bismarck (according to Rodney)	

Scale of Sea Miles

WIND
FROM 320°
FORCE 6-7

SEA 45

Longitude 16° West from Greenwich

ACTION AGAINST BISMARCK, 27 MAY 1941

ABOVE: Chart of British naval operations by *King George V*, *Rodney*, *Norfolk* and *Dorsetshire* against the German battleship *Bismarck* in the North Atlantic on 27 May 1941. *Bismarck* and her sister ship *Prinz Eugen* sailed from Gotenhaven on 18 May intending to break out into the Atlantic. They were detected by British reconnaissance aircraft on the 21st. The British Home Fleet under Admiral Tovey, which included the capital ships *Hood* and *Prince of Wales*, sailed to intercept and engaged on 24 May. In the ensuing battle Hood was sunk with a massive loss of life (only three out of a complement of 1,421 survived) and the *Prince of Wales* damaged, while *Bismarck*'s fuel tanks were ruptured and *Prinz Eugen*

escaped to the south. After having been engaged by Swordfish torpedo bombers from HMS *Victorious*, contact with the German ships was lost on 25 May and regained the next day. She was engaged the next day by a powerful force of ships made up of Force H which was based in Gibraltar and whose ships included *Renown* and carrier *Ark Royal*, and the battleships *King George V* and *Rodney*, recalled from convoy duties. Bismarck was reduced to a blazing wreck, finally sunk by torpedoes from the cruiser HMS *Dorsetshire* at 10.36am on the 27th. CAB 106/333.

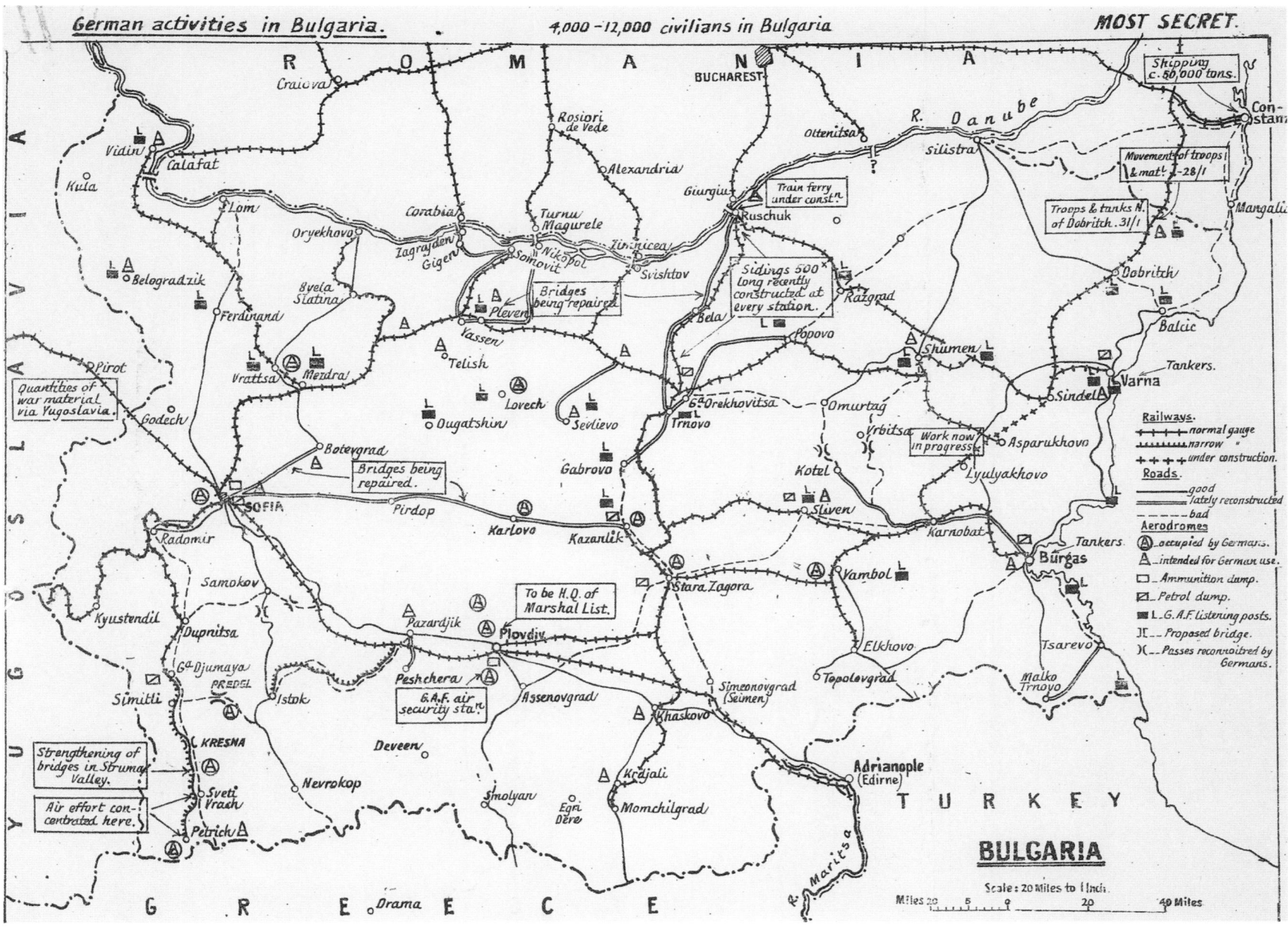

BULGARIA, FEBRUARY 1941

Bulgaria was an ally of Germany during the First World War, and in the interwar years a strong friendship with the Third Reich was fostered by the grant of territory belonging to Romania. In March 1941 it formally joined the Axis and participated in the invasion of Yugoslavia. This British map is based on intelligence received in the months leading up to those events, and shows the build up of forces in the areas bordering Yugoslavia. Note the legend at bottom left, which reports on the strengthening of bridges in the Struma Valley, a clear indication that this will be the route of an armoured thrust. MPH 1130 (2)

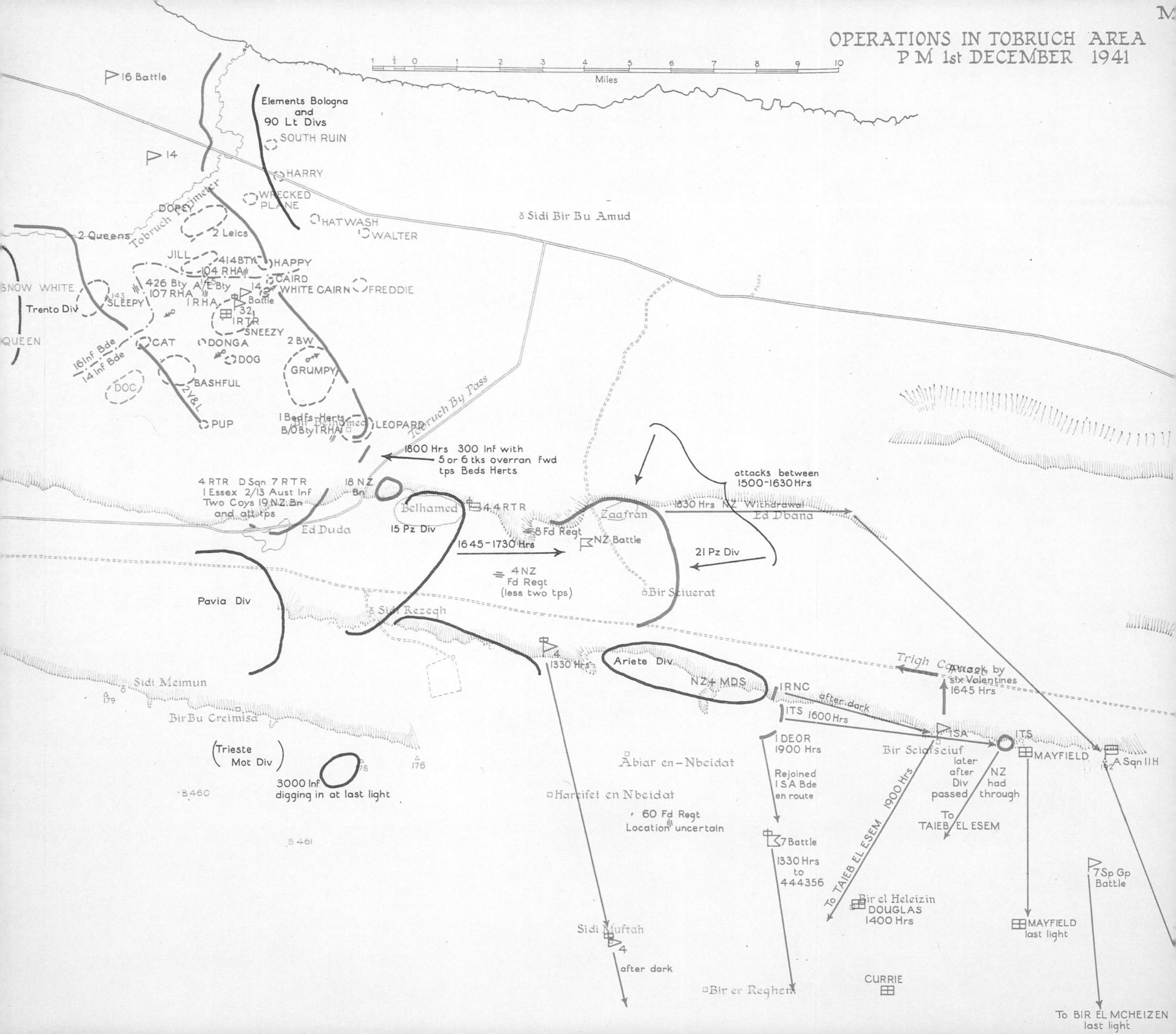

OPERATIONS IN TOBRUCH AREA
PM 1st DECEMBER 1941

Miles

⊐16 Battle

⊐14

Elements Bologna
and
90 Lt Divs
SOUTH RUIN

⊙ Sidi Bir Bu Amud

◌ HARRY

◌ WRECKED PLANE

DOC Perimeter

◌ HATWASH
◌ WALTER

2 Queens

2 Leics

JILL

414 BTY
104 RHA

HAPPY

SNOW WHITE

426 Bty A/E Bty
107 RHA 1 RHA

CAIRD
WHITE CAIRN

◌ FREDDIE

Trento Div

143
SLEEPY

143
Battle

32 I RTR

Trieste

SNEEZY

QUEEN

16 Inf Bde
14 Inf Bde

CAT

◌ DONGA
◌ DOG

2 BW

DOC

BASHFUL

GRUMPY

2 Y & L

⊐ PUP

1 Bedfs Herts
B/O Bty 1 RHA

LEOPARD

Tobruch By Pass

1600 Hrs 300 Inf with
5 or 6 tks overran fwd
tps Beds Herts

attacks between
1500-1630 Hrs

4 RTR D Sqn 7 RTR
1 Essex 2/13 Aust Inf
Two Coys 19 NZ Bn
and att tps

18 NZ
Bn

Belhamed

4.4 RTR

Zaafran

1630 Hrs NZ Withdrawal

Ed Dbana

Ed Duda

15 Pz Div

8 Fd Regt

NZ Battle

1645-1730 Hrs

21 Pz Div

4 NZ
Fd Regt
(less two tps)

⊙ Bir Sciuerat

Pavia Div

⊙ Sidi Rezegh

Trigh Capuzzo

Attack by
six Valentines
1645 Hrs

Sidi Meimun

4
1330 Hrs

Ariete Div

NZ + MDS

1 RNC

179

1 TS 1600 Hrs

after dark

Bir Bu Creimisa

1 DEOR
1900 Hrs

1 SA

1 TS

MAYFIELD

A Sqn 11 H

(Trieste
Mot Div)

178

176

Abiar en-Nbeidat

Bir Sciafsciuf

NZ
had
passed
through

To
TAIEB EL ESEM

152

B 460

3000 Inf
digging in at last light

Hartsfet en Nbeidat

60 Fd Regt
Location uncertain

Rejoined
1 SA Bde
en route

later
after
Div

B 461

7 Battle

1330 Hrs
to
444356

To TAIEB EL ESEM 1900 Hrs

Bir el Heleizin
DOUGLAS
1400 Hrs

MAYFIELD
last light

Sidi Muftah

4

after dark

Bir er Reghem

CURRIE

7 Sp Gp
Battle

To BIR EL MCHEIZEN
last light

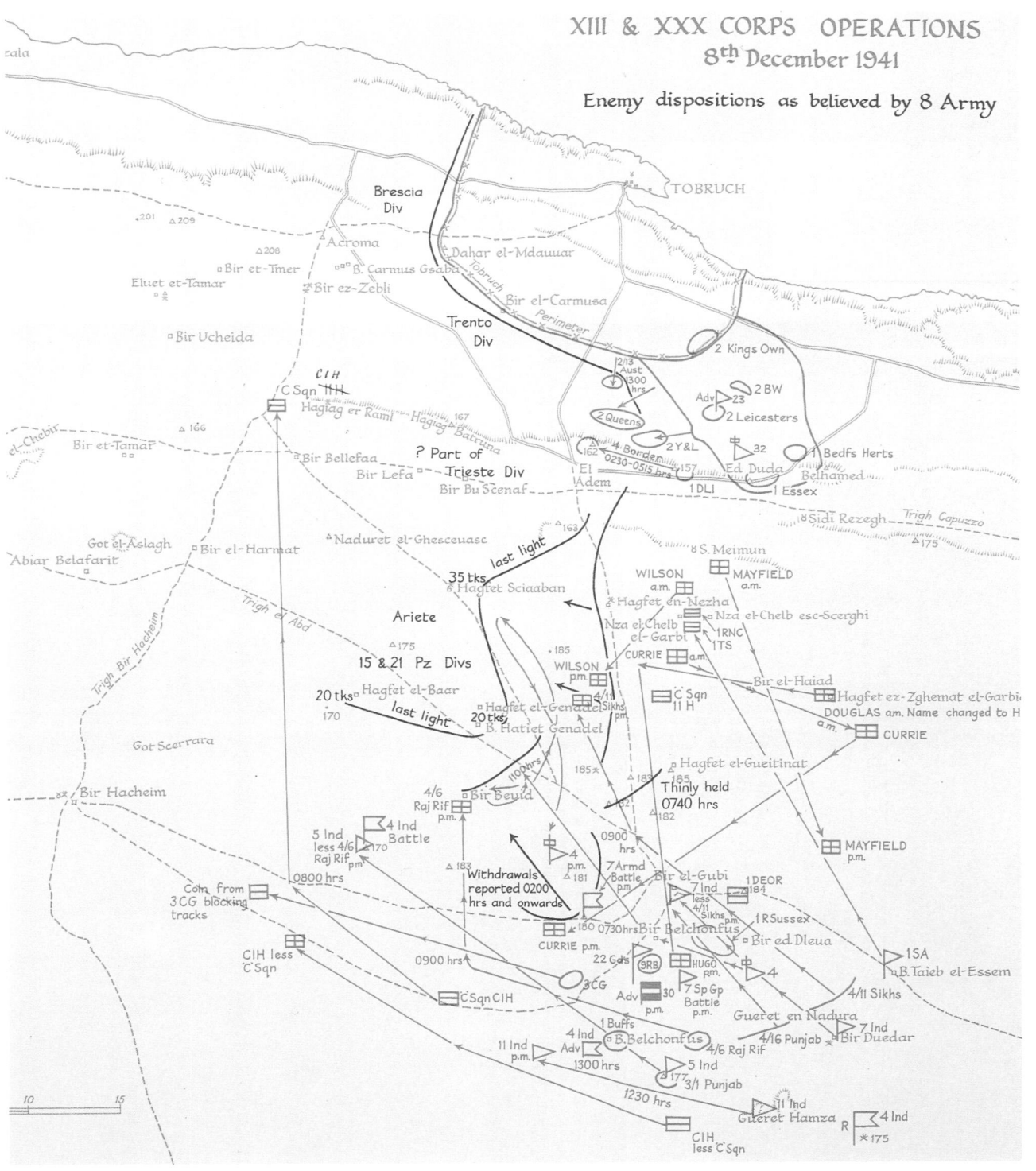

XIII & XXX CORPS OPERATIONS
8th December 1941

Enemy dispositions as believed by 8 Army

TOBRUK: OPERATION 'CRUSADER', DECEMBER 1941

LEFT AND FAR LEFT: Maps showing troop movements and enemy dispositions during the third week of Operation 'Crusader'. This had been planned by Auchinleck as a large-scale sweep by armoured elements of the Eighth Army towards the besieged port of Tobruk from the south, while infantry forces pinned down Axis-held positions on the Libya/Egypt frontier. Seen at the top left-hand corner of the map on page 34 is the southwest perimeter of the defensive line held by British and Commonwealth troops around the port, which had been encircled during Rommel's westward drive through North Africa. After strong counter-attacks had blunted the advance of the Eighth Army and threatened the frontier, matériel losses forced Rommel to order a withdrawal to positions west of El Agheila, and Tobruk was relieved. CAB 44/93 (1B) (10)

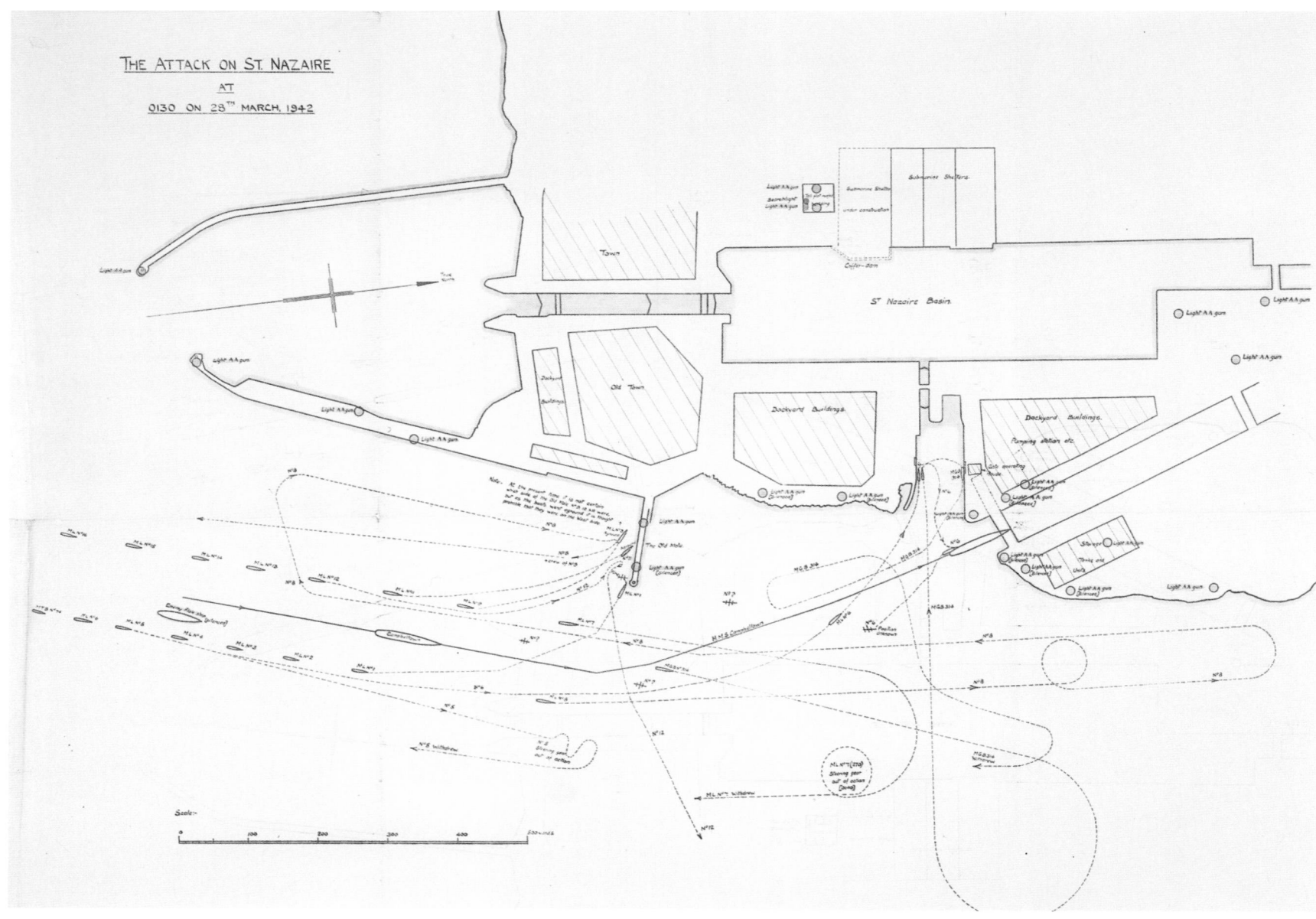

THE ATTACK ON ST. NAZAIRE
AT
0130 ON 28TH MARCH, 1942

ST. NAZAIRE, 27–28 MARCH 1942

The port of St. Nazaire on the French Atlantic coast possessed the only dry dock capable of mooring the giant German battleships *Bismarck* and *Tirpitz* should they venture into the Atlantic. On the night of 27-28 March 1942 a spectacular combined operations attack by Allied forces disabled the dry dock by ramming its gates with the old destroyer *Campbeltown*, which was packed with three tons of explosives timed to explode later.

Commandos destroyed the winding gear which operated the gates and also tried unsuccessfully to attack the U-boat pens. This map shows the planned route of the destroyer and the escorting vessels. Although the raid denied the use of the dry dock to the German navy, losses to the attackers were heavy. MFQ 306 (8)

BREST, AUGUST 1941

BELOW: Map showing flak concentrations around the French port of Brest, which was used as a base for by the German surface ships, including the *Scharnhorst*, *Gneisenau* and *Prinz Eugen*, and submarines from mid-1940. Brest was bombed repeatedly by the RAF until September 1944, when it fell to U.S. invasion forces and was found to be in unworkable condition.

51

FLAK MAPS ISSUED BY M.I.14(e) (FLAK INTELLIGENCE) AS AT 24.8.41

BREST — SECRET

Scale 1 : 80,000

'CHANNEL DASH', 12 FEBRUARY 1942

RIGHT: Map showing the track of the German battleships *Scharnhorst* and *Gneisenau* during Operation 'Cerberus', the codename for the so-called 'Channel Dash' on 12 February 1942. At the beginning of the war both these ships had operated successfully against British shipping in the Atlantic but after docking at Brest in February 1941 remained for a year under increasingly heavy bombardment by the RAF. Then on the morning of the 12 February both ships left the port and, hugging the French coast under the protection of an air umbrella organised by Adolf Galland, ran the gauntlet of the English Channel under the noses of the RAF and Royal Navy to Wilhelmshaven. The fact they were able to do so unscathed exposed severe weaknesses in the British Channel defences, although neither ship was able to break out again to the Atlantic. *Gneisenau* was badly bombed while in Kiel and did not see action again. *Scharnhorst* was sunk off North Cape on 26 December 1943. ADM 186/203

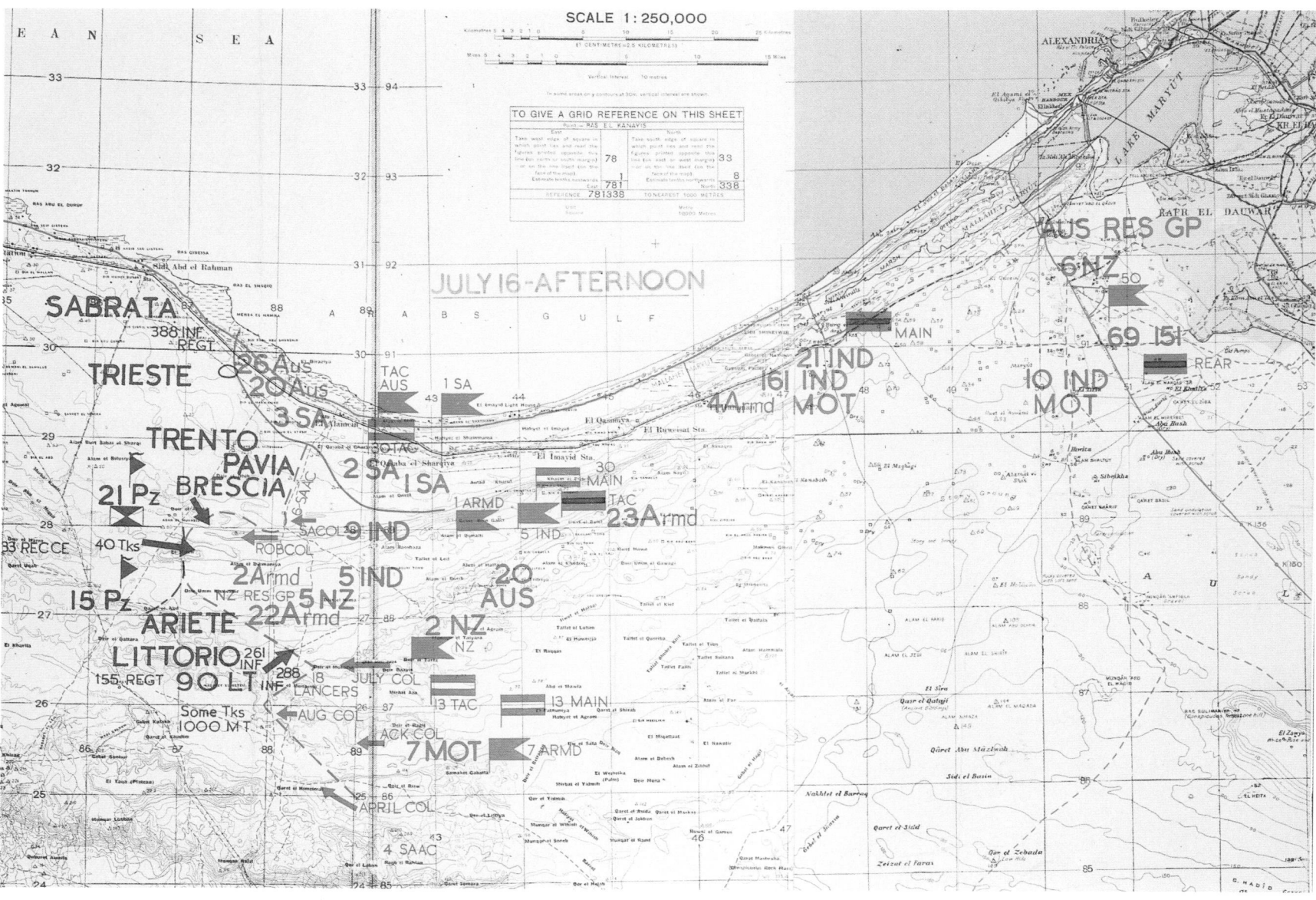

ALAM HALFA, 16 JULY 1942

This map shows the Allied and Axis positions at El Alamein in North Africa on the afternoon of 16 July 1942. By this stage in the Desert War the British Eighth Army — which included a large proportion of troops from the Commonwealth — under Claude Auchinleck had twice fallen back through Cyrenaica. However, the attack on the Alamein line by Rommel's depleted forces at the beginning of July had been repulsed by a well-organised defence. On the night of 30 August Rommel attacked the British position at Alam Halfa, which was guarded by the 22nd Armoured Brigade. He was driven back and, in many senses, this marked the turning point in the Desert War. In October the British and Commonwealth troops would get onto the offensive with dramatic effect (see pages 45–47). Note the geography of the impassable Qattara depression to the south of the line. WO 234/110 (15)

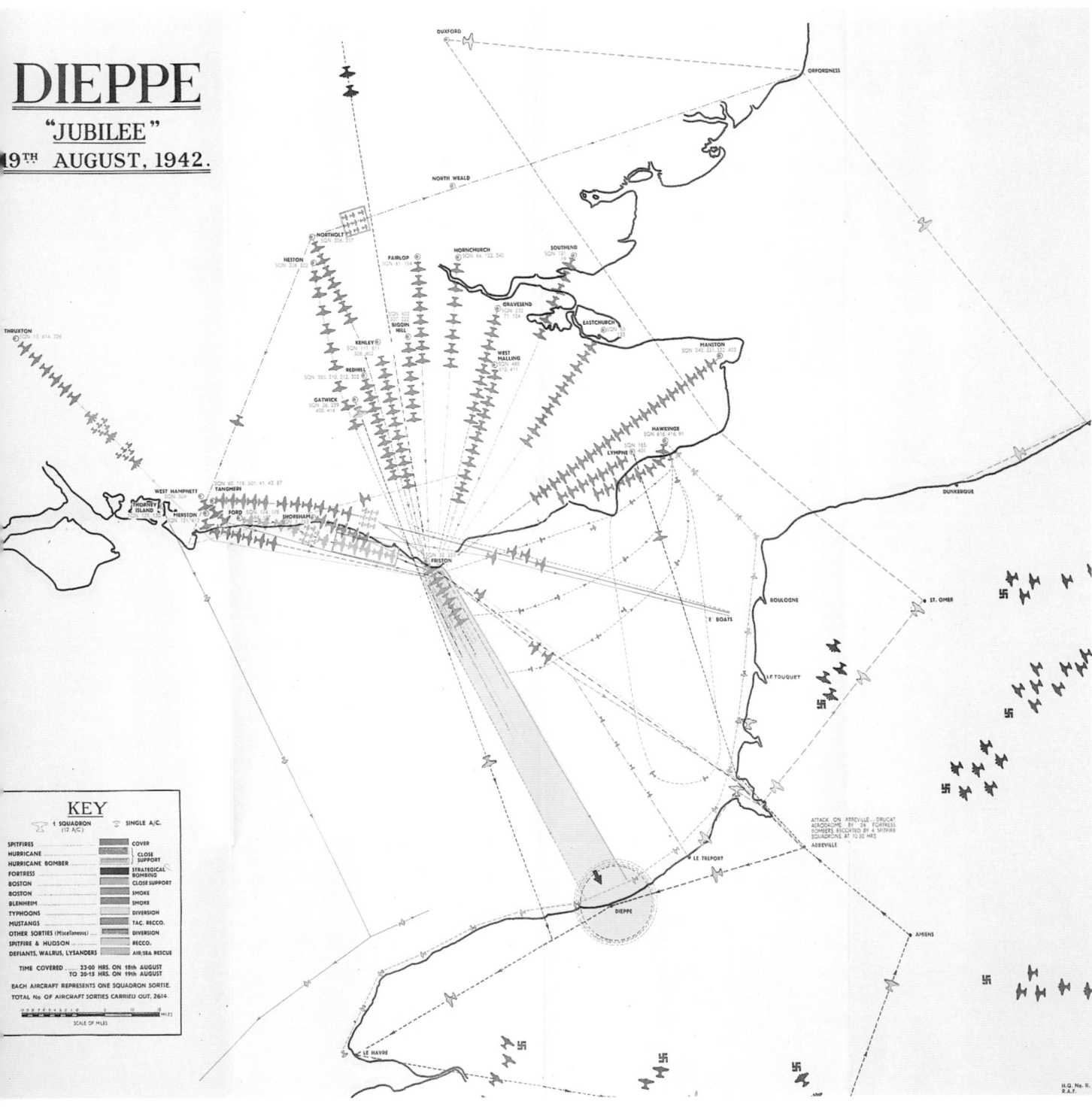

DIEPPE
"JUBILEE"
19ᵀᴴ AUGUST, 1942.

DIEPPE: OPERATION 'JUBILEE', 19 AUGUST 1942

The disastrous Dieppe raid was one of the most controversial military operations of the war. It was planned as an experiment in landing technique, in anticipation of the opening of the Second Front. The objective was to take and briefly hold the French port of Dieppe with a mixed force of 5,000 Canadian and 1,000 British troops. The force was landed on 19 August 1942 and was immediately subjected to intensive air and sea attacks. Once ashore the raiders had only intermittent close air support and within a few hours the operation had become a disaster. Of the 6,000 Allied troops involved, 4,000 were killed, captured or wounded. This chart shows RAF operations during the raid, and the location of German units in France. The air battle over the beachheads was the most intensive of the war in the West. DEFE 2/551

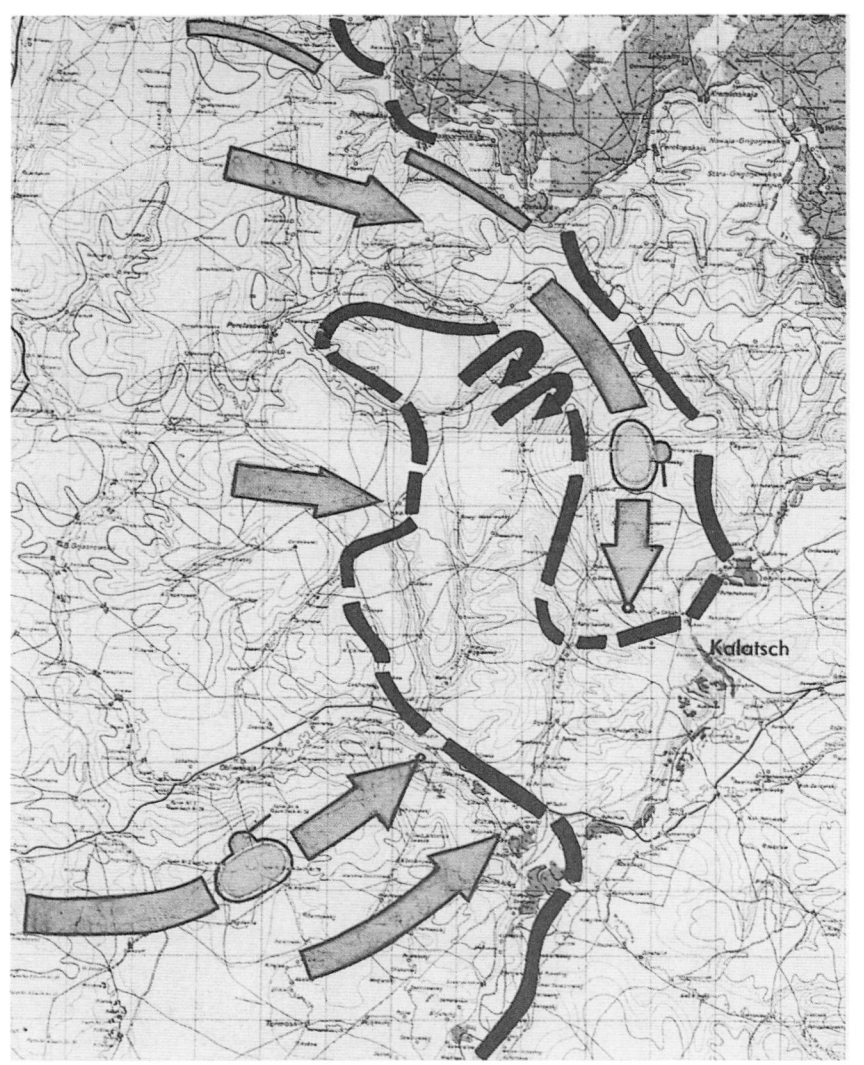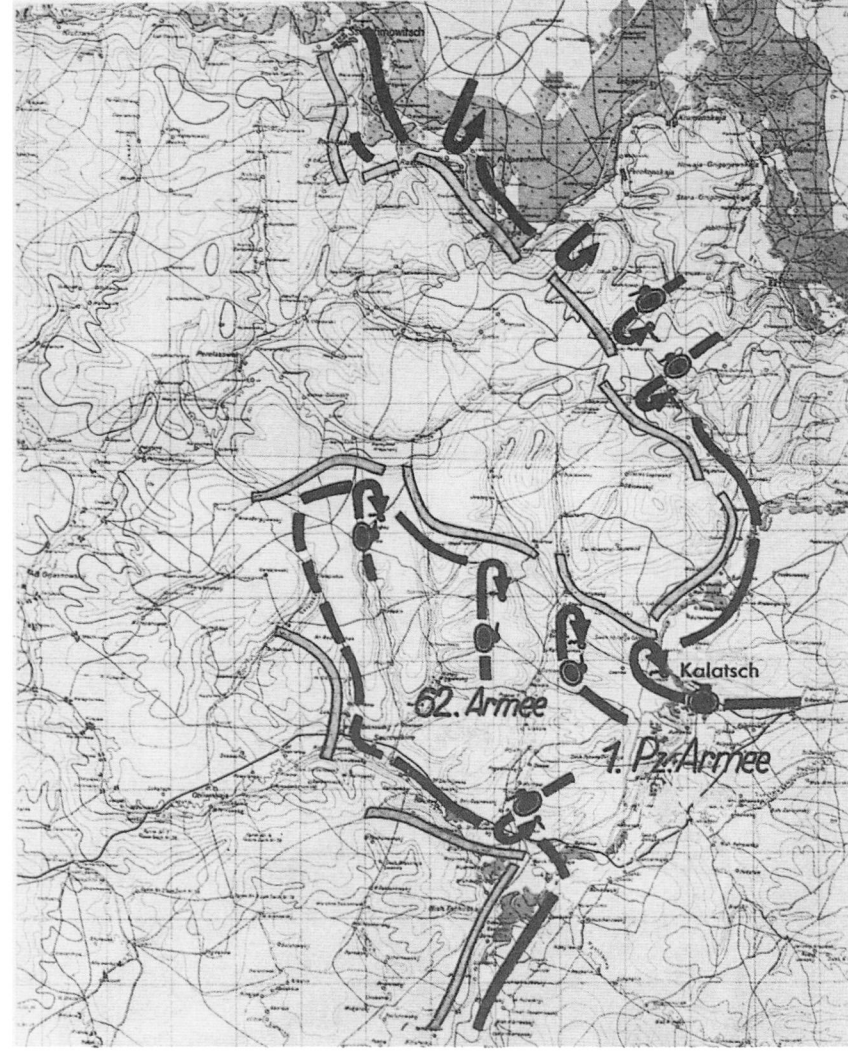

RUSSIA: KALACH
24 JULY–10 AUGUST 1942

ABOVE AND RIGHT: This series of maps was published in Signal, the official magazine of the German armed forces for the duration of the war, although there were others for each of the naval, air and land forces. Its pages contained details of the great battles, albeit in 'edited' form. This series shows what Signal identified as the destruction of the Soviet Sixty-second Army in a great encirclement battle west of Kalach. The maps illustrate well the way that Operation 'Barbarossa' and German operations in Russia were fought in 1941–42: In the first (above), the wings circle around the Soviet forces; in the second, Soviet counter-attacks to relieve the salient are beaten off (above right); in the third (opposite, left), the encirclement is completed; and then in the fourth (opposite, right) the pocket — the Germans called it the 'Kessel' (cauldron), an apt name — is squeezed and the forces within destroyed. Typically, those who survived the battle had little chance of surviving the march to the rear and captivity thereafter. After this victory, the German forces headed toward Stalingrad, which would become the anvil that blunted their hammer blows. WO 208/1819

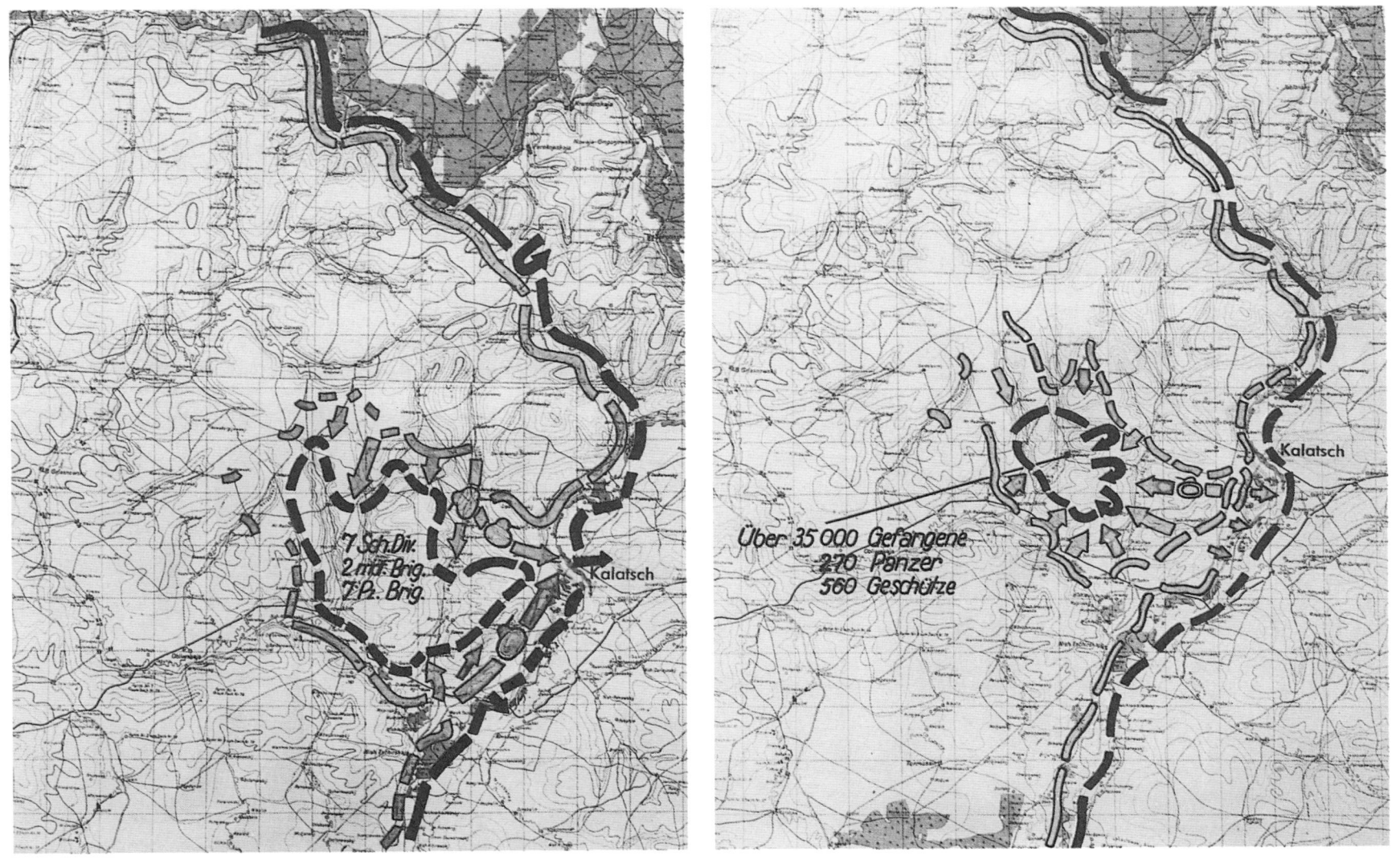

7.Sch.Div.
2.mot.Brig.
7.Pz.Brig.

Kalatsch

Über 35 000 Gefangene
270 Panzer
560 Geschütze

Kalatsch

SOUTHWEST RUSSIA AND THE CAUCASUS, 14 AUGUST 1942 – 10 OCTOBER 1942

RIGHT AND FAR RIGHT: The shifting front line on the southern sector of the Eastern Front, between mid-August and mid-October 1942. The Caucasus, situated between the Black and Caspian Seas, was a strategically highly important region as it contained the oilfields and a huge pipeline that supplied the Red Army with much of its fuel. Control of the region was bitterly disputed between July 1942 and mid-1943. The battle for Stalingrad was the decisive battle of the war on the Eastern Front — and, possibly, the decisive battle of the war against Germany — and the primary objective of the July 1942 German offensive in the south. The city was attacked by the Sixth Army on 19 August and by September had almost fallen, although at enormous cost **(see also map on page 53).** WO 208/1768

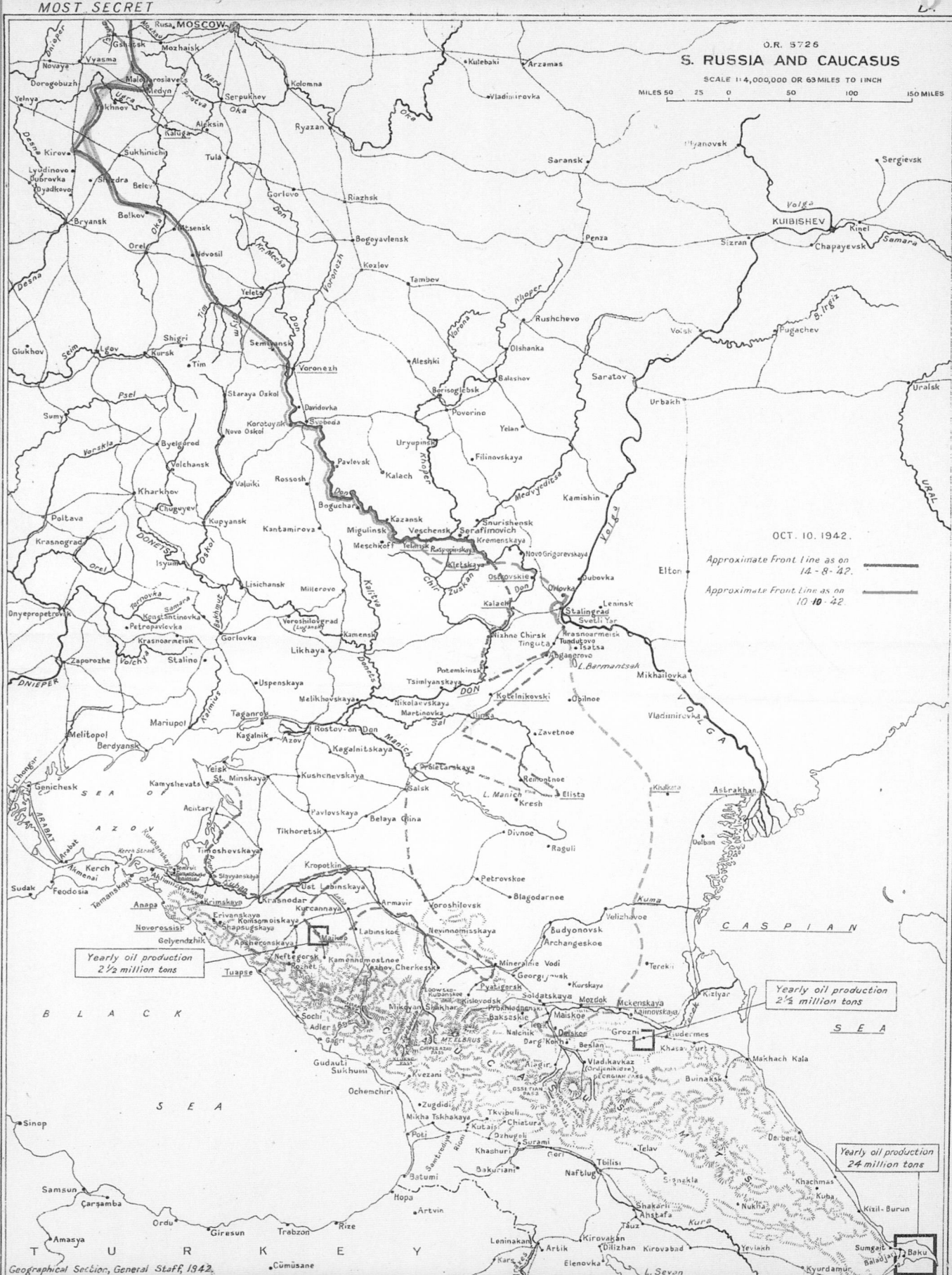

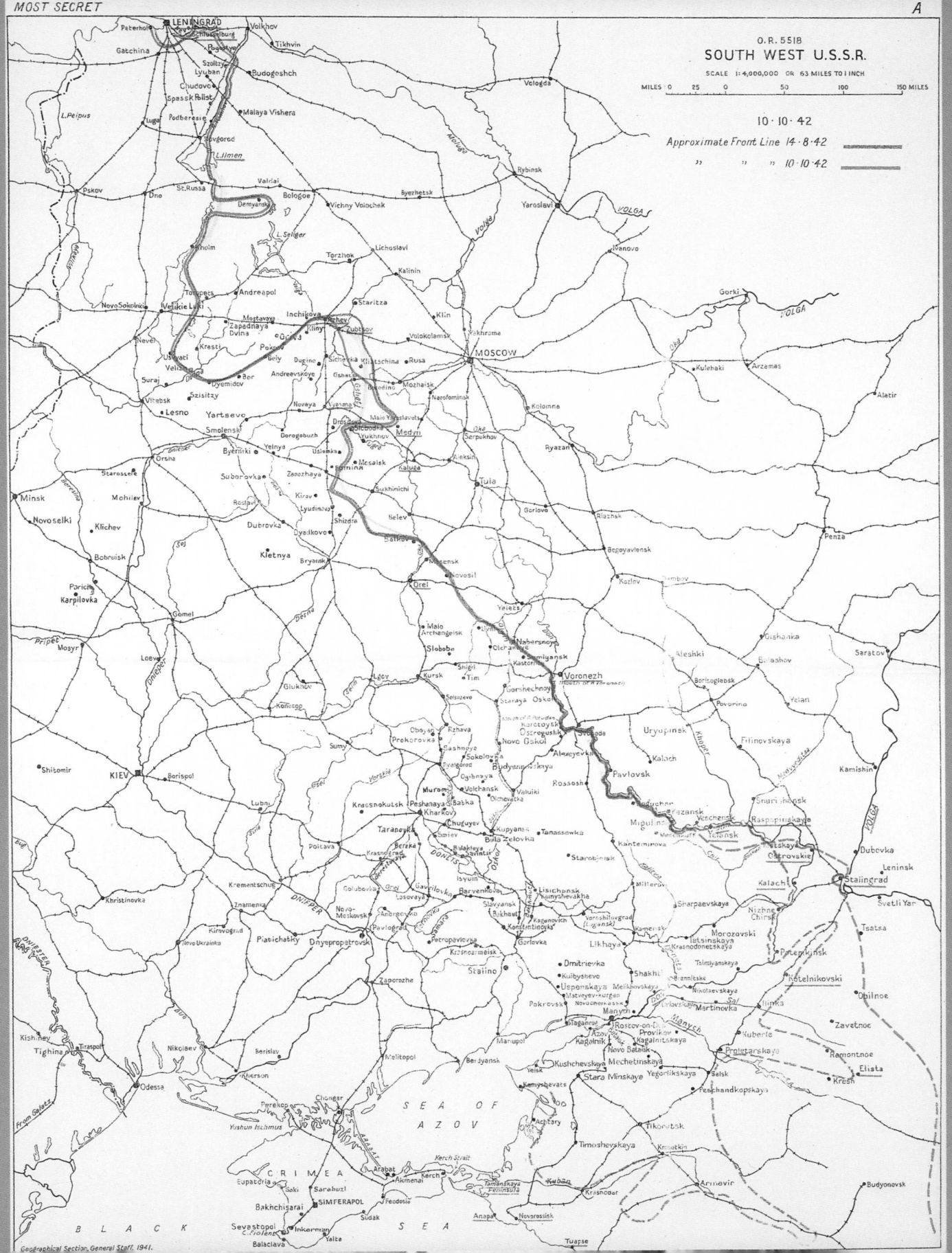

O.R. 5518
SOUTH WEST U.S.S.R.
SCALE 1:4,000,000 OR 63 MILES TO 1 INCH

MILES 0 25   0   50   100   150 MILES

10·10·42
Approximate Front Line 14·8·42
"   "   " 10·10·42

Geographical Section, General Staff, 1941.

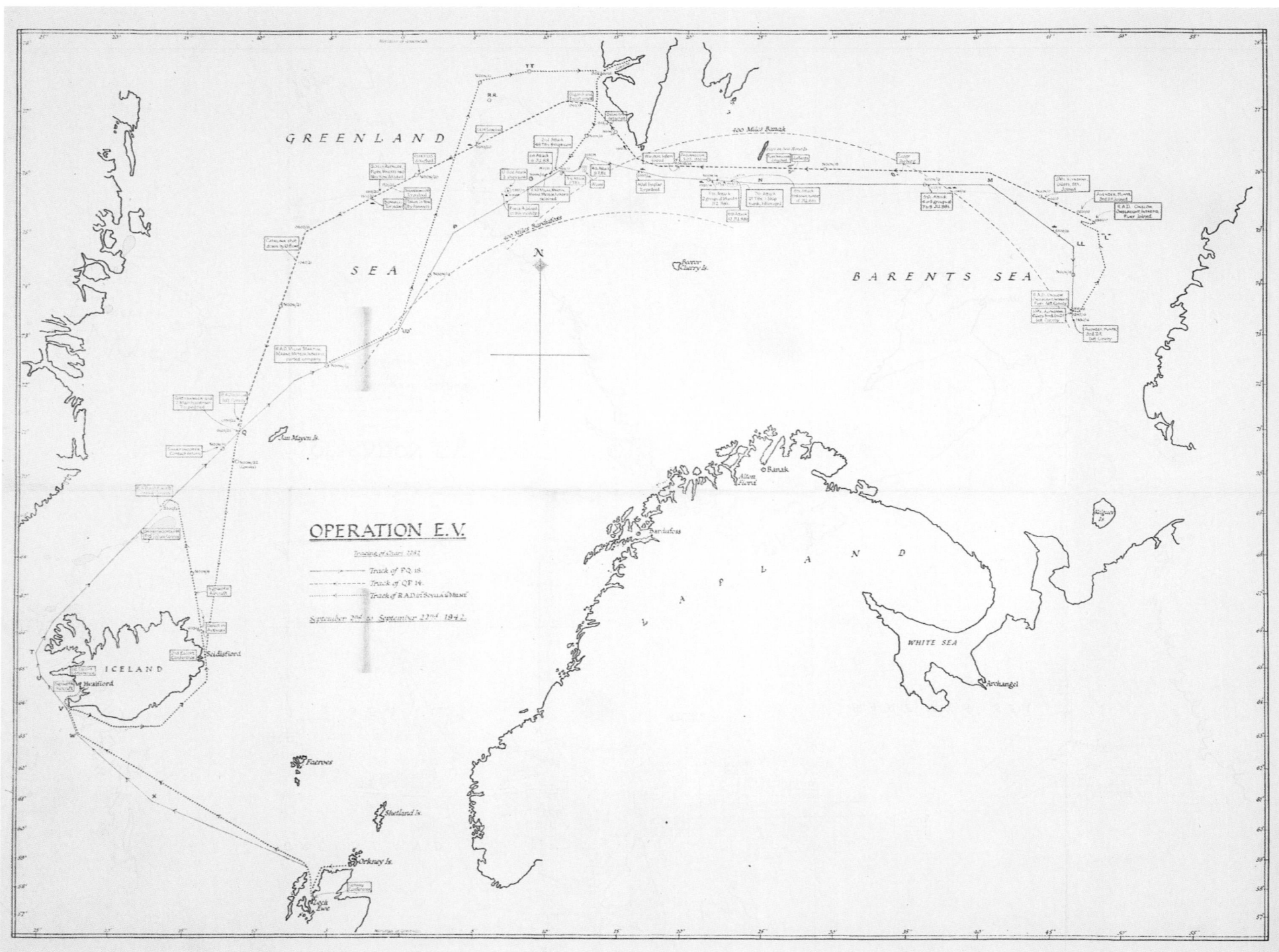

OPERATION E.V.

Tracking of Albert 1242

—————— *Track of PQ 18.*

— — — — *Track of QP 14.*

.... *Track of R.A.D.or Scylla & Milne*

September 2nd to September 27th 1942.

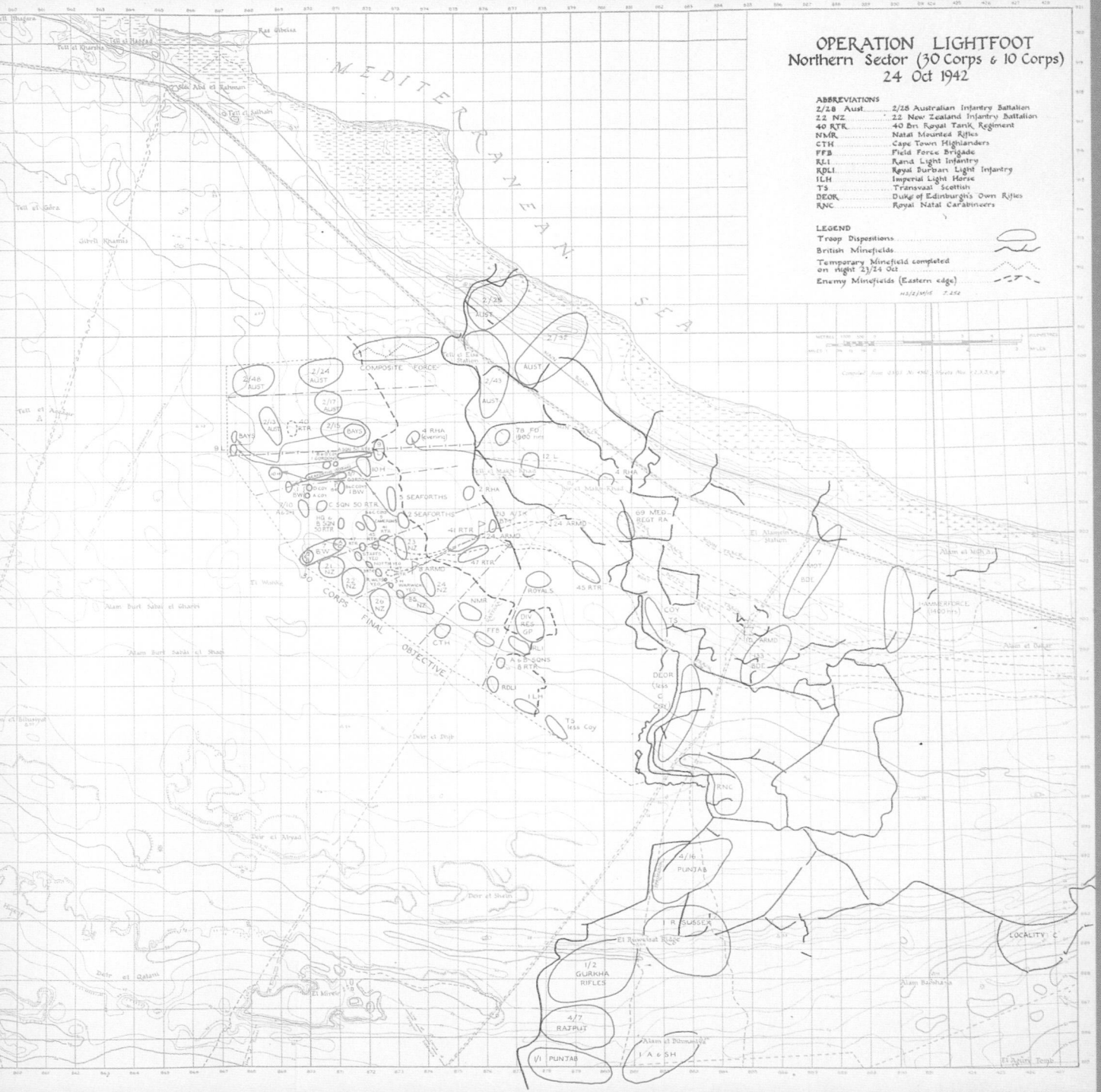

OPERATION LIGHTFOOT
Northern Sector (30 Corps & 10 Corps)
24 Oct 1942

ABBREVIATIONS

2/28 Aust .... 2/28 Australian Infantry Battalion
22 NZ .... 22 New Zealand Infantry Battalion
40 RTR .... 40 Bn Royal Tank Regiment
NMR .... Natal Mounted Rifles
CTH .... Cape Town Highlanders
FFB .... Field Force Brigade
RLI .... Rand Light Infantry
RDLI .... Royal Durban Light Infantry
ILH .... Imperial Light Horse
TS .... Transvaal Scottish
DEOR .... Duke of Edinburgh's Own Rifles
RNC .... Royal Natal Carabineers

LEGEND
Troop Dispositions
British Minefields
Temporary Minefield completed
on night 23/24 Oct
Enemy Minefields (Eastern edge)

CONVOY PQ18, 2 SEPTEMBER 1942

FAR LEFT: The route taken by Convoy PQ18 as it travelled from Liverpool to the Russian White Sea port of Archangel in the weeks following 2 September 1942. The Arctic convoys were particularly hazardous. The merchantmen had to contend with U-boats and long-range Focke-Wulf Condor aircraft, as well as sub-Arctic weather conditions. MFQ 90 (6)

EL ALAMEIN, 24–25 OCTOBER 1942

LEFT AND PAGES 46 AND 47: Maps of the northern and southern sectors of the British Eighth Army positions at El Alamein, showing the positions of X, XIII and XXX Corps prior to Operation 'Lightfoot'. Montgomery, who in August had replaced Auchinleck as C-in-C in North Africa, had built up a force that included 230,000 men and 1,200 tanks. Opposing this force across the minefields, Rommel's Deutsches Afrika Korps had only 540 tanks (most of them obsolete Italian types) and 80,000 men. Another of his problems was a critical shortage of fuel.

The main British attack was opened by a massive artillery barrage along the southern sector on the evening of the 23rd, followed by an infantry assault at 0200hrs on the 24th. The attack was concentrated along a narrow front a few miles south of the coast, which is shown in more detail on the later map **(page 47).** This drove a wedge into the German positions but became bogged down by minefields and defensive fire, and the diversionary attack to the south by the 4th Indian Division and XIII Corps broke down. CAB 44/102

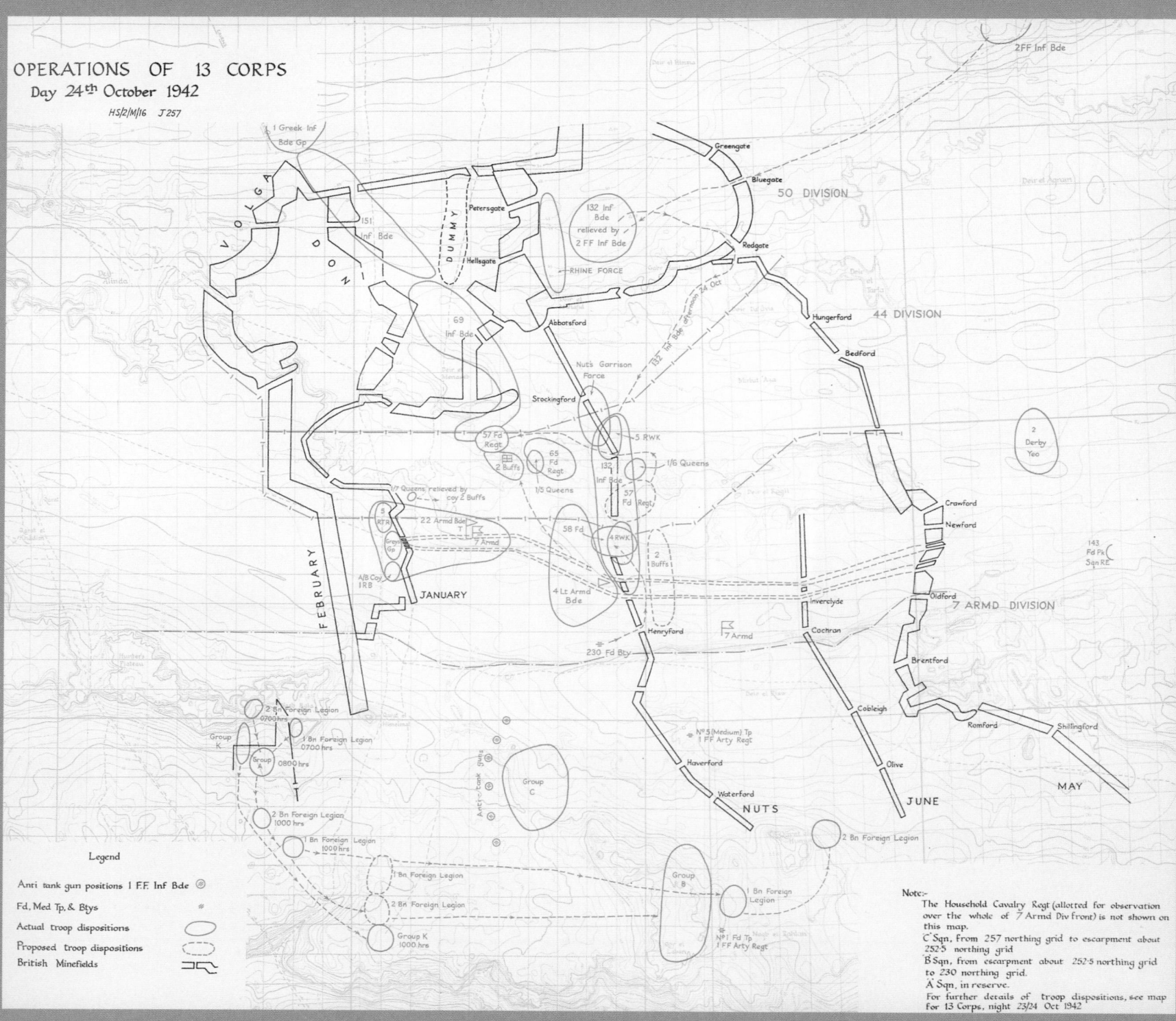

OPERATIONS OF 13 CORPS
Day 24th October 1942

HS/2/M/16   J257

Legend

Anti tank gun positions 1 F.F. Inf Bde

Fd, Med Tp, & Btys

Actual troop dispositions

Proposed troop dispositions

British Minefields

Note:-

The Household Cavalry Regt (allotted for observation over the whole of 7 Armd Div front) is not shown on this map.

C Sqn, from 257 northing grid to escarpment about 252·5 northing grid

B Sqn, from escarpment about 252·5 northing grid to 230 northing grid.

A Sqn, in reserve.

For further details of troop dispositions, see map for 13 Corps, night 23/24 Oct 1942

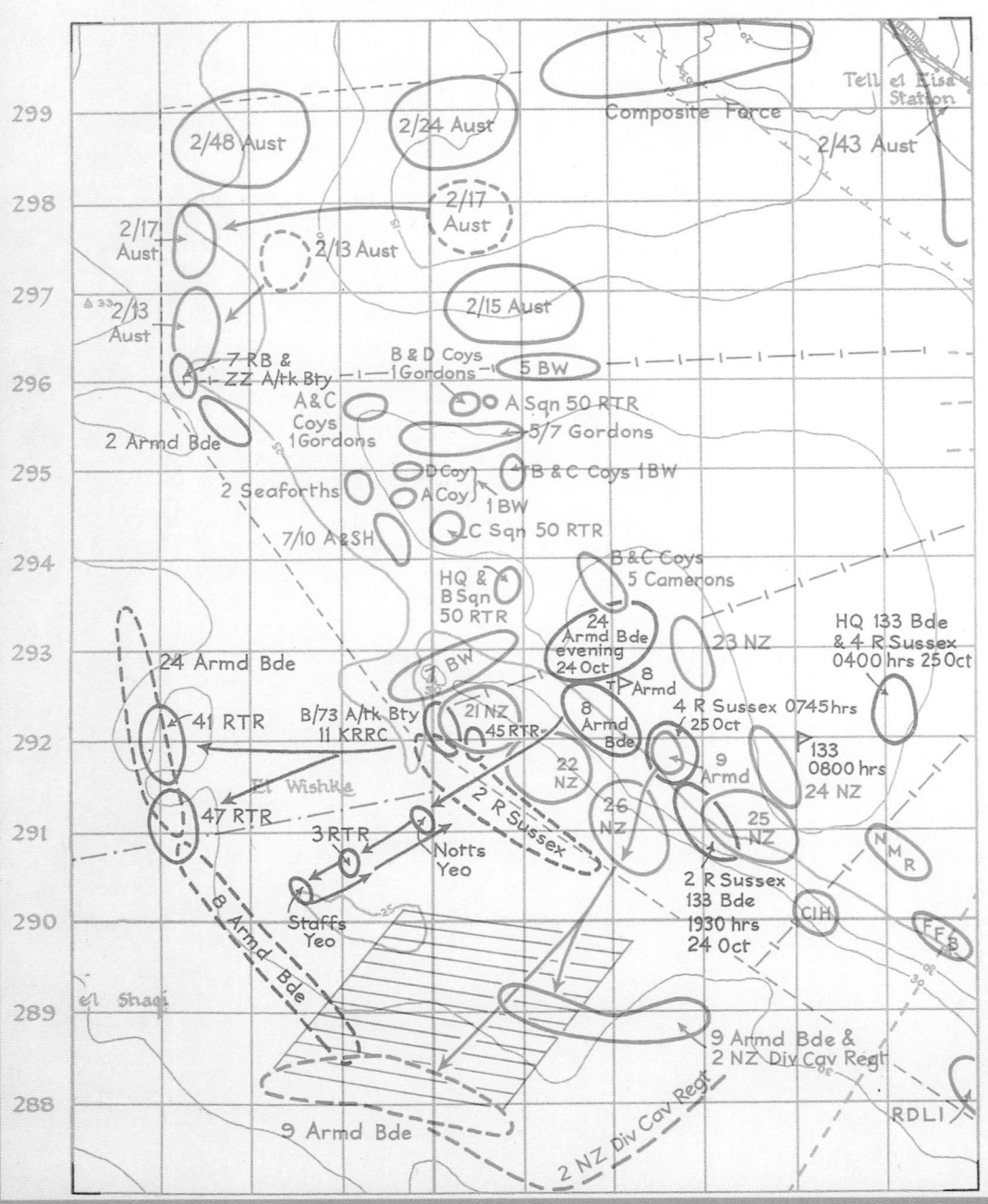

OPERATIONS on 30 CORPS FRONT
Night 24/25 Oct 1942

Note:- Operations on 4 Ind Div Front on night 24/25 Oct are shown on a separate map.

Tell el Eisa Station

Composite Force

2/43 Aust

2/48 Aust
2/24 Aust
2/17 Aust
2/13 Aust
2/17 Aust
2/13 Aust
2/15 Aust

7 RB & ZZ A/tk Bty
B & D Coys 1 Gordons
5 BW

A & C Coys 1 Gordons
A Sqn 50 RTR
5/7 Gordons

2 Armd Bde
D Coy
A Coy
B & C Coys 1 BW
1 BW

2 Seaforths
7/10 A & SH
C Sqn 50 RTR

B & C Coys 5 Camerons

HQ & B Sqn 50 RTR

24 Armd Bde evening 24 Oct
23 NZ
HQ 133 Bde & 4 R Sussex 0400 hrs 25 Oct

24 Armd Bde
8 Armd
4 R Sussex 0745 hrs 25 Oct

41 RTR
B/73 A/tk Bty 11 KRRC
21 NZ
45 RTR
8 Armd Bde
9 Armd
133 0800 hrs 24 NZ

47 RTR
El Wishka
22 NZ
26 NZ
25 NZ
NMR

3 RTR
Notts Yeo
2 R Sussex
2 R Sussex 133 Bde 1930 hrs 24 Oct
CIH
FFR

Staffs Yeo

8 Armd Bde
el Shaqi
9 Armd Bde & 2 NZ Div Cav Regt
RDLI

9 Armd Bde
2 NZ Div Cav Regt

Legend

Troops of 30 Corps { planned / actual

Troops of 10 Corps { planned / actual

Artillery barrage

Final objective of 30 Corps

HS/2/M/19   J.261

47

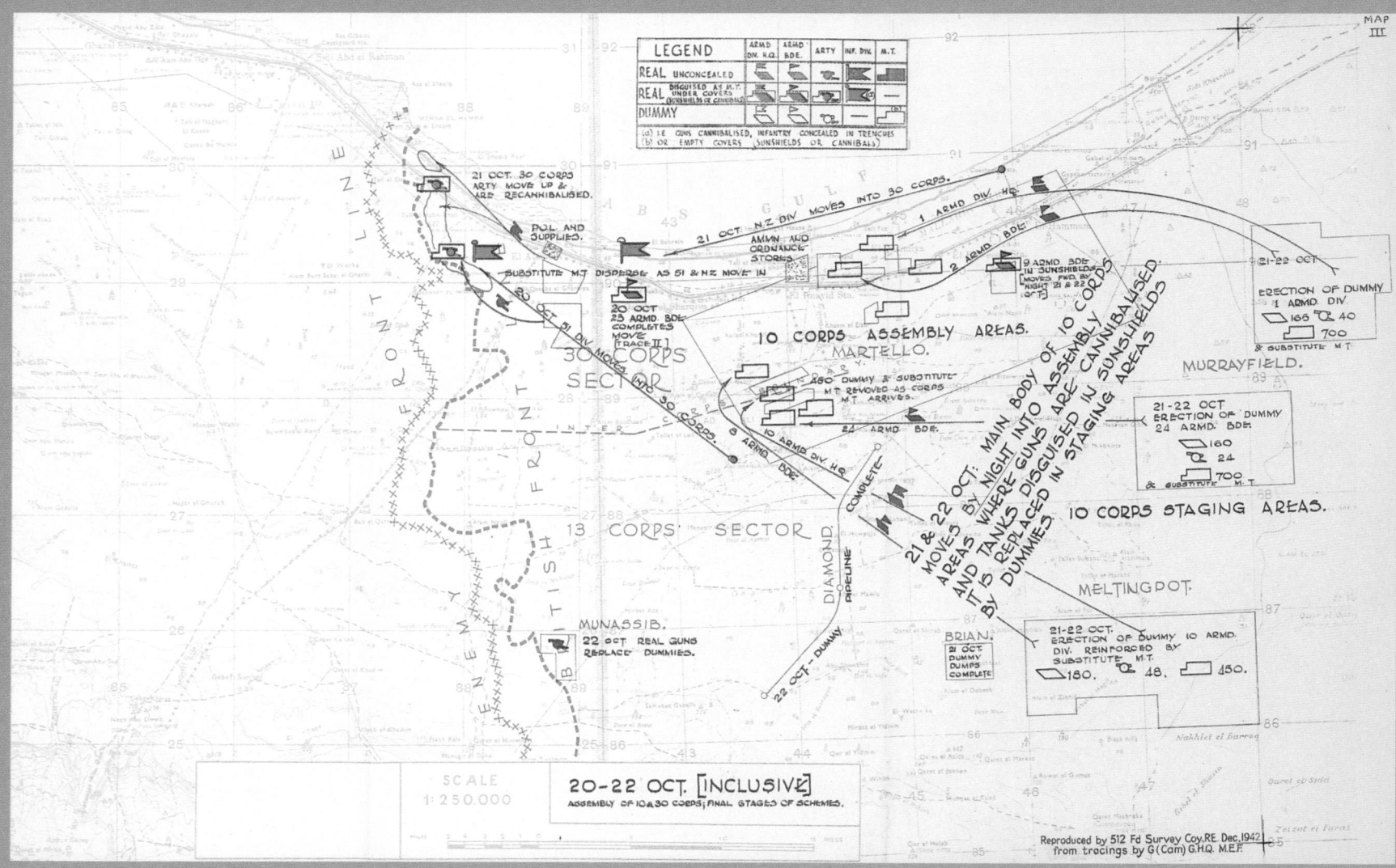

DECEPTION PRIOR TO EL ALAMEIN, 21–23 OCTOBER 1942

ABOVE AND RIGHT: Prior to the battle of El Alamein (Operation 'Lightfoot'), in order to fool enemy reconnaissance and intelligence operations, the Eighth Army put in place a number of deception plans. At their most basic, these plans saw lorries disguised to look like tanks, false gun emplacements and tanks disguised as motor vehicles ('Sunshields' and 'Cannibals'). On the day of the attack, and during the battle, there were feint attacks and diversions. These maps show the extent of the deception operations. WO 201/2024 (IV) (V)

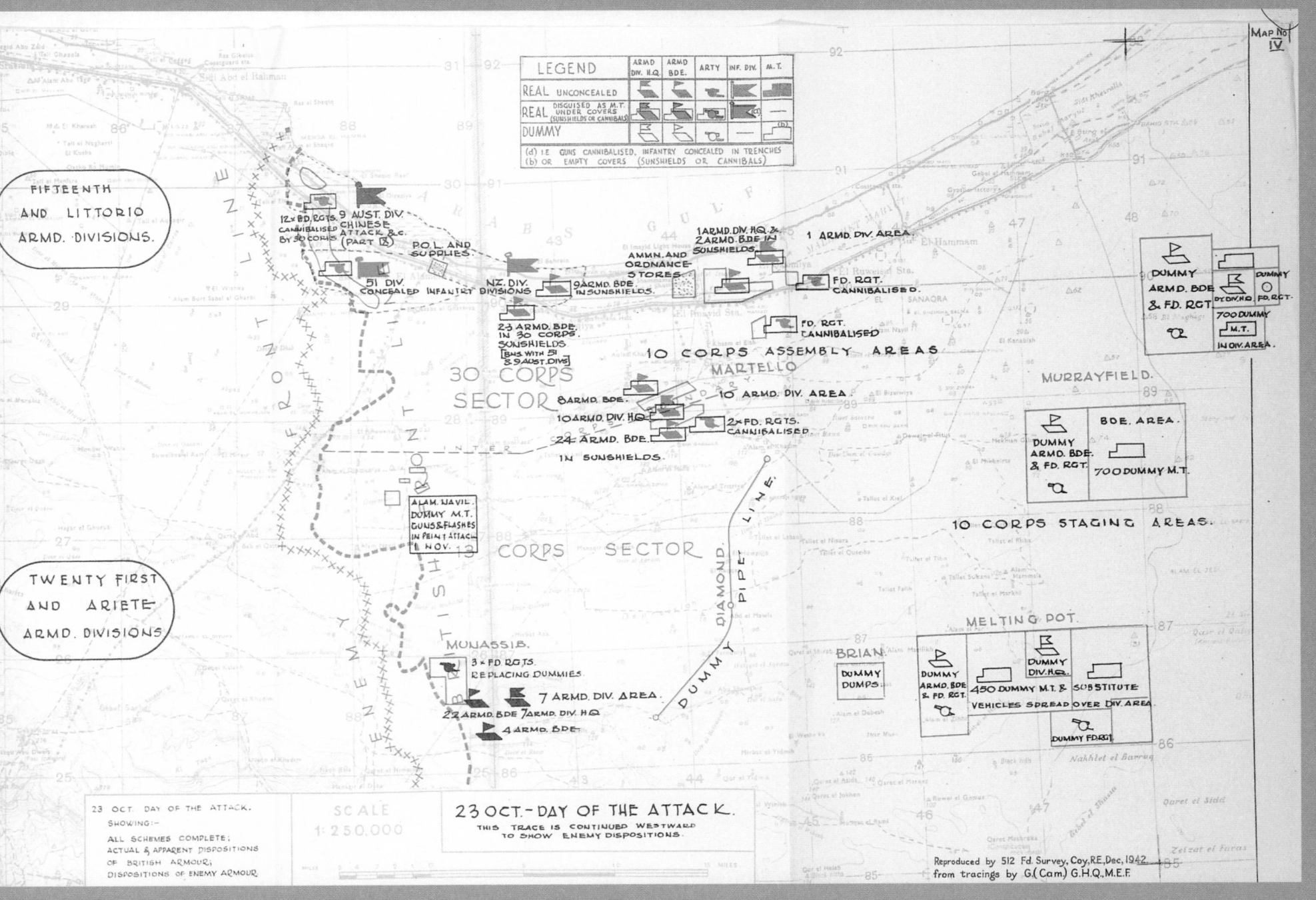

FIFTEENTH AND LITTORIO ARMD. DIVISIONS.

TWENTY FIRST AND ARIETE ARMD. DIVISIONS.

LEGEND	ARMD. DIV. H.Q.	ARMD. BDE.	ARTY.	INF. DIV.	M.T.
REAL UNCONCEALED					
REAL DISGUISED AS M.T. UNDER COVERS (SUNSHIELDS OR CANNIBALS)					
DUMMY					

(d) I.E. GUNS CANNIBALISED, INFANTRY CONCEALED IN TRENCHES
(b) OR EMPTY COVERS (SUNSHIELDS OR CANNIBALS)

12 × FD. RGTS. CANNIBALISED BY 30 CORPS

9 AUST. DIV. CHINESE ATTACK &c. (PART X)

P.O.L. AND SUPPLIES.

51 DIV. CONCEALED INFANTRY DIVISIONS

N.Z. DIV.

9 ARMD. BDE. IN SUNSHIELDS.

AMMN. AND ORDNANCE STORES

1 ARMD. DIV. HQ. & 2 ARMD. BDE. IN SUNSHIELDS

1 ARMD. DIV. AREA

FD. RGT. CANNIBALISED

DUMMY ARMD. BDE. & FD. RGT.

DUMMY

DY. DIV. H.Q.   FD. RGT.

700 DUMMY M.T. IN DIV. AREA.

23 ARMD. BDE. IN 30 CORPS. SUNSHIELDS
[BNS. WITH 51 & 9 AUST. DIVS.]

FD. RGT. CANNIBALISED

10 CORPS ASSEMBLY AREAS

MARTELLO

MURRAYFIELD.

30 CORPS SECTOR

8 ARMD. BDE.

10 ARMD. DIV. H.Q.

24 ARMD. BDE. IN SUNSHIELDS.

10 ARMD. DIV. AREA

2 × FD. RGTS. CANNIBALISED.

BDE. AREA.

DUMMY ARMD. BDE. & FD. RGT.

700 DUMMY M.T.

10 CORPS STAGING AREAS.

ALAM. NAYIL. DUMMY M.T. GUNS & FLASHES IN PRELIM. ATTACK 1 NOV.

13 CORPS SECTOR

DIAMOND PIPE LINE.

DUMMY PIPE LINE.

MELTING POT.

MUNASSIB.

3 × FD. RGTS. REPLACING DUMMIES.

7 ARMD. DIV. AREA

22 ARMD. BDE. 7 ARMD. DIV. H.Q

4 ARMD. BDE.

BRIAN

DUMMY DUMPS.

DUMMY ARMD. BDE. & FD. RGT.

DUMMY DIV. H.Q.

450 DUMMY M.T. & SUBSTITUTE VEHICLES SPREAD OVER DIV. AREA.

DUMMY FD. RGT.

23 OCT. DAY OF THE ATTACK. SHOWING:—
ALL SCHEMES COMPLETE;
ACTUAL & APPARENT DISPOSITIONS OF BRITISH ARMOUR;
DISPOSITIONS OF ENEMY ARMOUR.

SCALE 1:250,000

23 OCT.—DAY OF THE ATTACK.
THIS TRACE IS CONTINUED WESTWARD TO SHOW ENEMY DISPOSITIONS.

Reproduced by 512 Fd. Survey, Coy, RE, Dec, 1942. from tracings by G.(Cam) G.H.Q., M.E.F.

GERMAN NIGHT AIR DEFENCES, DECEMBER 1942

ABOVE AND RIGHT: Three maps showing the most heavily defended areas of northwest Europe at the end of 1942. The first **(above)** shows that the Dutch coast (the point where Allied bombers crossed into occupied Europe on the outbound leg of their night missions) and the industrial Ruhr region of Germany were particularly heavily defended by searchlight belts, flak units and radar stations, all of which fell under the jurisdiction of Generalfeldmarschall Goering's Luftwaffe. As the Allied bomber offensive against German cities intensified, more and more German aircraft were committed to the defence of the Homeland. The fighter defences became increasingly sophisticated, with ground-based radar operators coordinating attacks by specialised night fighters.

The second map **(above right)** shows the areas patrolled by the four main Nachtgeschwader (nightfighter wings) charged with the night defence of Germany. These units were equipped with Junkers Ju88 and Messerschmitt Bf110 aircraft that were increasingly obsolescent.

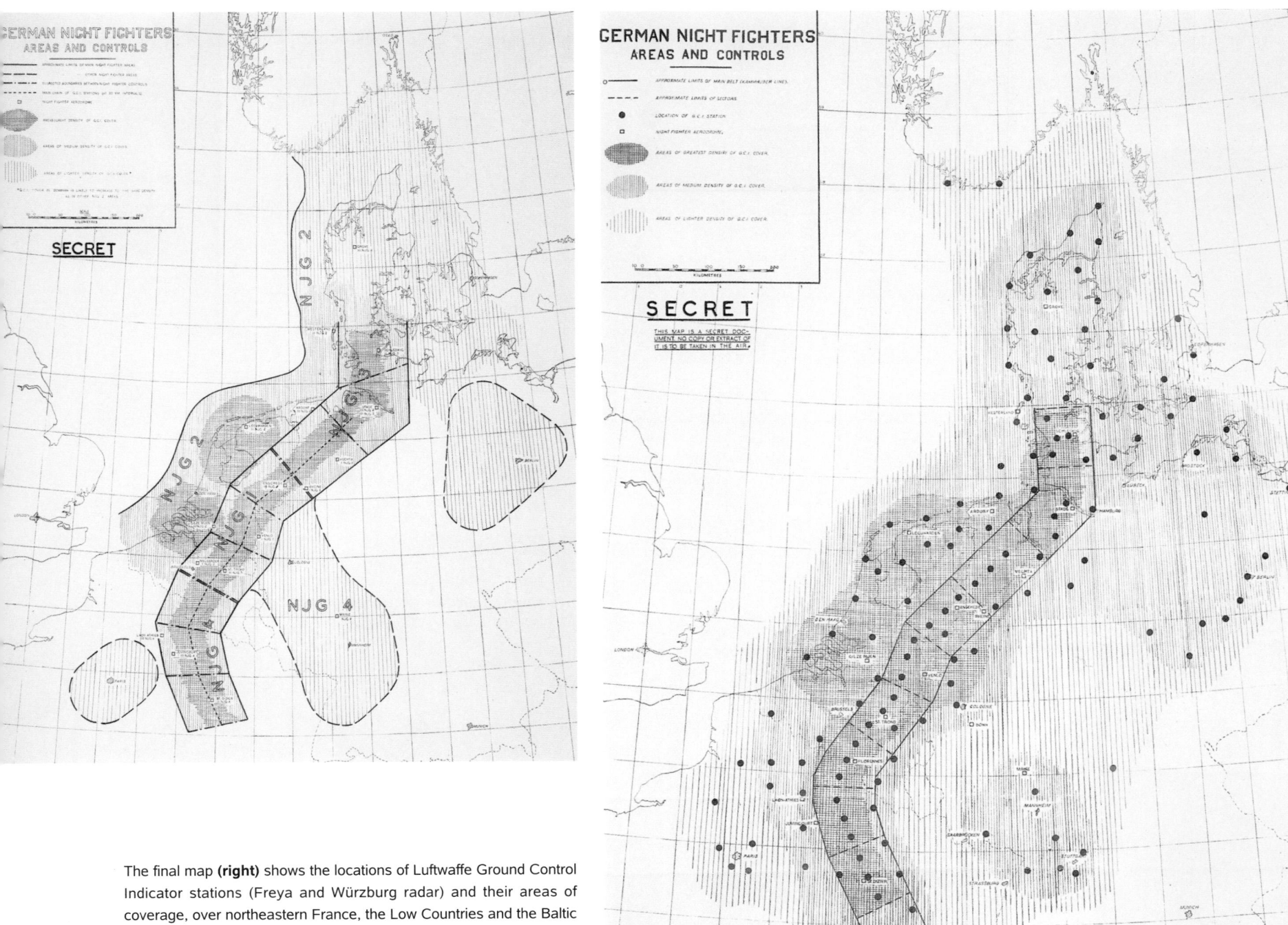

The final map **(right)** shows the locations of Luftwaffe Ground Control Indicator stations (Freya and Würzburg radar) and their areas of coverage, over northeastern France, the Low Countries and the Baltic Coast. This defensive belt was known as the 'Kammhuber Line' after the major-general promoted General der Nachtflieger (General of Nightfighters) in October 1940. MPI 668 (6) MPI 467 (2) MPI 467 (1)

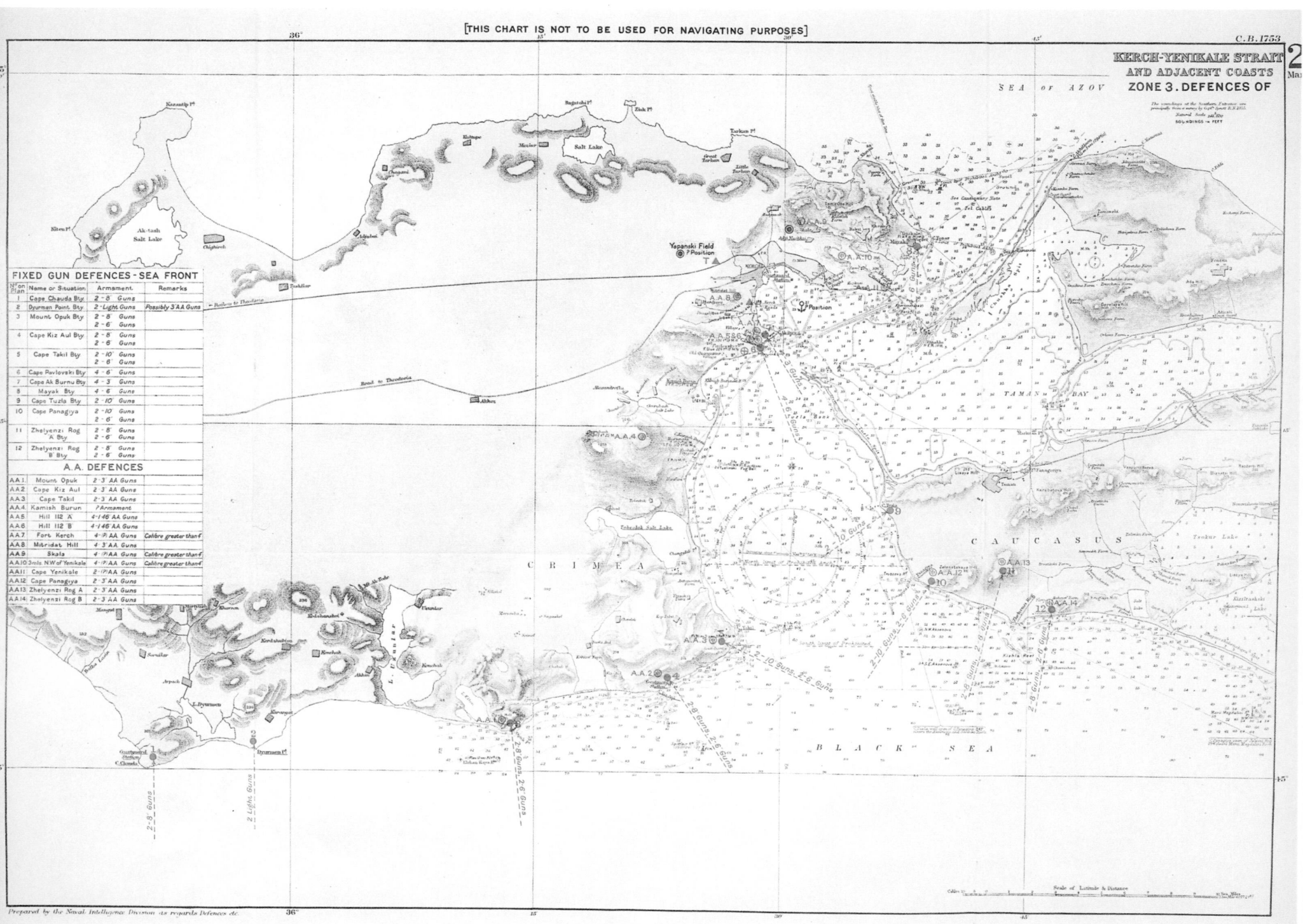

Map: MOST SECRET — O.R. 5720 — S. RUSSIA AND CAUCASUS. SCALE 1:4,000,000 OR 63 MILES TO 1INCH

RUSSIAN FORCES

Front Line 19 Nov. 1942	————	
" " 7 Feb. 1943	– – – –	
Army Groups or Fronts	·········	
Armoured Armies		(5т)
Guards Armies		(3G)
Ordinary Armies		(6)
Reserve Armies		(10R)
Cavalry Army		(1C)
"Popov" Armoured Group		(P)
Armies grouped into one command after reorganisation of fronts		(24)

Geographical Section, General Staff, 1943.

SOUTHWEST RUSSIA AND THE CAUCASUS, 19 NOVEMBER 1942 – 7 FEBRUARY 1943

LEFT: The Soviet counter-attack at Stalingrad, codenamed Operation 'Uranus', was launched by Southwestern Front forces under Zhukov and Vasilkevsky on 19 November. This was followed by attacks in the northern and southern sectors of the German salient at Stalingrad which trapped von Paulus's Sixth Army, which stood firm by Hitler's orders rather than retreat. An attempt to resupply the trapped army by air during the winter completely failed and at the end of January von Paulus surrendered the 94,000 survivors. WO 208/1768

CRIMEA, 1942

FAR LEFT: German sea and air defences on and around the Kerch Peninsula (the eastern tip of the Crimean peninsula in southwestern Russia). On 20 October 1941 German forces under Manstein attacked the Soviet lines across the five-mile wide gateway to the Crimea, the Perekop Isthmus, aiming towards Sevastopol in the west and the Kerch Peninsula in the east. In December Soviet forces launched attacks on the Kerch to divert German forces attacking Sevastopol, and there followed a bitter series of battles on the peninsula, which was taken by von Manstein in mid-May 1942 at a cost to the Soviets of two whole armies. Sevastopol fell on 4 July. It would be retaken by the Russians in May 1944. WO 208/1783

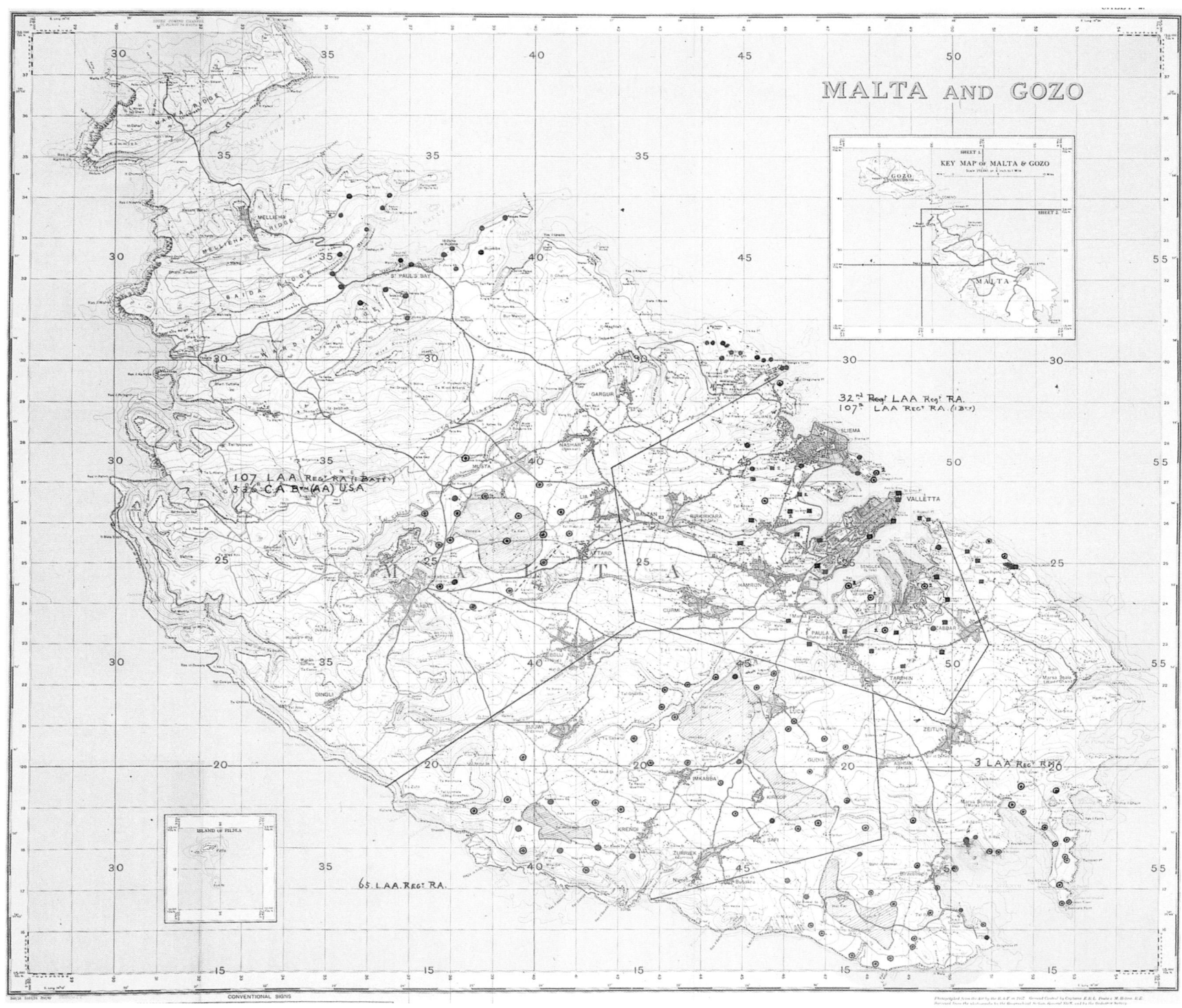

MALTA AND GOZO

32nd Regt LAA Regt RA.
107th LAA Regt RA. (1 Bty)

107. LAA Regt RA (1 Batty)
536 CA B₁ (AA) USA

3 LAA Regt RMO

65. LAA. Regt. RA.

CONVENTIONAL SIGNS

54

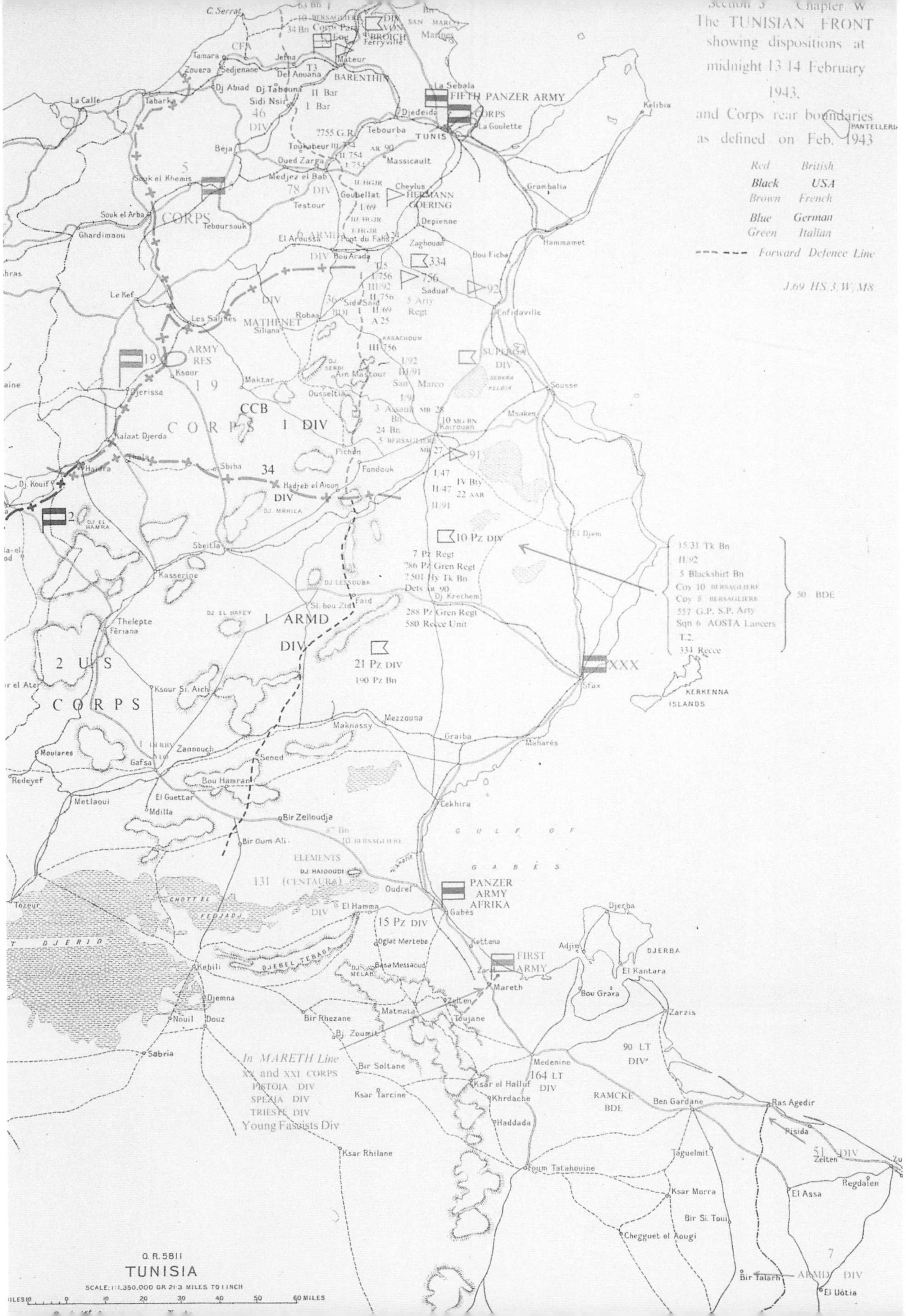
The TUNISIAN FRONT
showing dispositions at
midnight 13/14 February
1943,
and Corps rear boundaries
as defined on Feb. 1943
Red British
Black USA
Brown French
Blue German
Green Italian
Forward Defence Line
J.69 HS/3/W/M8
FIFTH PANZER ARMY
TUNIS
La Goulette
Kelibia
PANTELLERIA
Grombalia
Hammamet
Bou Ficha
Enfidaville
Sousse
Msaken
Kairouan
El Djem
Sfax
KERKENNA
ISLANDS
Mahares
Graiba
Mezzouna
Maknassy
Sened
Gafsa
Zannouch
Moulares
Redeyef
Metlaoui
El Guettar
Bou Hamran
Bir Zelloudja
Bir Oum Ali
Cekhira
G U L F O F
G A B E S
PANZER
ARMY
AFRIKA
Gabès
El Hamma
Oudref
15 Pz DIV
Kettana
FIRST
ARMY
Mareth
Djerba
DJERBA
El Kantara
Bou Grara
Zarzis
Medenine
164 LT
DIV
90 LT
DIV
RAMCKE
BDE
Ben Gardane
Ras Agedir
Foum Tatahouine
Ksar Rhilane
Kebili
Douz
Sabria
Tozeur
Sbeitla
Kasserine
Thelepte
Fériana
Ksour Si. Aich
2 US
CORPS
1 ARMD
DIV
21 Pz DIV
10 Pz DIV
Faid
Sidi bou Zid
Pichon
Fondouk
Sbiba
Hadjeb el Aioun
Maktar
Ousseltia
CCB
1 DIV
34
DIV
Souk el Arba
Souk el Khemis
Beja
Medjez el Bab
Testour
Goubellat
HERMANN
GOERING
Depienne
Zaghouan
Massicault
Tebourba
Djedeida
La Sebala
Mateur
Ferryville
Tabarka
La Calle
Sedjenane
Ghardimaou
Le Kef
Les Salines
Siliana
Robaa
Kalaat Djerda
Thala
Haidra
Dj Kouif
5
CORPS
78 DIV
46 DIV
19
XXX
50 BDE
In MARETH Line
XX and XXI CORPS
PISTOIA DIV
SPEZIA DIV
TRIESTE DIV
Young Fascists Div
Matmata
Toujane
Bir Soltane
Ksar Tarcine
Ksar el Hallouf
Khrdache
Haddada
Zeltene
Taguelmit
Ksar Morra
Bir Si Toui
Chegguet el Aougi
Bir Tlarh
El Assa
Regdalen
Zelten
51 DIV
7 ARMD DIV
El Uotia
O.R.5811
TUNISIA
SCALE: 1:1,350,000 OR 21·3 MILES TO 1 INCH
MILES 10 0 10 20 30 40 50 60 MILES

TUNISIA, 13/14 FEBRUARY 1943

LEFT AND PAGE 56: The port of Tunis was a major supply point for the Axis armies in North Africa, and likewise a major objective for Allied attacks. The slow advance of American forces after the landings in Morocco (Operation 'Torch') allowed the Axis to resupply through Tunis and, until February 1943, they held out against attacks from the west. Rommel's forces had, by this time, been pushed back all the way across Libya. In mid-February Rommel and von Arnim launched an attack from southern Tunisia through the Kasserine Pass at the U.S. II Army Corps positions along the Western Dorsale, trying to split the mass of men and material between the Tunisian front and the Allied bases at Bone **(see top left of map at left)** and Constantine. Despite some success, by the afternoon of 22 February Rommel had lost faith in the attack and began to withdraw. CAB 44/115

MALTA, AIR DEFENCES 1943

FAR LEFT: This map shows the light anti-aircraft defences on the Mediterranean islands of Malta and Gozo, which were vital bases for Allied aircraft and shipping during the Desert War. Because of its strategic importance, and relative proximity to Axis airfields in Sicily and southern Italy, Malta was subjected to intensive aerial bombardment. These air defences — along with, initially, three Gloster Gladiator biplanes named Faith, Hope and Charity — allowed British forces on the islands to hold out and earn the people of Malta a George Cross for their heroism. MFQ 469

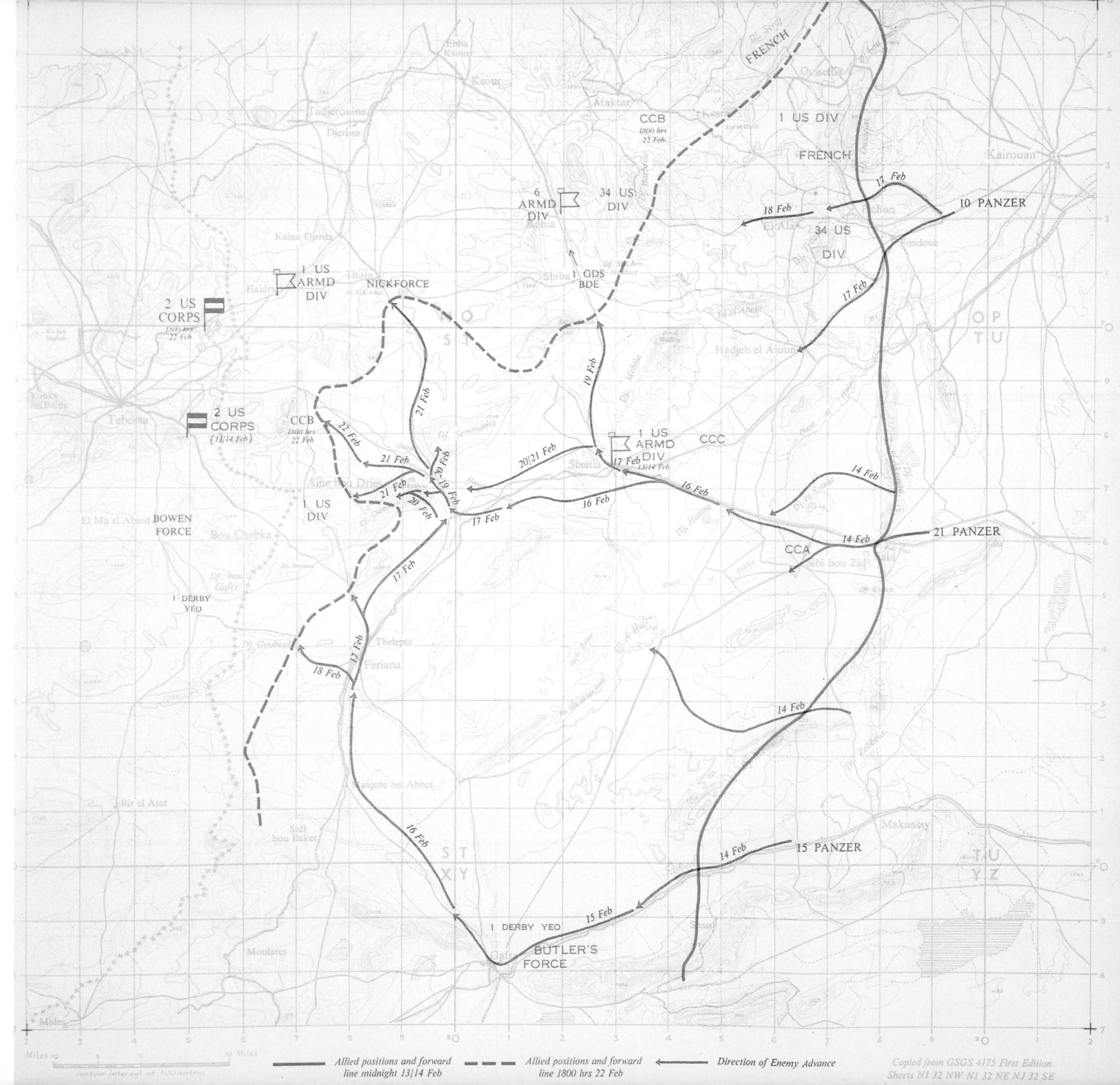

Allied positions and forward line midnight 13/14 Feb

Allied positions and forward line 1800 hrs 22 Feb

Direction of Enemy Advance

Copied from GSGS 4175 First Edition
Sheets NI 32 NW NI 32 NE NJ 32 SE

Miles 10   5   0   10 Miles

contour interval at 100 metres

TUNISIA, 18 FEBRUARY– 15 MARCH 1943

LEFT: Map showing the relocation of air and headquarters units as the Allied forces began to retake ground lost to the Germans during during the last great Axis offensive in North Africa against the Allied First Army. Tebessa **(at centre left)** was one of the major Allied supply centres along with Thela, and the route to them was guarded by the Kasserine Pass. Initial German successes against inexperienced U.S. forces saw the U.S. IInd Corps take a battering, but Rommel was forced to retreat by the size of the Allied force and, having won the battle of Kasserine, the German regrouping on the Mareth Line was a strategic failure. AIR 41/33

MÖHNE DAM, MAY 1943

The primary target for the legendary Dambusters raid in May 1943 was the Möhne dam **(centre)**, which encloses the valley of the Möhne and Hever rivers. It was hoped that by breaching this structure, and the dams on the Eder, Sorpe, Lister and Schwelme Lake, vital water supplies to the industrial heartland of the Ruhr could be disrupted. In the event only the Möhne and Eder were breached, and although the raid interrupted the German war machine for a short time and represented a major propaganda coup for the Allies, its long-term strategic effect was negligible. MPI 668 (5)

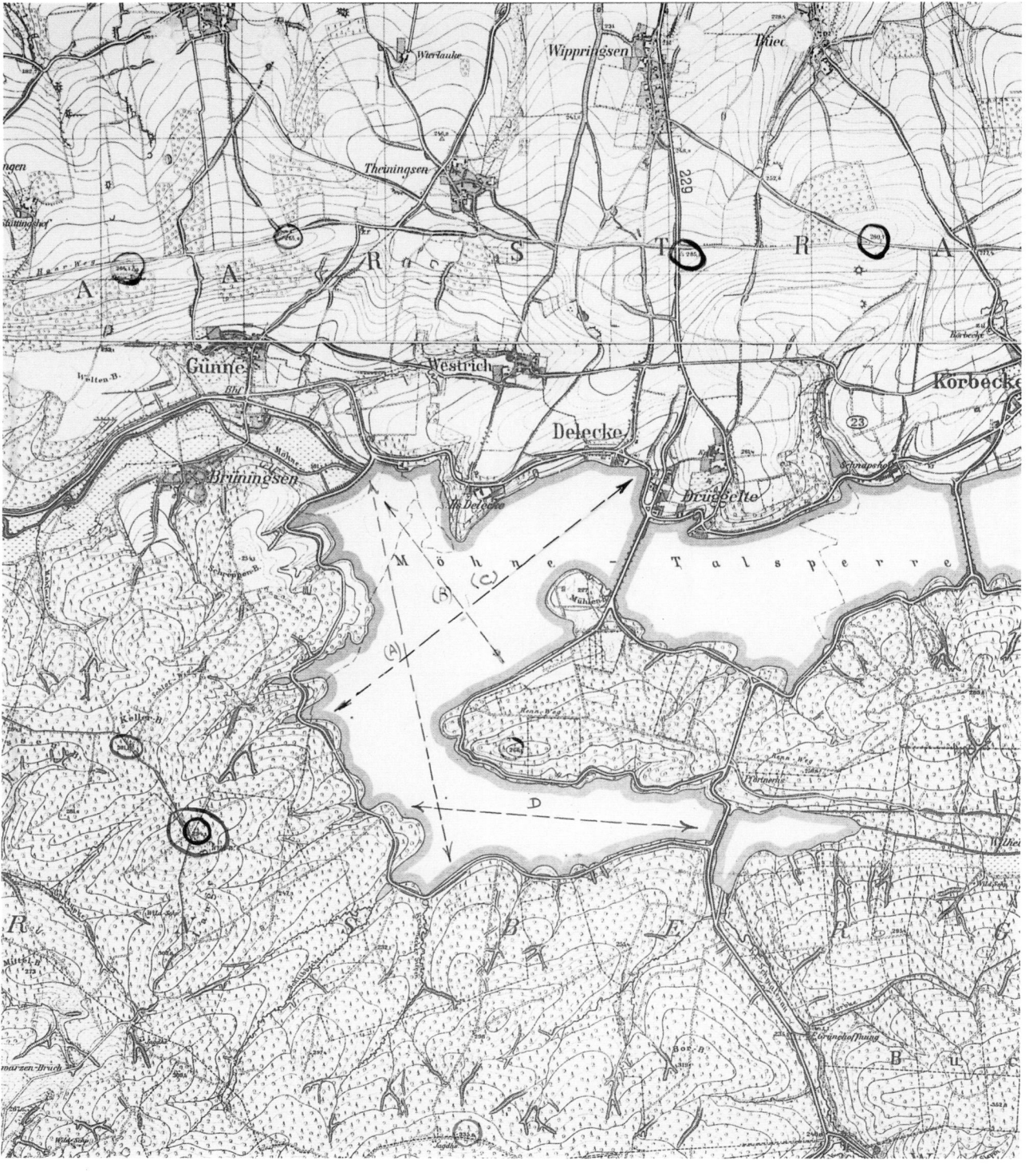

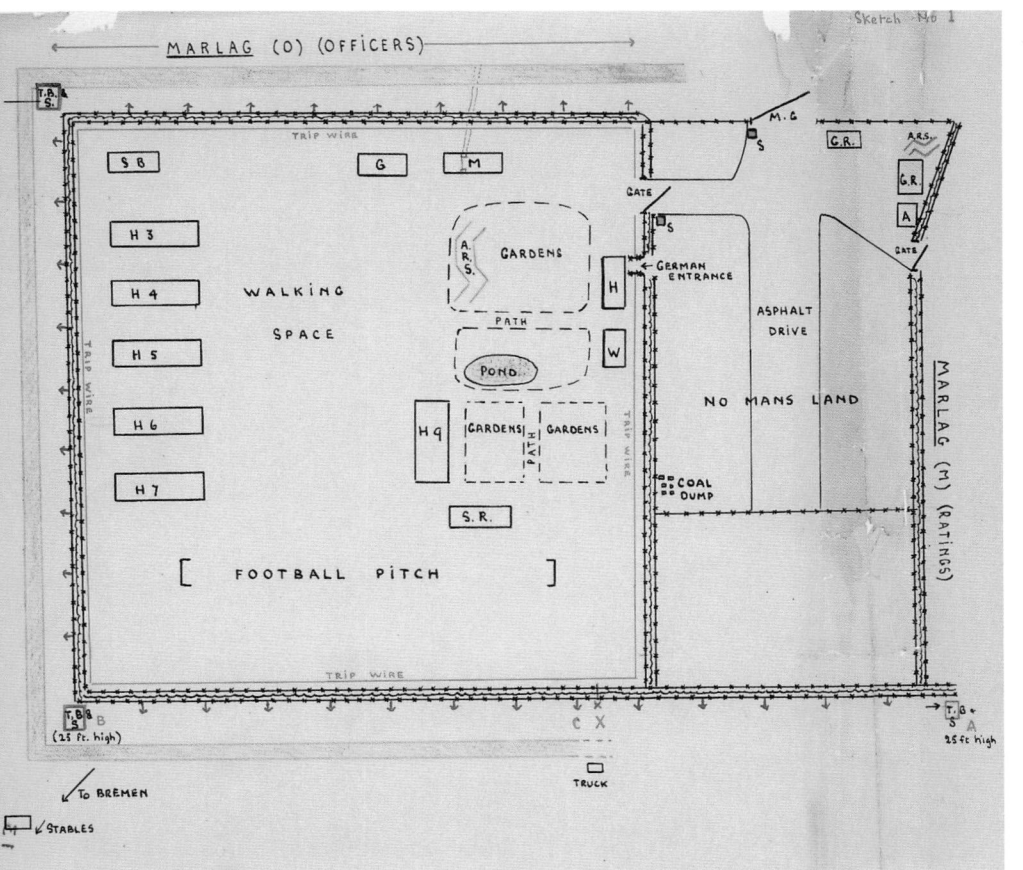

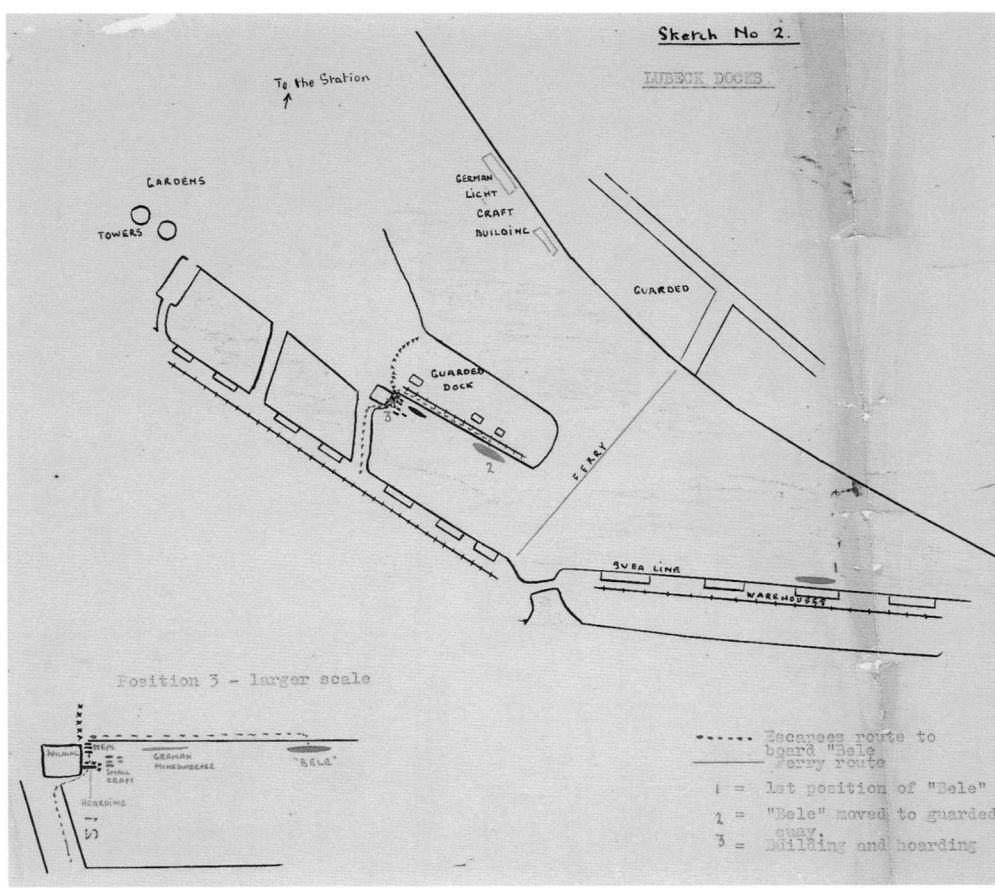

MARLAG, LÜBECK, JANUARY 1944

ABOVE: These two sketch maps, one of Marlag POW camp **(left)** and the other of the docks at the German Baltic port of Lübeck **(right),** record one of the most remarkable escape stories of the war. In January 1944 Royal Navy Lt. Cambell and Rating Kellehers began planning a breakout from Marlag. Five possible schemes were proposed to the camp escape committee, until they settled on a break through the wire, disguised as Dutch seamen, from where they would make their way to the port of Lübeck. In the ensuing weeks appropriate clothing was produced, German lessons taken and the all important Ausweis (identity cards) forged. On the night of 20 February the wire was cut for the escapers, but as they were making their way through, searchlights suddenly flicked on and began to probe the shadows. Camp guards came out with torches, but failed to discover the breach. Once outside, Cambell and Kellehers made their way to a nearby barn, where they hid for the night before making for Bremen on foot. In Bremen they took a train to Hamburg, overcoming the suspicions of the train guard with a letter claiming they were replacement crew for the SS *Waal*. From Hamburg they travelled to Lübeck, but failed to find a neutral ship on which they could stow away. The pair decided to travel to Rostock, by way of Wismar, but again could find no suitable ship and were forced to return to Lübeck on 24 February. On their return, they discovered a Swedish collier had docked and after watching it closely, were able to board without difficulty. Once on the ship they hid in a pool of water under one of the engines for five days, with the assistance of a helpful sailor, until the ship sailed. Out at sea they emerged from their hiding place and were treated well by the captain, who gave them food, warm clothing and comfortable berths. Finally, on 2 March 1944, they sailed into Stockholm and made their way to the British consulate, from where they returned to the UK. ADM 1/16842

RUSSIA,
1 JUNE 1943

RIGHT: Front line and Russian order of battle for 1 June 1943. Note the Kursk salient (marked Voronezh on the map): what this map does not show is the massive work that the Russians had put in to build defence works in this area. On 5 July 1943 the Germans initiated Operation 'Zitadelle' (Citadel) and one of the biggest and most important of all World War II battles. The Germans lost over 500 tanks and 35,000 men in the battles around Kursk and the Russian counter-offensive, launched on 12 July, saw the start of a long German retreat that would end in Berlin in 1945. WO 208/1768

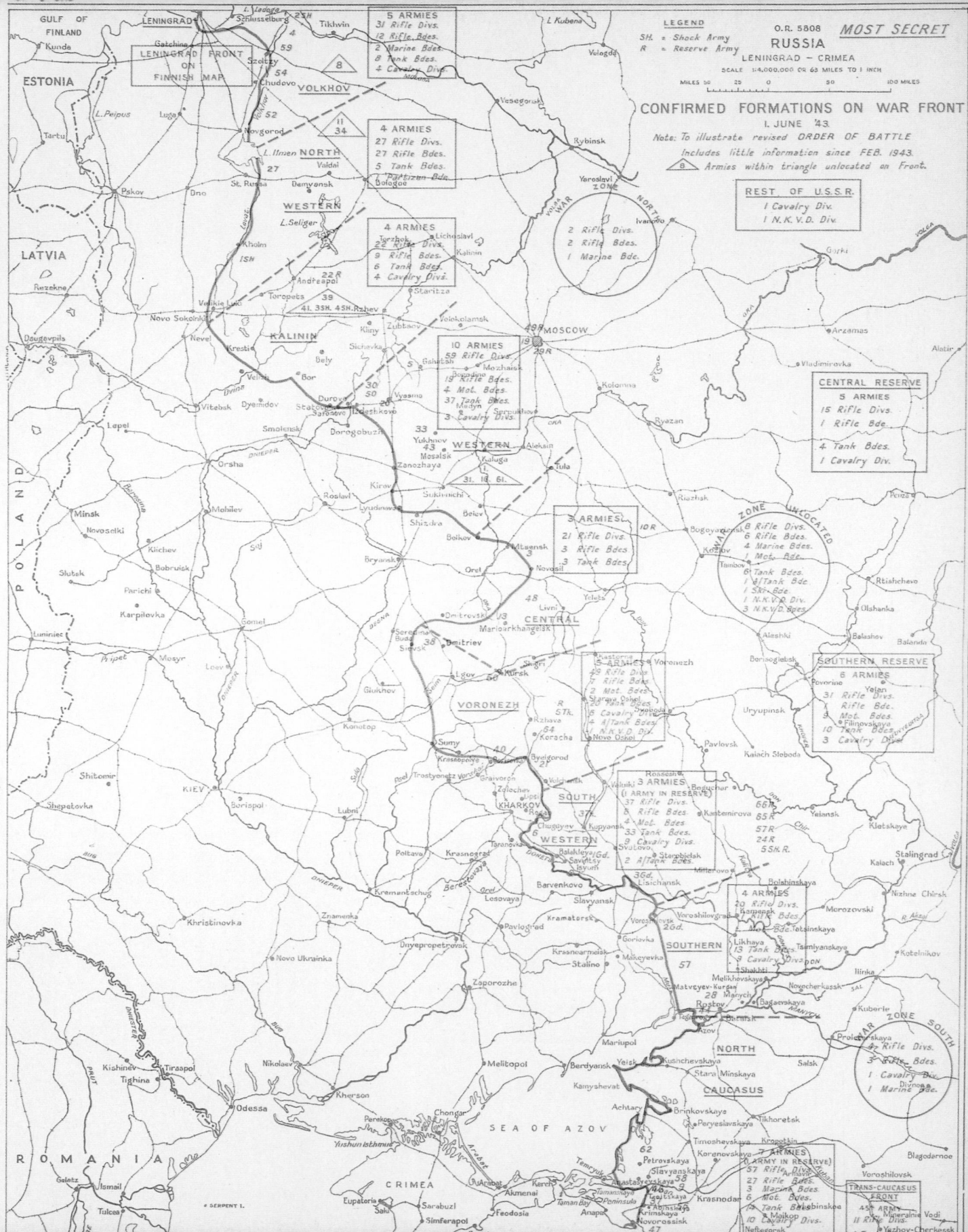

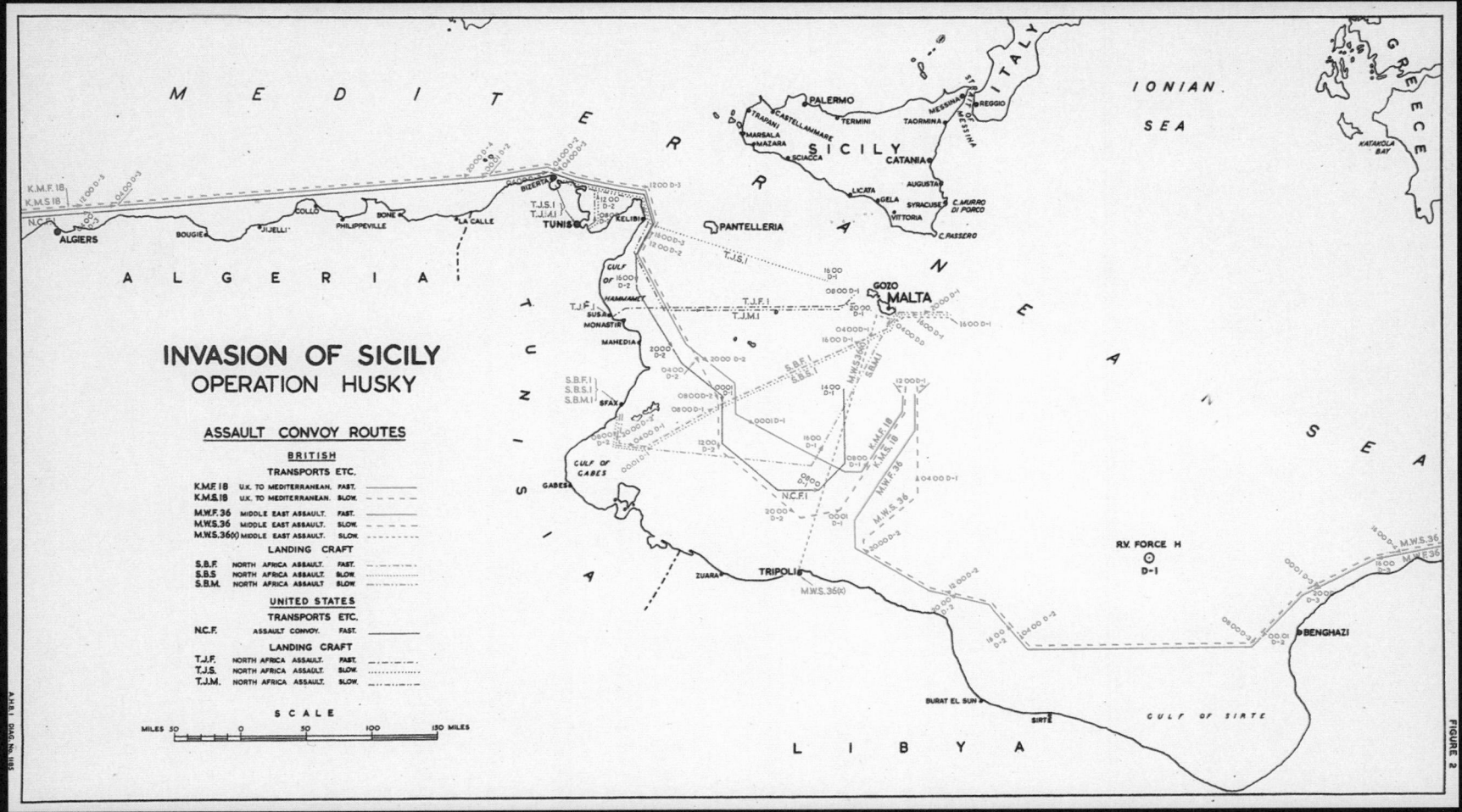

SICILY, OPERATION 'HUSKY' 10 JUNE 1943

ABOVE: Naval chart showing the movements of British and U.S. ships from North Africa, the British Isles and the Middle East in preparation for Operation 'Husky', the Allied invasion of Sicily, which was launched on 10 June 1943. 'Husky' was the greatest amphibious assault of the war in terms of initial assault strength, and involved nearly half a million men deployed in eight divisions. AIR 41/54

DEFENCES OF
THE FARO OR MESSINA STRAIT

From Admiralty Chart Nᵒ 177.
Natural Scale 1 : 30,350.
Figures on the land express the heights in feet above the sea.
SOUNDINGS IN FATHOMS.

FIXED GUN DEFENCES
COAST.

Nᵒ on Chart	Name or Situation	Armament	Remarks	Nᵒ on Chart	Name or Situation	Armament	Remarks
1	Battery	7 ~ 6" Guns	Tractor drawn battery provisionally installed 1935	14	Pietrazza Battery	4 ~ 11" Howitzers	Old work
2	Matiniti Lower Battery	6 ~ 11" Howitzers	Old work Armed in 1935	15	Messina Citadel	4 ~ 6" Guns	Provisional Battery installed in 1935 and since maintained
3	Matiniti Upper Battery	8 ~ 11" Howitzers	Old work Armed in 1935	16	Fort San Salvatore	4 ~ 4·7 Guns	
4	Poggia Pignatelli Battery	6 ~ 11" Howitzers	Old work Armed in 1935	17	Ogliastri Battery	6 ~ 7·6" Guns	Old work re-armed with present armament
5	Telegrafo Battery	8 ~ 9·4 Howitzers	Old work Armed in 1935	18	San Iachiddo Battery	6 ~ 11" Howitzers	Old work
6	Pta Pezzo Battery	6 ~ 4·7 Guns		19	Menaja Battery	6 ~ 11" Howitzers	Old work
7	Arghilla Battery	8 ~ 11" Howitzers	Old work Possibly mountings only	20	Polvereva Battery	8 ~ 11" Howitzers 2 ~ 6" Guns	Old work
8	Catona Battery	6 ~ 9·4 Howitzers	Old work	21	Serra della Croce Battery	4 ~ 11" Howitzers	Old work
9	Pentimele North Battery	4 ~ 11" Howitzers	Old work	22	Cape Pelaro Battery	4 ~ 6" or 4·7 Guns	
10	Pentimele South Battery	4 ~ 11" Howitzers	Old work Armed	23	Fort Spuria	4 ~ 6" Guns 4 ~ 4·7 Guns	
11	Monte Gallo Battery	4 ~ 11" Howitzers	Old work	24	Monte Dei Centri Battery	4 ~ 6" Guns	
12	Giulitta Battery	6 ~ 4·7 Guns	Old work re-armed with present armament	25	Monte Campore Battery	4 ~ 6" Guns	For Land Defence of East Coast Batteries
13	Mangialupi Battery	6 ~ 9·4 Howitzers		26	Puntal Ferraro Battery	6 ~ 4·7 Guns	For Land Defence of East Coast Batteries

A. A. DEFENCES

Nᵒ on Chart	Name or Situation	Armament	Remarks
A.A.1	Battery	? Armament	

SICILY, OPERATION 'HUSKY' 10 JUNE 1943

ABOVE: Detailed map of the gun emplacements and anti-aircraft batteries guarding the Messina Strait separating Sicily from Italy. The original plan for Operation 'Husky' called for the U.S. Seventh Army to land near Palermo in the northwest of the island. Some military historians suggest that, had they done so, four German divisions under Kesselring could have been prevented from escaping across the Strait during

RIGHT AND PAGES 64 AND 65: Maps showing the final plan for the assault on Sicily by Allied forces and the U.S. Seventh Army radio network on the day that German resistance effectively ended (18 August). The landings, made under conditions of almost total air superiority, were conducted with a great deal of success, also due in some part to the employment of new landing craft. The worst casualties were suffered by the Allied

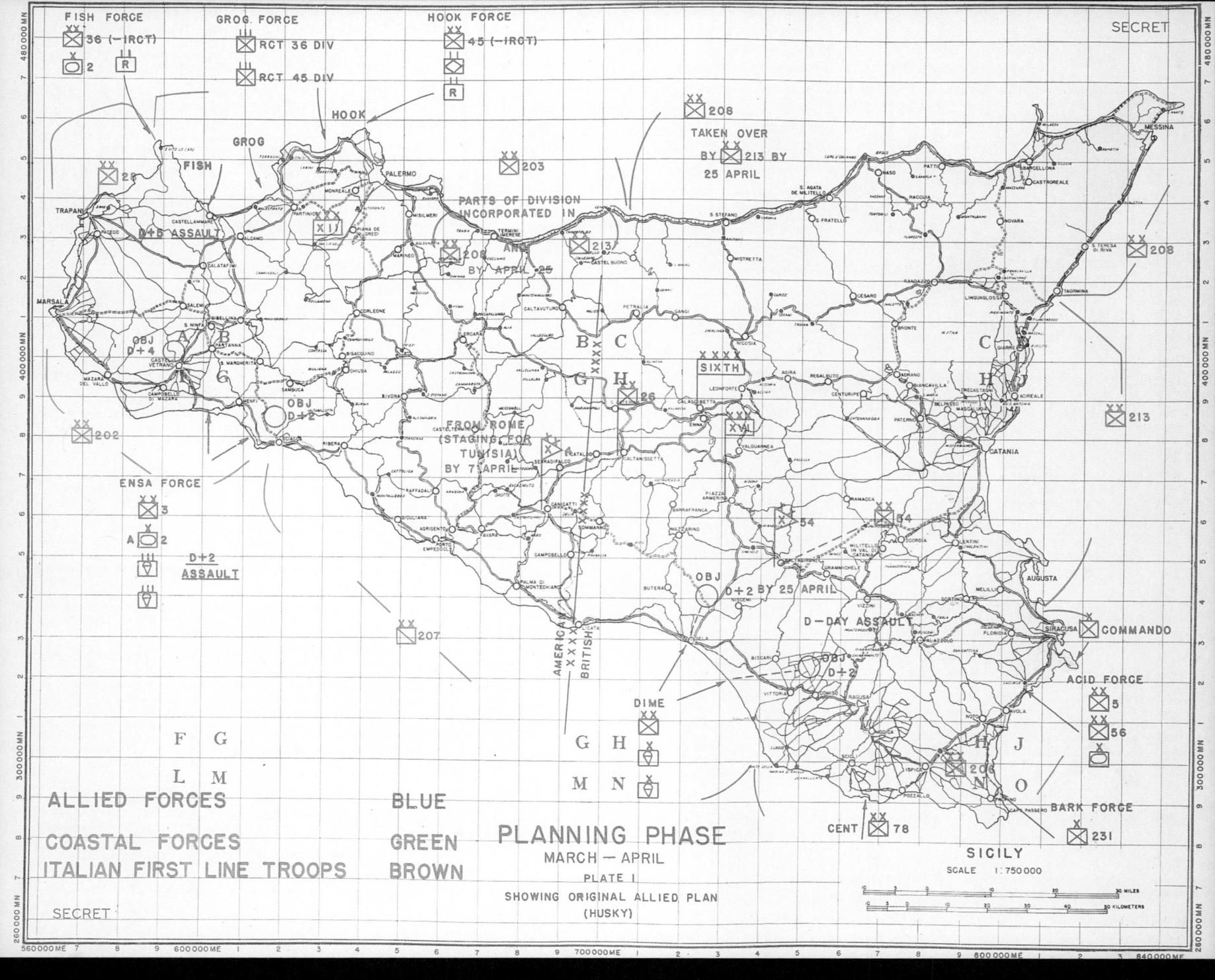

PLANNING PHASE

MARCH — APRIL

PLATE I

SHOWING ORIGINAL ALLIED PLAN

(HUSKY)

SICILY

SCALE 1:750 000

ALLIED FORCES .... BLUE

COASTAL FORCES ...... GREEN

ITALIAN FIRST LINE TROOPS .. BROWN

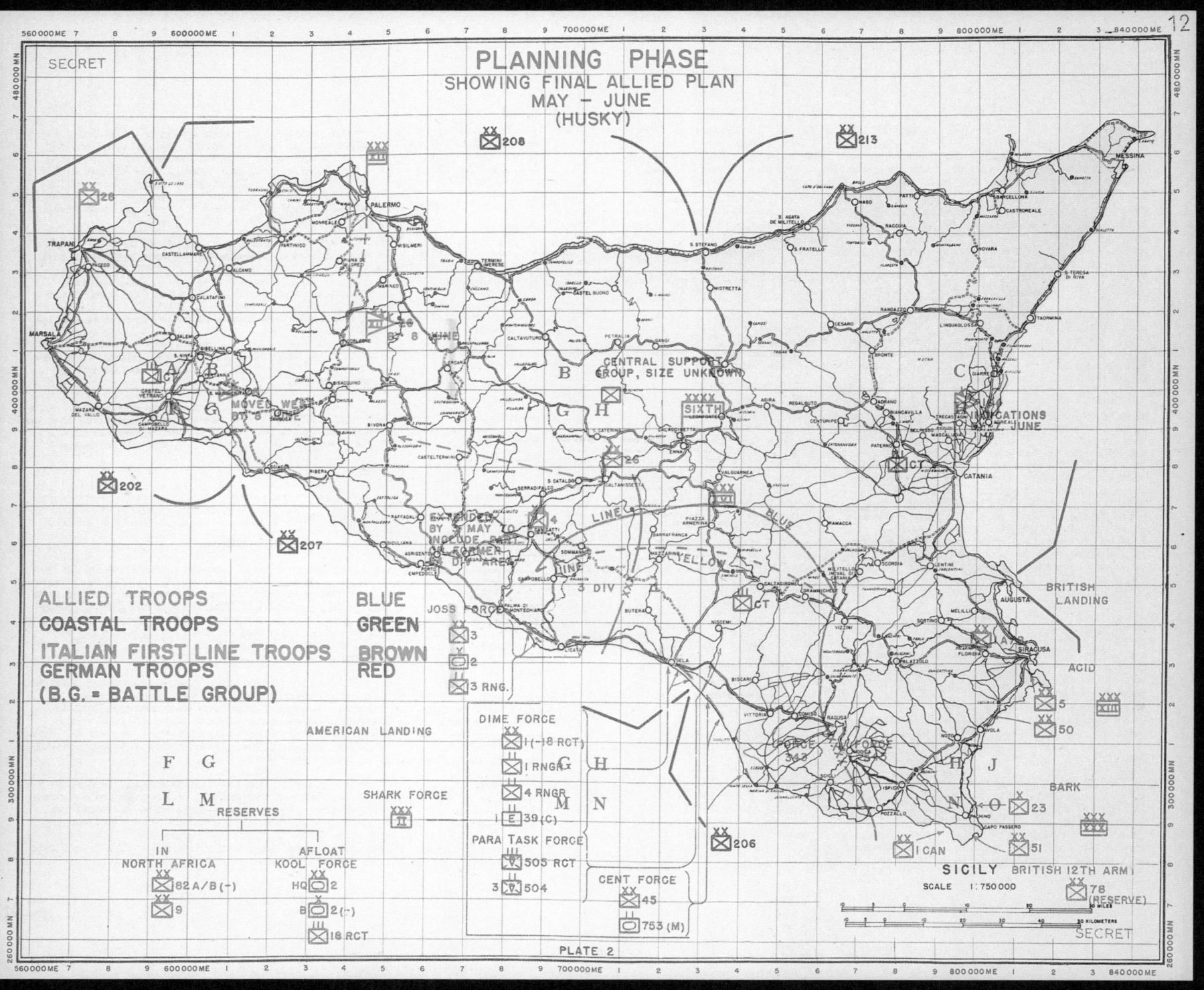

PLANNING PHASE
SHOWING FINAL ALLIED PLAN
MAY — JUNE
(HUSKY)

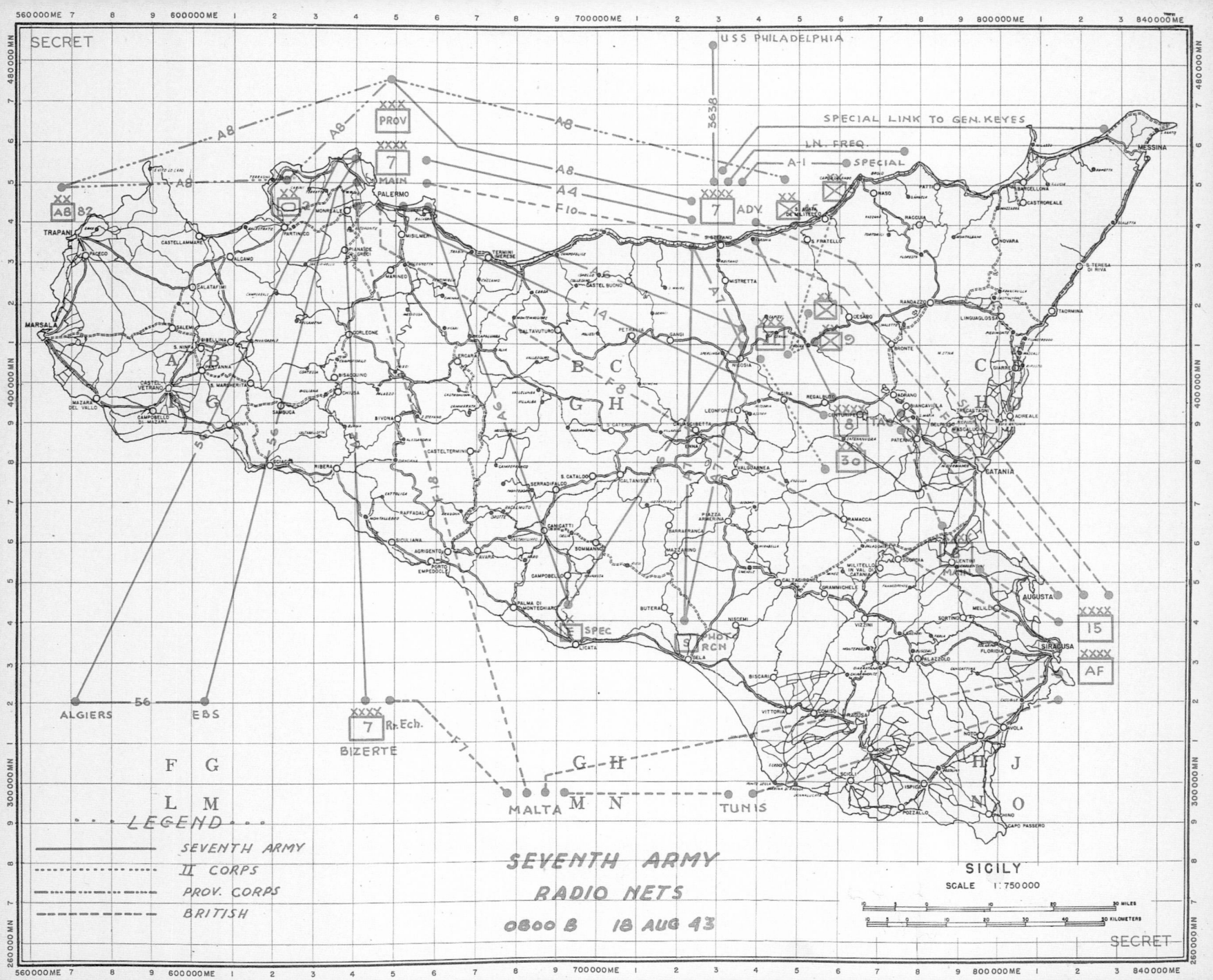

SEVENTH ARMY
RADIO NETS
0800 B   18 AUG 43

SICILY
SCALE 1:750 000

SALERNO, OPERATION 'AVALANCHE', 9 SEPTEMBER 1943

RIGHT AND FAR RIGHT: Detailed plans of coastal defence batteries around Salerno, Naples and Gaeta, on the south-western coast of Italy, and planned landing zones and objectives around Salerno, which were prepared for Operation 'Avalanche'. Salerno was assaulted from the sea on 9 September 1943 by the U.S. Fifth Army, under Mark Clark, at the start of the Allied invasion of Italy. The choice of Salerno for the landings was both predictable and cautious and, lacking the element of surprise, the U.S. forces suffered heavy casualties both on the beach-heads and during six days of heavy fighting inland. ADM 199/949

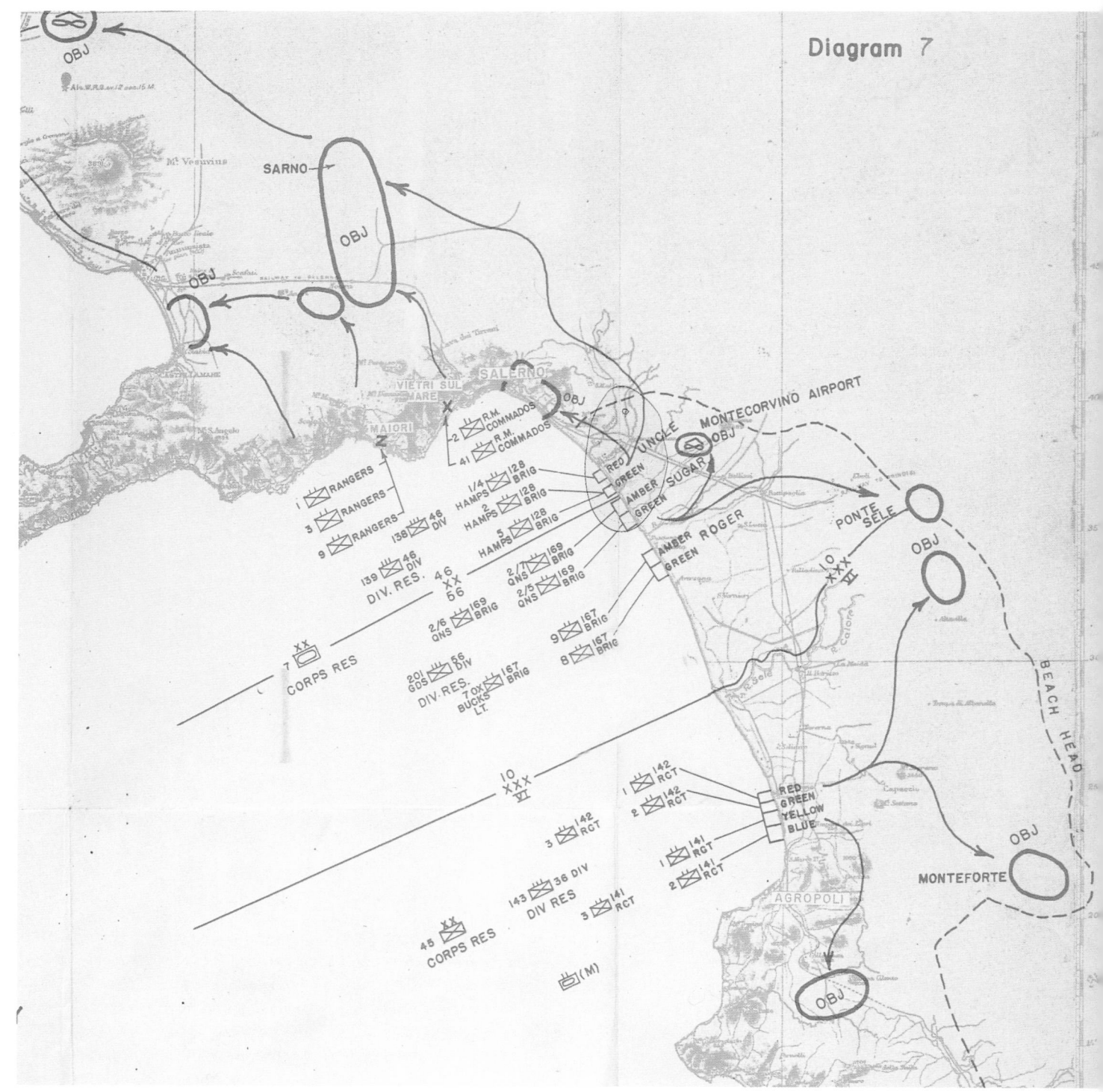

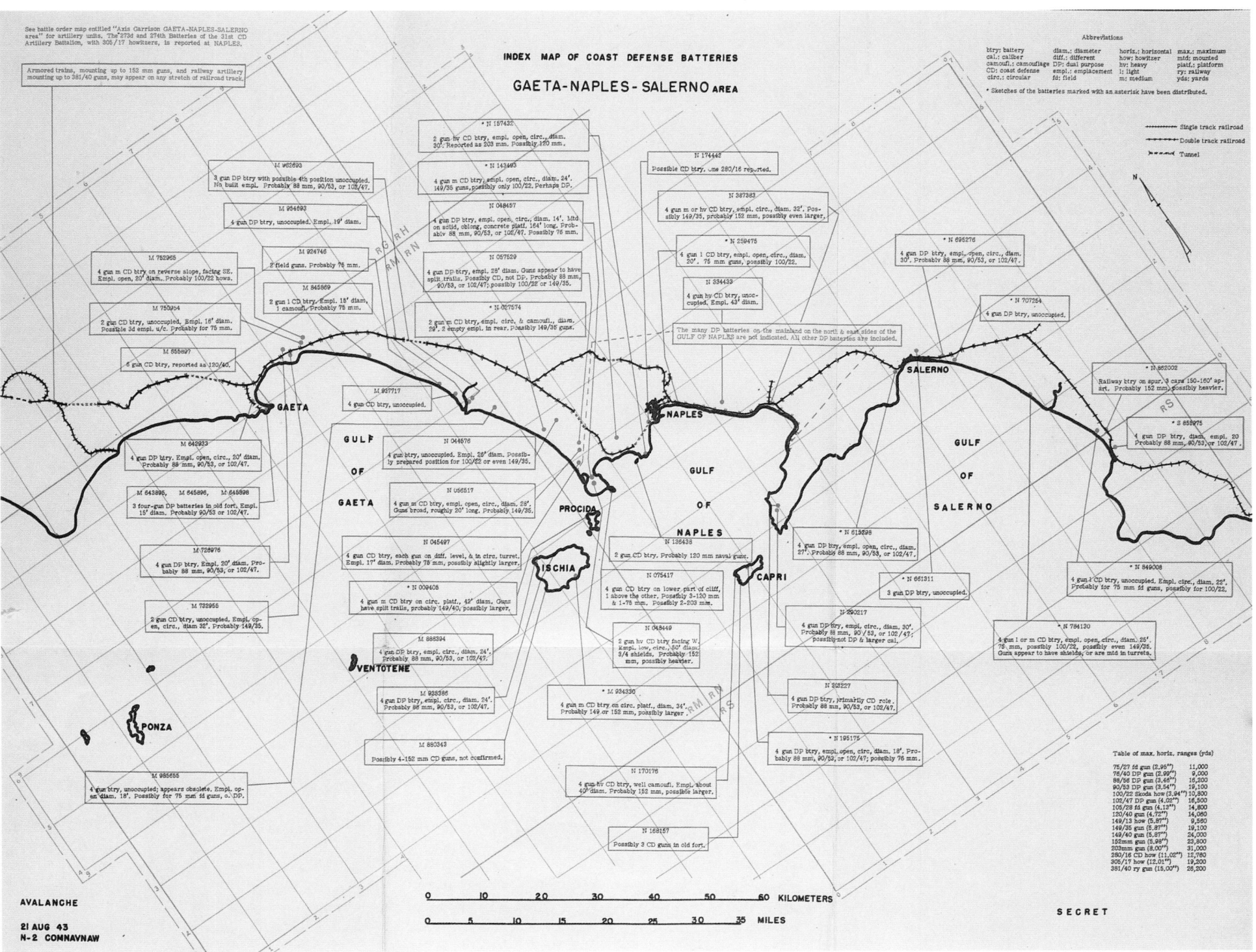

INDEX MAP OF COAST DEFENSE BATTERIES

GAETA-NAPLES-SALERNO AREA

See battle order map entitled "Axis Garrison GAETA-NAPLES-SALERNO area" for artillery units. The 273d and 274th Batteries of the 31st CD Artillery Battalion, with 305/17 howitzers, is reported at NAPLES.

Armored trains, mounting up to 152 mm guns, and railway artillery mounting up to 381/40 guns, may appear on any stretch of railroad track.

Abbreviations

btry: battery	diam.: diameter	horiz.: horizontal	max.: maximum
cal.: caliber	diff.: different	how: howitzer	mtd: mounted
camoufl.: camouflage	DP: dual purpose	hv: heavy	platf.: platform
CD: coast defense	empl.: emplacement	ll: light	ry: railway
circ.: circular	fd: field	m: medium	yds: yards

* Sketches of the batteries marked with an asterisk have been distributed.

········· Single track railroad
━━━━━━ Double track railroad
▸◂▸◂▸◂ Tunnel

Battery annotations

* N 157432 — 2 gun hv CD btry, empl. open, circ., diam. 30'. Reported as 203 mm. Possibly 120 mm.

N 174442 — Possible CD btry, one 280/16 reported.

* N 143493 — 4 gun m CD btry, empl. open, circ., diam. 24'. 149/35 guns, possibly only 100/22. Perhaps DP.

N 387383 — 4 gun m or hv CD btry, empl. open, circ., diam. 32'. Possibly 149/35, probably 152 mm, possibly even larger.

M 962693 — 3 gun DP btry with possible 4th position unoccupied. No built empl. Probably 88 mm, 90/53, or 102/47.

M 954693 — 4 gun DP btry, unoccupied. Empl. 19' diam.

N 048457 — 4 gun DP btry, empl. open, circ., diam. 14'. Mtd. on solid, oblong, concrete platf. 164' long. Probably 88 mm, 90/53, or 102/47. Possibly 76 mm.

* N 259475 — 4 gun l CD btry, empl. open, circ., diam. 20'. 75 mm guns, possibly 100/22.

* N 695276 — 4 gun DP btry, empl. open, circ., diam. 30'. Probably 88 mm, 90/53, or 102/47.

M 924746 — 2 field guns. Probably 76 mm.

N 057529 — 4 gun DP btry, empl. 28' diam. Guns appear to have split trails. Possibly CD, not DP. Probably 88 mm, 90/53, or 102/47; possibly 100/22 or 149/35.

N 334433 — 4 gun hv CD btry, unoccupied. Empl. 43' diam.

M 752965 — 4 gun m CD btry on reverse slope, facing SE. Empl. open, 20' diam. Probably 100/22 hows.

M 845869 — 2 gun l CD btry. Empl. 18' diam. 1 camoufl. Probably 75 mm.

* N 027574 — 2 gun m CD btry, empl. circ. & camoufl., diam. 29'. 2 empty empl. in rear. Possibly 149/35 guns.

* N 707254 — 4 gun DP btry, unoccupied.

M 750954 — 2 gun CD btry, unoccupied. Empl. 18' diam. Possible 3d empl. u/c. Probably for 75 mm.

The many DP batteries on the mainland on the north & east sides of the GULF OF NAPLES are not indicated. All other DP batteries are included.

M 655897 — 6 gun CD btry, reported as 120/40.

* N 852002 — Railway btry on spur. 3 cars 150'-160' apart. Probably 152 mm, possibly heavier.

M 937717 — 4 gun CD btry, unoccupied.

* S 859975 — 4 gun DP btry, diam. empl. 20'. Probably 88 mm, 90/53, or 102/47.

M 642933 — 4 gun DP btry. Empl. open, circ., 20' diam. Probably 88 mm, 90/53, or 102/47.

N 044876 — 4 gun btry, unoccupied. Empl. 28' diam. Possibly prepared position for 100/22 or even 149/35.

M 643895, M 645896, M 645898 — 3 four-gun DP batteries in old fort. Empl. 15' diam. Probably 90/53 or 102/47.

N 066517 — 4 gun m CD btry, empl. open, circ., diam. 28'. Guns broad, roughly 20' long. Probably 149/35.

* N 615298 — 4 gun DP btry, empl. open, circ., diam. 27'. Probably 88 mm, 90/53, or 102/47.

* N 849008 — 4 gun l CD btry, unoccupied. Empl. circ., diam. 25'. Probably for 75 mm fd guns, possibly for 100/22.

M 728976 — 4 gun DP btry. Empl. 20' diam. Probably 88 mm, 90/53, or 102/47.

N 045497 — 4 gun CD btry, each gun on diff. level, & in circ. turret. Empl. 17' diam. Probably 75 mm, possibly slightly larger.

N 136438 — 2 gun CD btry. 120 mm naval guns.

N 075417 — 4 gun CD btry on lower part of cliff, 1 above the other. Possibly 3-120 mm & 1-75 mm. Possibly 2-203 mm.

* N 661311 — 3 gun DP btry, unoccupied.

M 732955 — 2 gun CD btry, unoccupied. Empl. open, circ., diam. 32'. Probably 149/35.

* N 009405 — 4 gun m CD btry on circ. platf., 42' diam. Guns have split trails, probably 149/40, possibly larger.

N 290217 — 4 gun DP btry, empl. circ., diam. 30'. Probably 88 mm, 90/53, or 102/47; possibly not DP & larger cal.

* N 784130 — 4 gun l or m CD btry, empl. open, circ., diam. 25'. 75 mm, possibly 100/22, possibly even 149/35. Guns appear to have shields, or are mtd in turrets.

M 888394 — 4 gun DP btry, empl. circ., diam. 24'. Probably 88 mm, 90/53, or 102/47.

N 048449 — 2 gun hv CD btry facing W. Empl. low, circ., 30' diam. 3/4 shields. Probably 152 mm, possibly heavier.

M 935386 — 4 gun DP btry, empl. circ., diam. 24'. Probably 88 mm, 90/53, or 102/47.

* M 934330 — 4 gun m CD btry on circ. platf., diam. 34'. Probably 149 or 152 mm, possibly larger.

N 302227 — 4 gun DP btry, primarily CD role. Probably 88 mm, 90/53, or 102/47.

M 880343 — Possibly 4-152 mm CD guns, not confirmed.

* N 195175 — 4 gun DP btry, empl. open, circ., diam. 18'. Probably 88 mm, 90/53, or 102/47; possibly 76 mm.

M 985655 — 4 gun btry, unoccupied; appears obsolete. Empl. open, diam. 18'. Possibly for 75 mm fd guns, o. DP.

N 170176 — 4 gun hv CD btry, well camoufl. Empl. about 40' diam. Probably 152 mm, possibly larger.

N 168157 — Possibly 3 CD guns in old fort.

Place labels

GAETA · GULF OF GAETA · VENTOTENE · PONZA · ISCHIA · PROCIDA · NAPLES · GULF OF NAPLES · CAPRI · SALERNO · GULF OF SALERNO

Table of max. horiz. ranges (yds)

75/27 fd gun (2.95")	11,000
76/40 DP gun (2.99")	9,000
88/56 DP gun (3.46")	16,200
90/53 DP gun (3.54")	19,100
100/22 Skoda how (3.94")	10,800
102/47 DP gun (4.02")	16,500
105/28 fd gun (4.13")	14,800
120/40 gun (4.72")	14,060
149/13 how (5.87")	9,560
149/35 gun (5.87")	19,100
149/40 gun (5.87")	24,000
152mm gun (5.98")	23,800
203mm gun (8.00")	31,000
280/16 CD how (11.02")	12,760
305/17 how (12.01")	19,200
381/40 ry gun (15.00")	26,200

0 10 20 30 40 50 60 KILOMETERS

0 5 10 15 20 25 30 35 MILES

AVALANCHE

21 AUG 43
N-2 COMNAVNAW

N

67

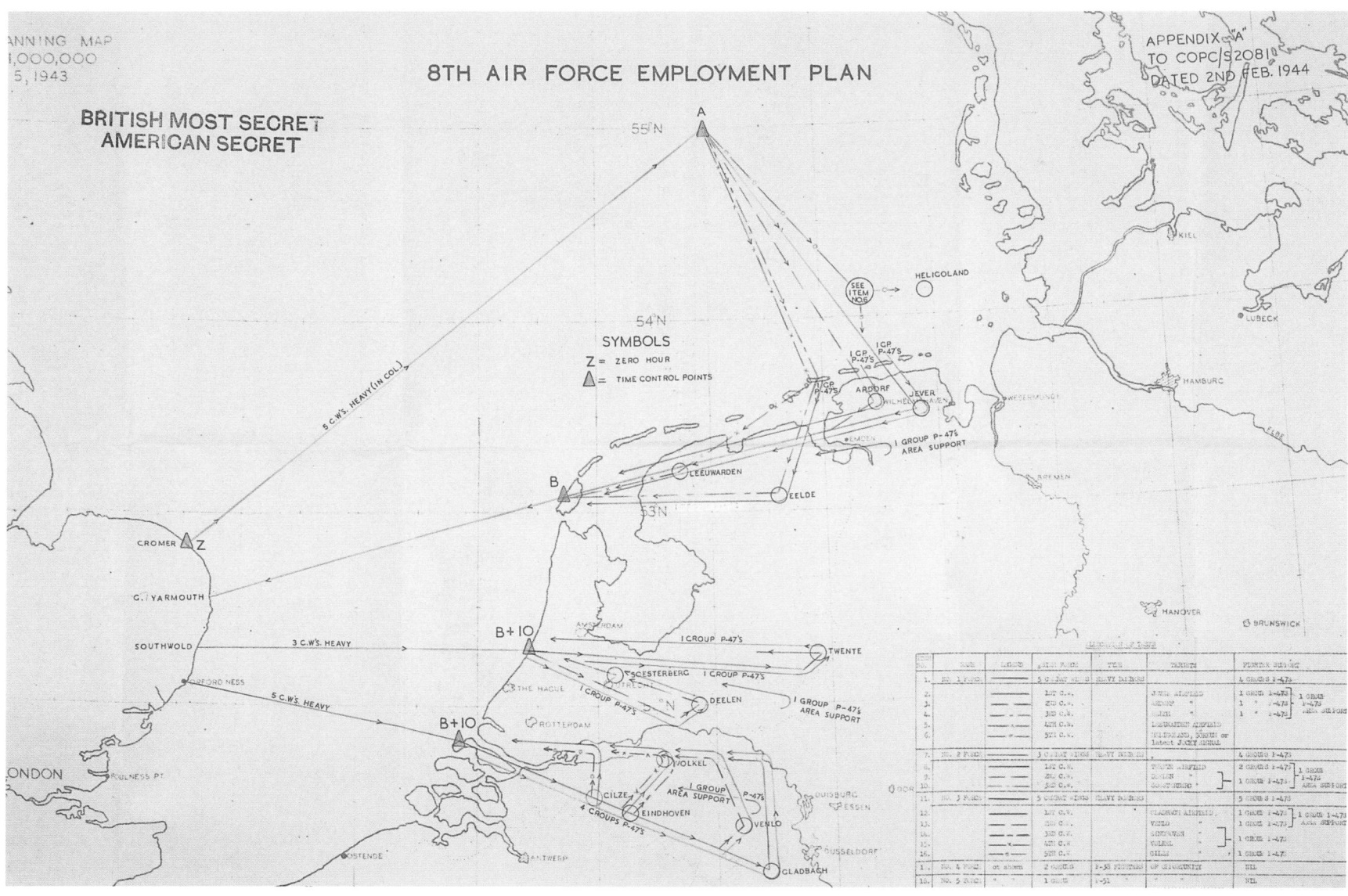

BRITISH MOST SECRET
AMERICAN SECRET

8TH AIR FORCE EMPLOYMENT PLAN

APPENDIX "A"
TO COPC/S2081
DATED 2ND FEB. 1944

USAAF EIGHTH AIR FORCE, 5 AUGUST 1943

ABOVE: Chart showing a raid by units of the Eighth Air Force on 5 August 1943. The Eighth Air Force was dedicated from its inception to the strategic bombing of targets in German-held territory and flew its first missions in August 1942. At the time of this raid the Eighth was suffering heavy losses to the German defences for lack of an effective long-range fighter escort (a problem solved by the advent of longer-range P-51 Mustangs), although interestingly, the relatively short-range raid planned for that day enjoyed fighter cover by P-47 Thunderbolts. AIR 42/2

ITALY: MONTE CASSINO, 11 MAY 1944

RIGHT: Map showing the front line in Italy on the day that Monte Cassino fell to Polish troops. In November 1943 German forces retreating up through Italy halted along a line straddling the country (the Gustav Line) south of Rome along the Garigliano and Rapido Rivers and prepared for a long defence. During the winter of 1943–44 they resisted all attacks by the Allied forces, but on 11 May a renewed Allied offensive finally broke the line. The monastery at Monte Cassino, occupying tactically vital high ground at the centre of the line, was reduced to rubble during the repeated attacks. AIR 23/8566

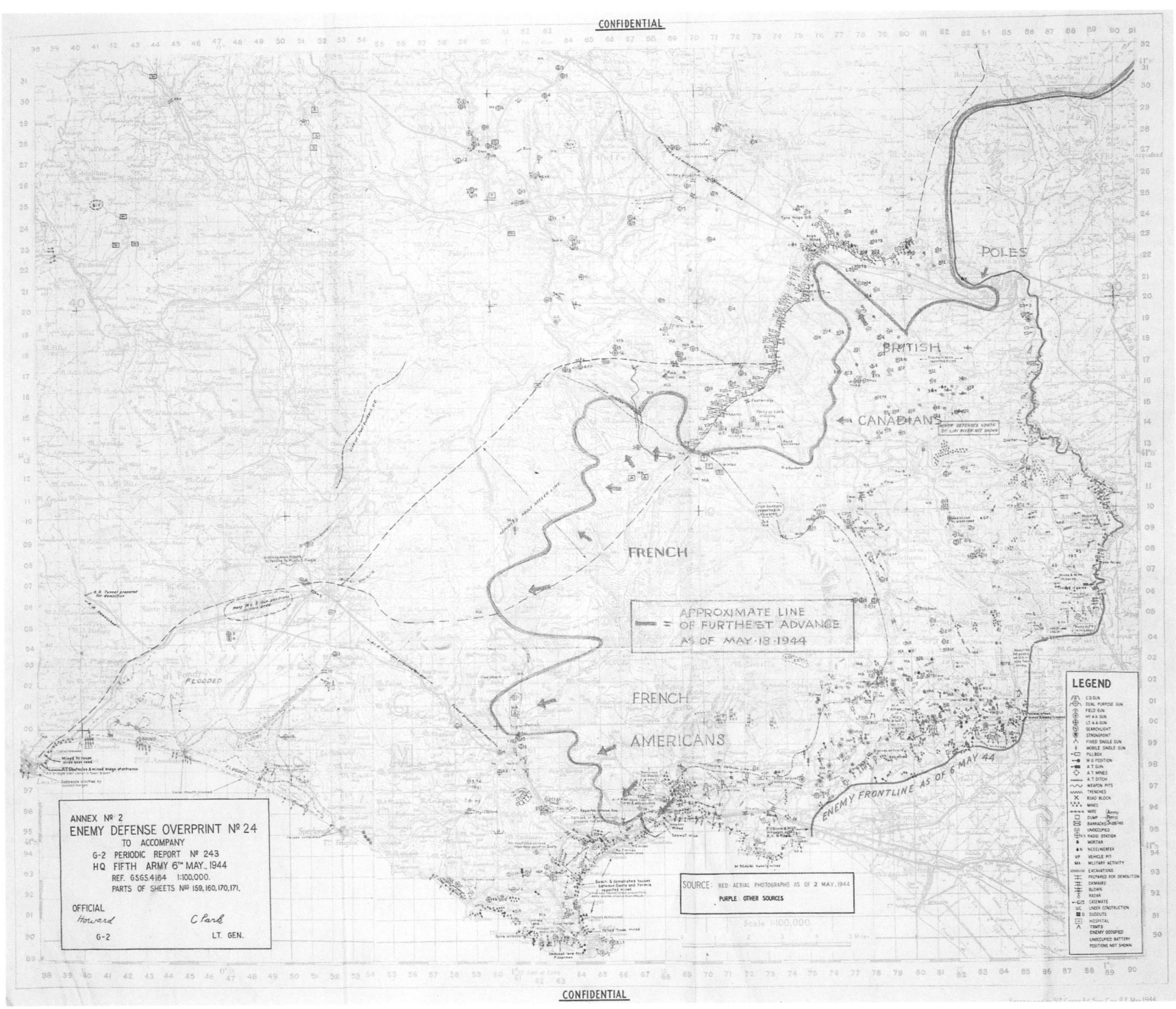

ANNEX Nº 2
ENEMY DEFENSE OVERPRINT Nº 24
TO ACCOMPANY
G-2 PERIODIC REPORT Nº 243
HQ FIFTH ARMY 6TH MAY, 1944
REF. GSGS 4164 1:100,000.
PARTS OF SHEETS Nºs 159, 160, 170, 171.

OFFICIAL

Howard   C Park
G-2   LT. GEN.

SOURCE: RED: AERIAL PHOTOGRAPHS AS OF 2 MAY, 1944
PURPLE: OTHER SOURCES

Scale 1:100,000

APPROXIMATE LINE
OF FURTHEST ADVANCE
AS OF MAY 18 1944

ENEMY FRONTLINE AS OF 6 MAY 44

POLES

BRITISH

CANADIAN

FRENCH

FRENCH

AMERICANS

LEGEND

ITALY: OPERATION 'SHINGLE', ANZIO JANUARY 1944

RIGHT AND FAR RIGHT: Maps detailing aspects of the Allied operation at Anzio, a small port on the west coast of Italy. It was hoped that the operation, codenamed 'Shingle', would cut the communications lines of the German Tenth Army and force it to retreat from its strongly held positions along the Gustav Line. The landings were made largely unopposed on 17–20 January 1944, but despite establishing a bridgehead, swift German counter-attacks forced the U.S. troops to fight one of the most bitter defensive battles of the war for nearly three months before advancing units of the Fifth Army were able to relieve them. In those three months the troops were resupplied by landing craft from Naples to the points shown on the second map. CAB 106/392

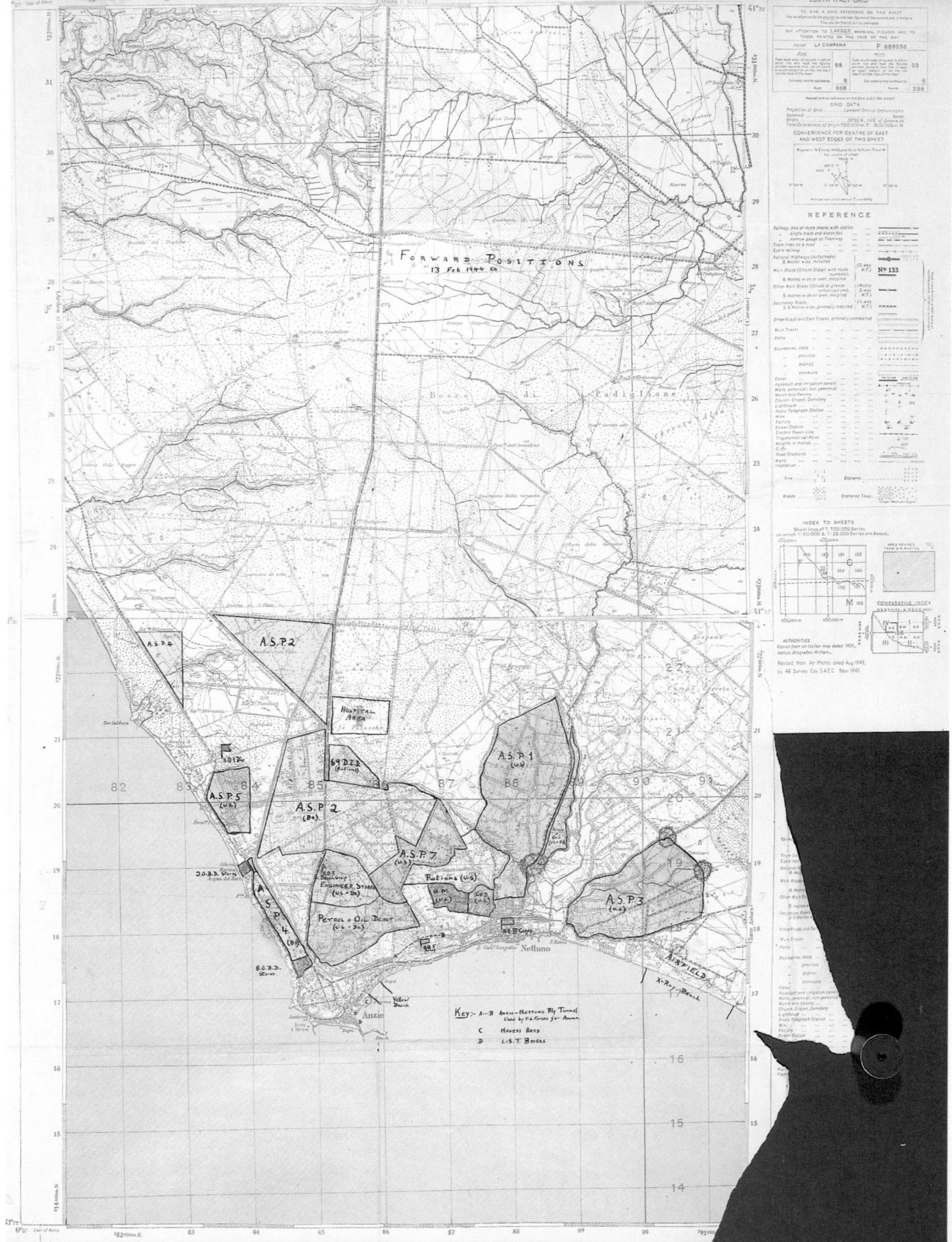

MOST SECRET

REFERENCE

CONTOURS AT 10 METRES INTERVAL.

NOTE

Scale :- 1:15,000

SITUATION IN YUGOSLAVIA
AS KNOWN AT 0500 HRS. B.S.T. 1 NOV. '43

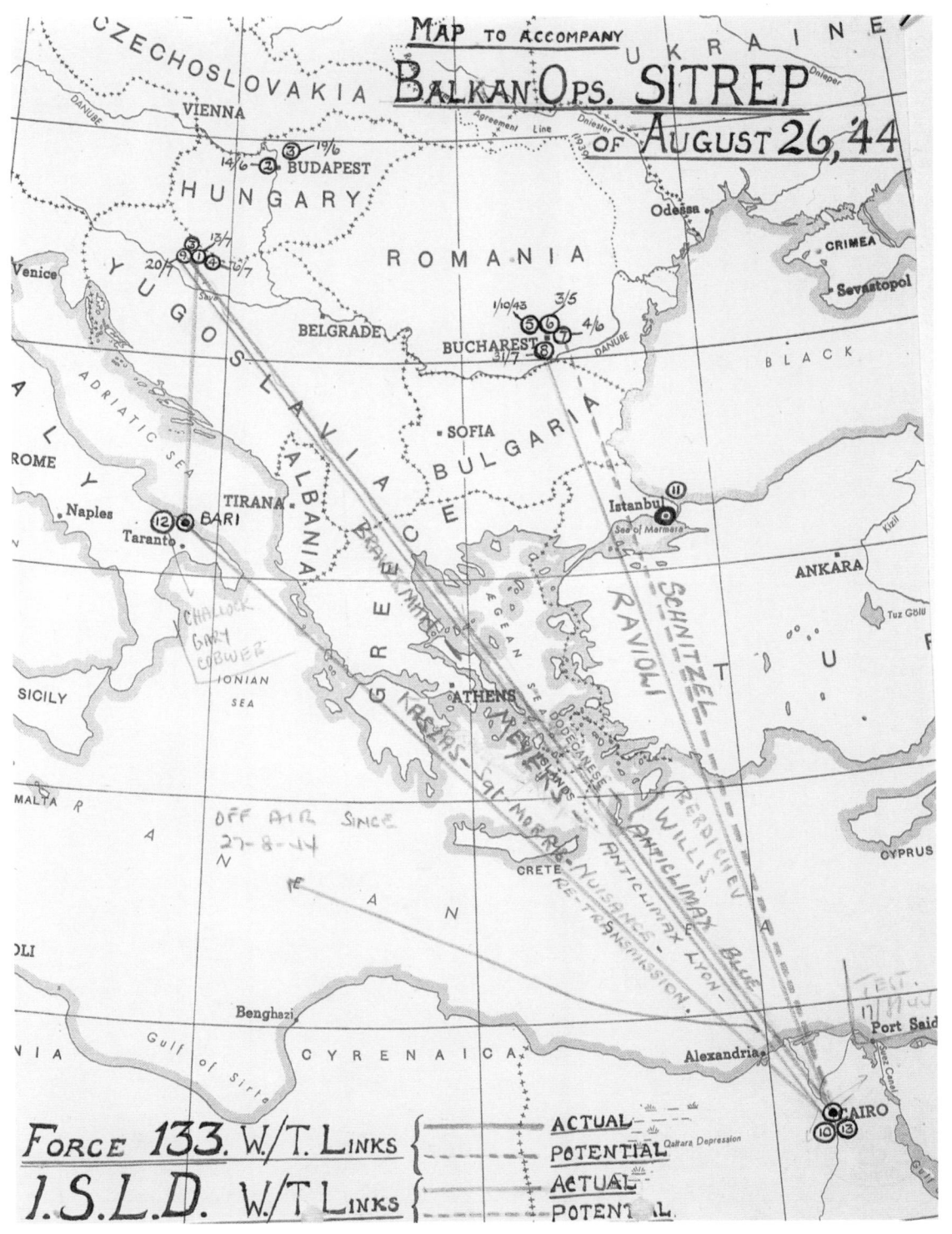

YUGOSLAVIA, 1 NOVEMBER 1943

FAR LEFT: Map showing the distribution of forces in Yugoslavia in late 1943. In April 1941, following a coup d'etat that deposed the pro-Axis regent, Yugoslavia was invaded by Axis forces. Two distinct resistance groups emerged, the Cetniks (led by Mihajlovic) and Partisans (led by Tito), but internecine tensions between the two leaders prevented any possibility of a cohesive resistance to the Axis. By mid-1942 the two sides were fighting openly against the other in an appallingly violent civil war. Between the autumn of 1943 and late 1944 the British slowly withdrew all support for the Cetniks, while Tito's forces swelled to nearly 300,000 men. When the German forces began their withdrawal, Tito's partisan army emerged from its mountain strongholds to fight alongside the liberating Red Army. MFQ 453 (1)

AGENTS IN THE BALKANS, 1944

LEFT: For the duration of the war Cairo was used as a base by the British Secret Service from which to control its agents in the Balkans and Mediterranean. The lines on this map, dated 26 August 1944, describe recent W/T (Wireless Transmission) links between Cairo and Allied agents in occupied Yugoslavia and Romania. The numbers and dates presumably represent individual agents and the time of their last transmission. WO 208/3383

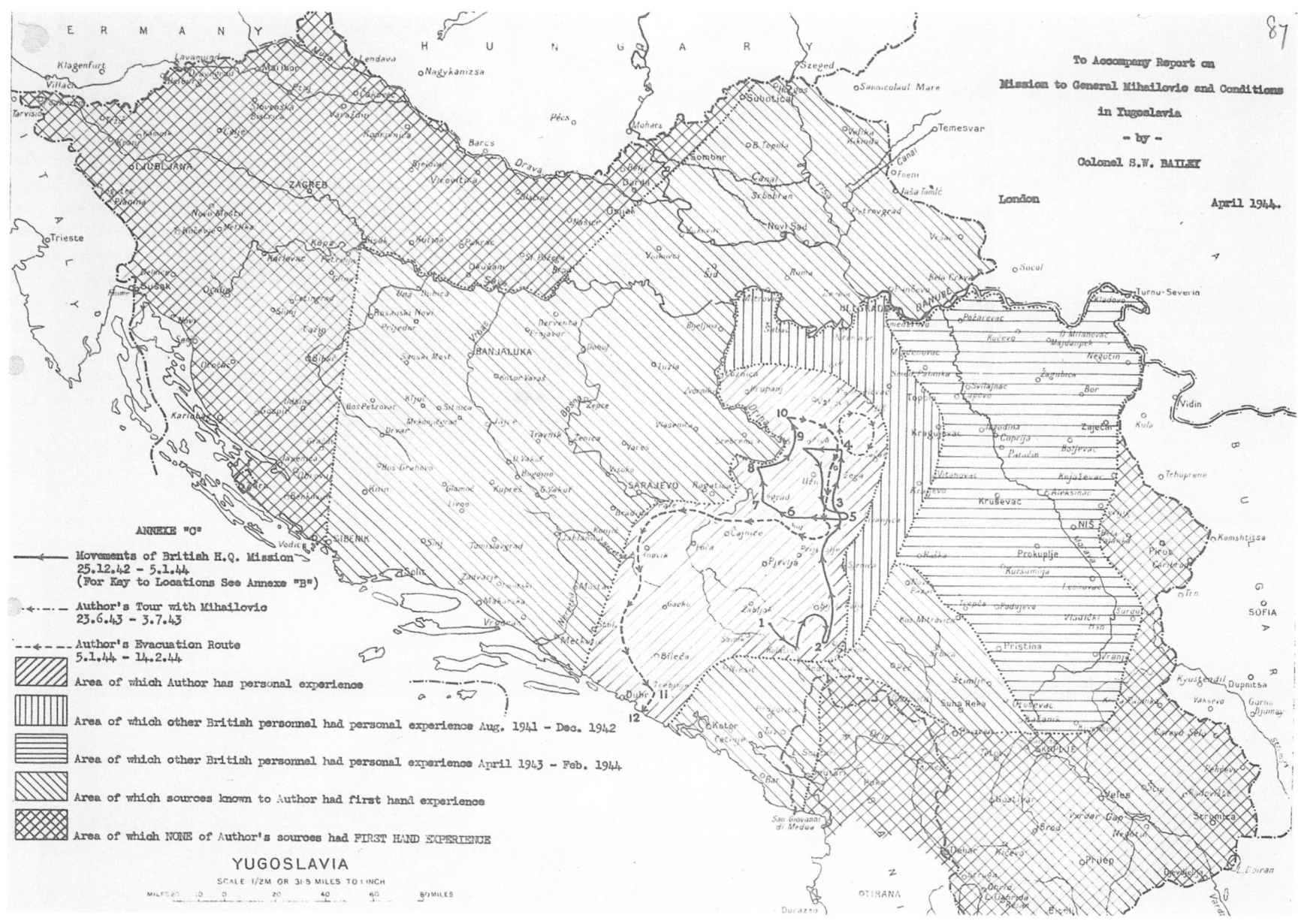

GUERRILLA MOVEMENTS WITHIN YUGOSLAVIA, APRIL 1944

ABOVE AND RIGHT: These two charts were produced in April 1944 as part of a report on the guerrilla movements within Yugoslavia. The author, Colonel S.V. Bailey, was an intelligence officer who spent a long time in the country working with both Tito and Mihailovic. The first map **(above)** records a personal tour of the borders with Mihailovic's group. The second shows both Bailey's movements and those of intelligence operatives in his group in 1943. MFQ 553 (1) (2)

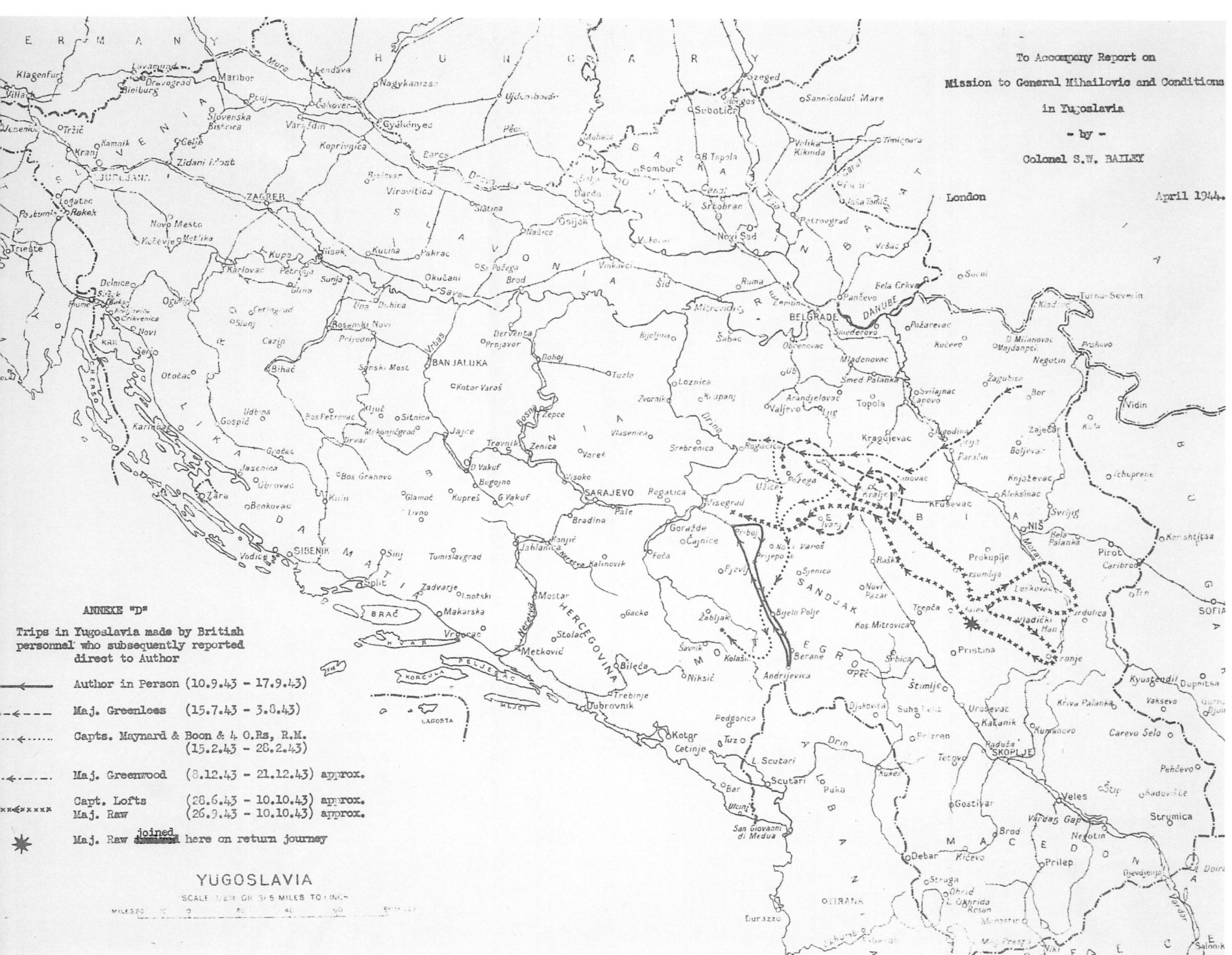

To Accompany Report on

Mission to General Mihailovic and Conditions

in Yugoslavia

– by –

Colonel S.W. BAILEY

London   April 1944.

ANNEXE "D"

Trips in Yugoslavia made by British
personnel who subsequently reported
direct to Author

⟶	Author in Person	(10.9.43 – 17.9.43)
– – – ◄	Maj. Greenlees	(15.7.43 – 3.8.43)
····◄····	Capts. Maynard & Boon & 4 O.Rs, R.M. (15.2.43 – 28.2.43)
–·–·–◄	Maj. Greenwood	(8.12.43 – 21.12.43) approx.
xx◄xxxx	Capt. Lofts	(28.6.43 – 10.10.43) approx.
	Maj. Raw	(26.9.43 – 10.10.43) approx.
✸	Maj. Raw joined here on return journey	

YUGOSLAVIA

SCALE 1/2M OR 3·5 MILES TO 1 INCH

MILES 20 10 0 20 40 60 80 MILES

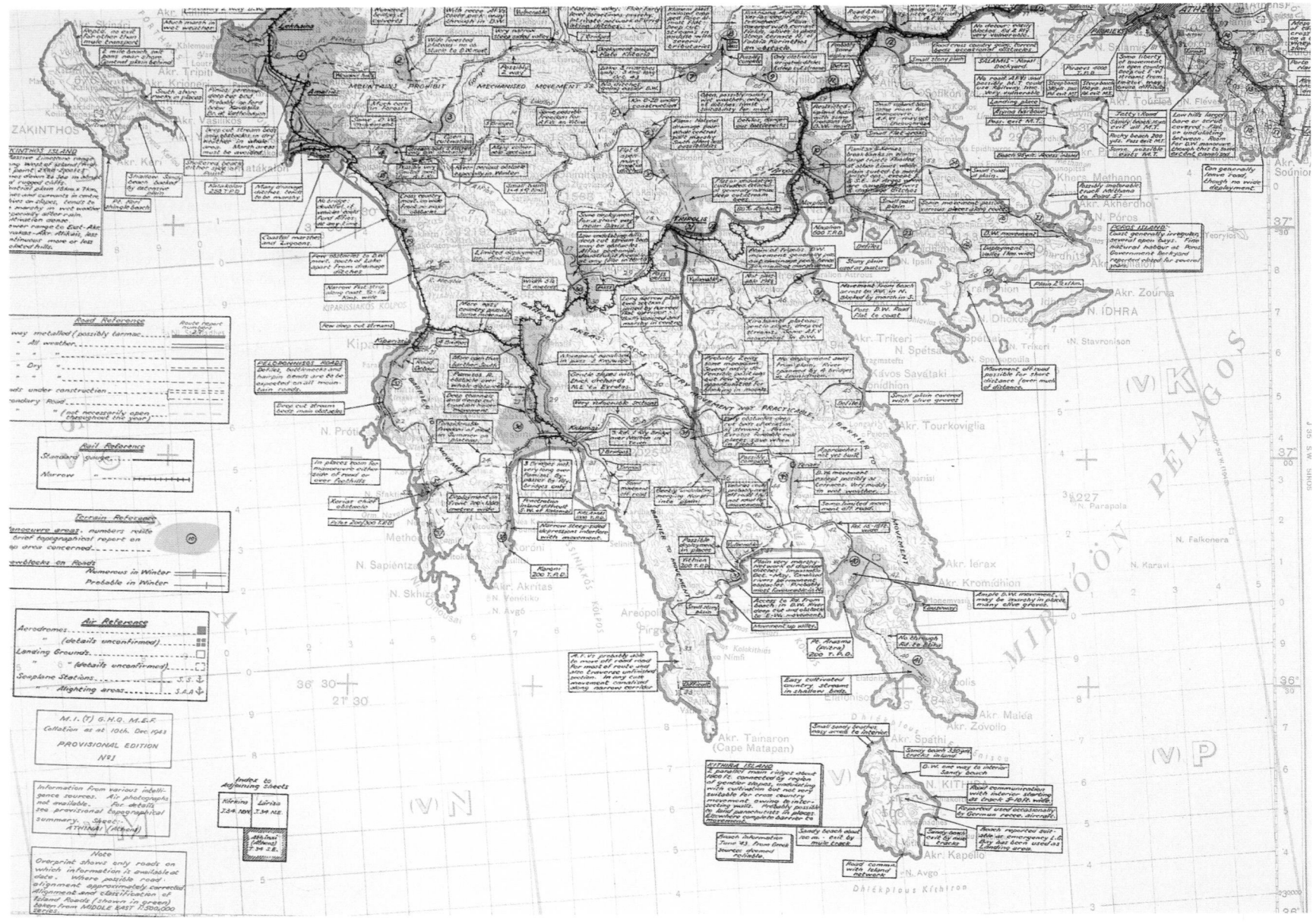

ATHENS, NOVEMBER 1943

The following maps **(pages 76–79)** illustrate the sort of geographical maps produced during the war by field survey companies. They show clearly that the Allies were able to obtain detailed intelligence of such regions, which could form the basis of detailed invasion plans. **Above:** The area surrounding Athens, the Greek capital, based on information collated up to 10 December 1943.

Greece was occupied by Germany and Italy in March 1941 and, in spite of British support for, and attempts to unite, Greek resistance movements, fought an underground civil war from October 1943 until the end of February 1944. In November the Germans began to withdraw and internecine fighting restarted as communist and nationalist forces fought over the country. MPH 897 (14)

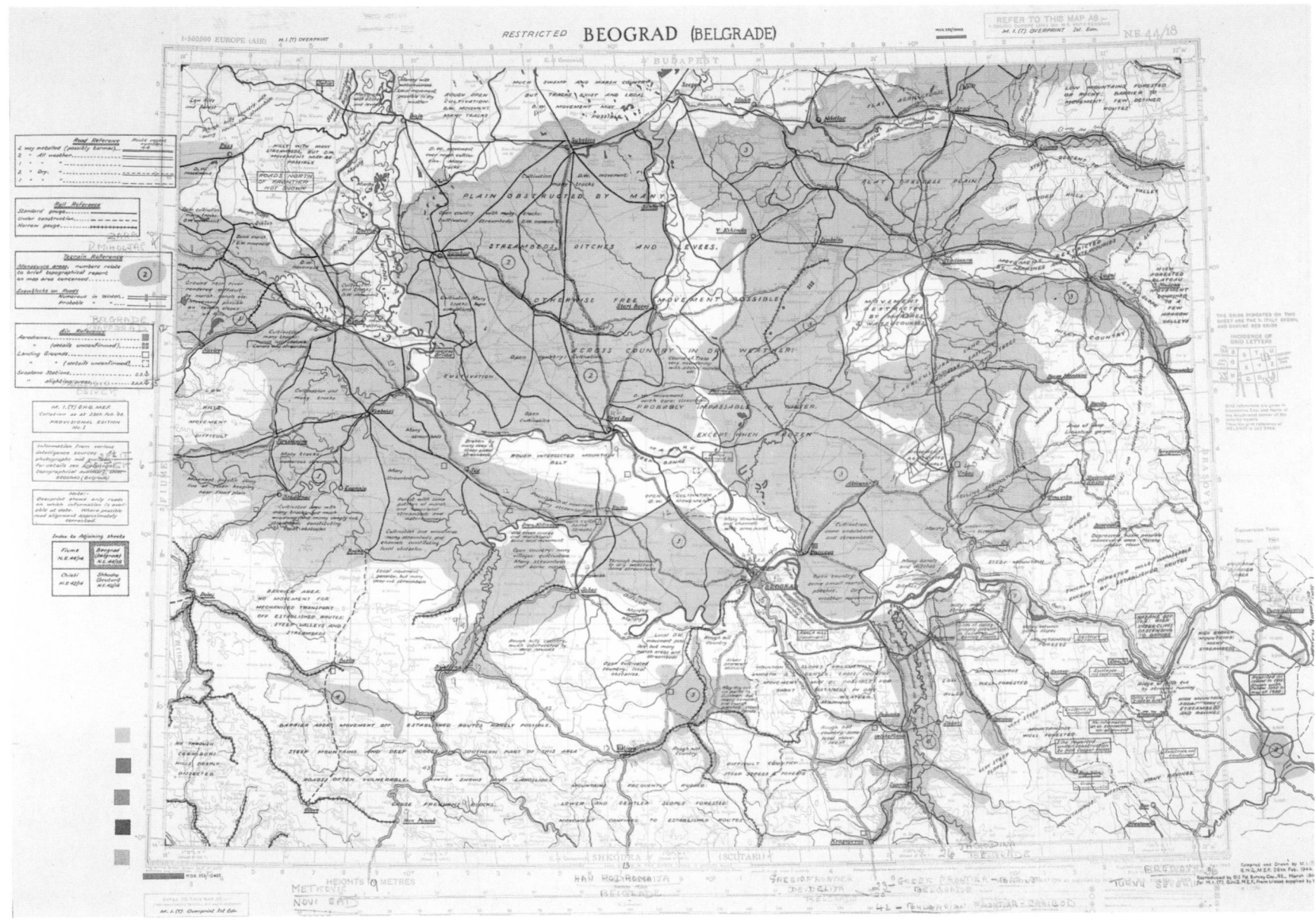

BELGRADE, FEBRUARY 1944

Geographical map of the region surrounding Belgrade, the Yugoslav capital, based on information collated up to 28 February 1944. Information on local topographical features and the status of the transport network is given, presumably based on information supplied by Tito's partisans. MPH 897 (12)

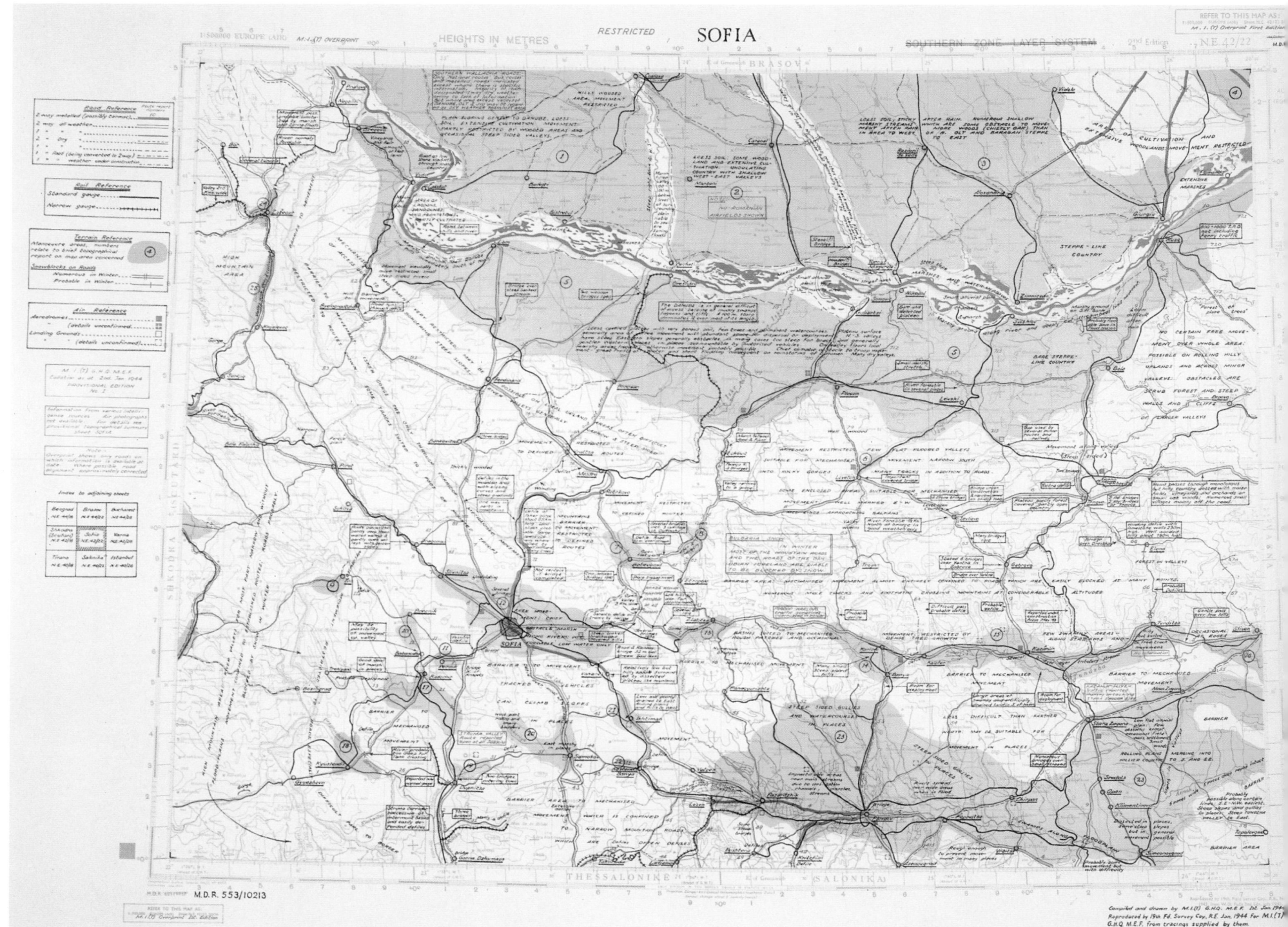

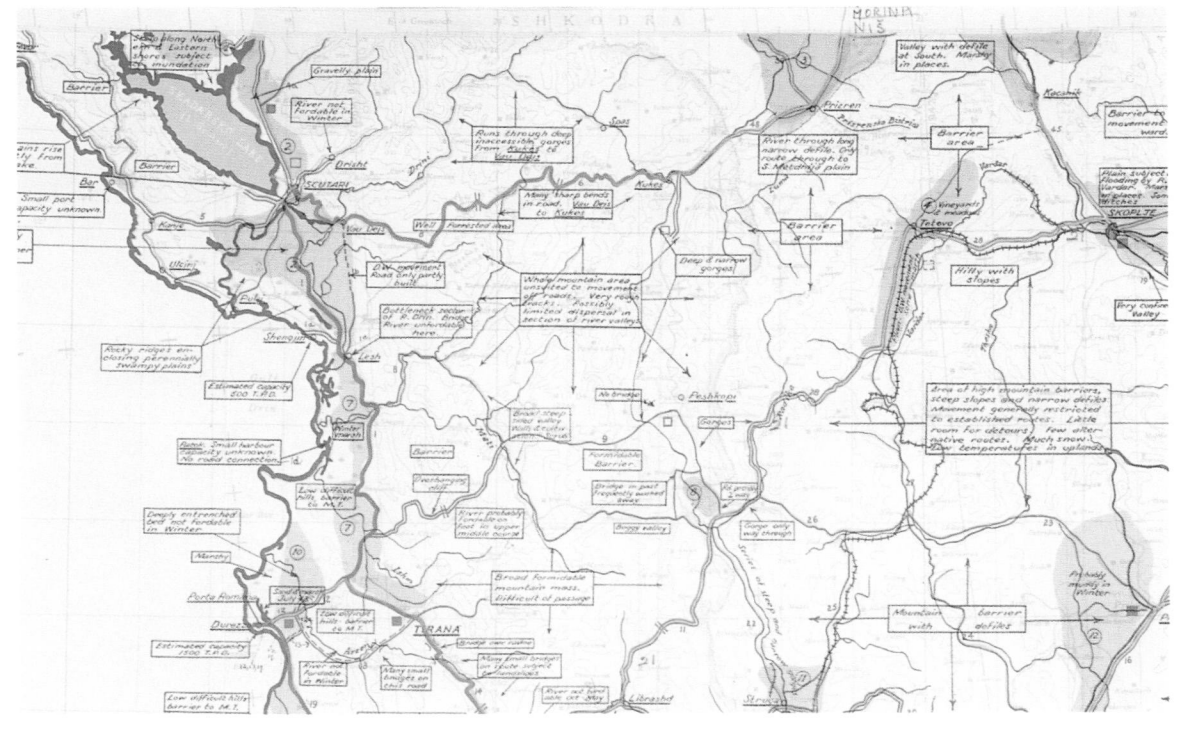

SOFIA, JANUARY 1944

FAR LEFT: Geographical map of the region surrounding Sofia, the Bulgarian capital, based on information collated up to 2 January 1944. The detailed annotation describes the many natural barriers to armour and mechanised transport around the city. Bulgaria joined the Axis in 1941 and, although it did not participate in Operation 'Barbarossa', it was invaded by the Red Army in September 1944. MPH 897 (5)

TIRANA, NOVEMBER 1943

ABOVE LEFT: Geographical map of the region surrounding Tirana in Albania based on information from sources on the ground, up until 18 November 1943. The detailed annotation describes local topographical features and potential landing zones on the coast. Also described are military installations. Italy invaded Albania on 7 April 1939, and from it launched attacks against Greece and Yugoslavia. After the capitulation of Italy in July 1943, Hitler restored Albanian independence, but by the end of the war communist partisans led by Enver Hoxha controlled most of the country. MPH 897 (2)

LJUBLJANA, 1944

LEFT: A French map from 1944 of Ljubljana province in southern Yugoslavia, which indicates the location of public and private buildings destroyed by the occupying Axis forces and through the actions of partisans. Also marked (by red crosses) are the scenes of atrocities against the local population, which were committed by all of those that fought in the violent war in Yugoslavia. MPK 512

BERLIN, RAF TARGET MAP, 1944

Detailed RAF map of Berlin, showing the main military and industrial targets, and residential areas. Note how the map has been divided into sectors showing building concentrations. At the end of 1941 the RAF's Strategic Bombing Offensive was achieving very little success in pinpoint attacks on predetermined military and industrial targets, and the controversial policy of 'area bombing' was adopted. Championed by the C-in-C of the Air Staff, Air Marshal Sir Charles Portal, and fully implemented from February 1942 by the head of Bomber Command, Air Marshal Arthur Harris, 'area bombing' gradually reduced Germany's cities to rubble. The aim was to bring the civilian population to its knees, but the extent to which this aim was achieved is still a hotly-disputed topic. MFQ 446 (2) (3)

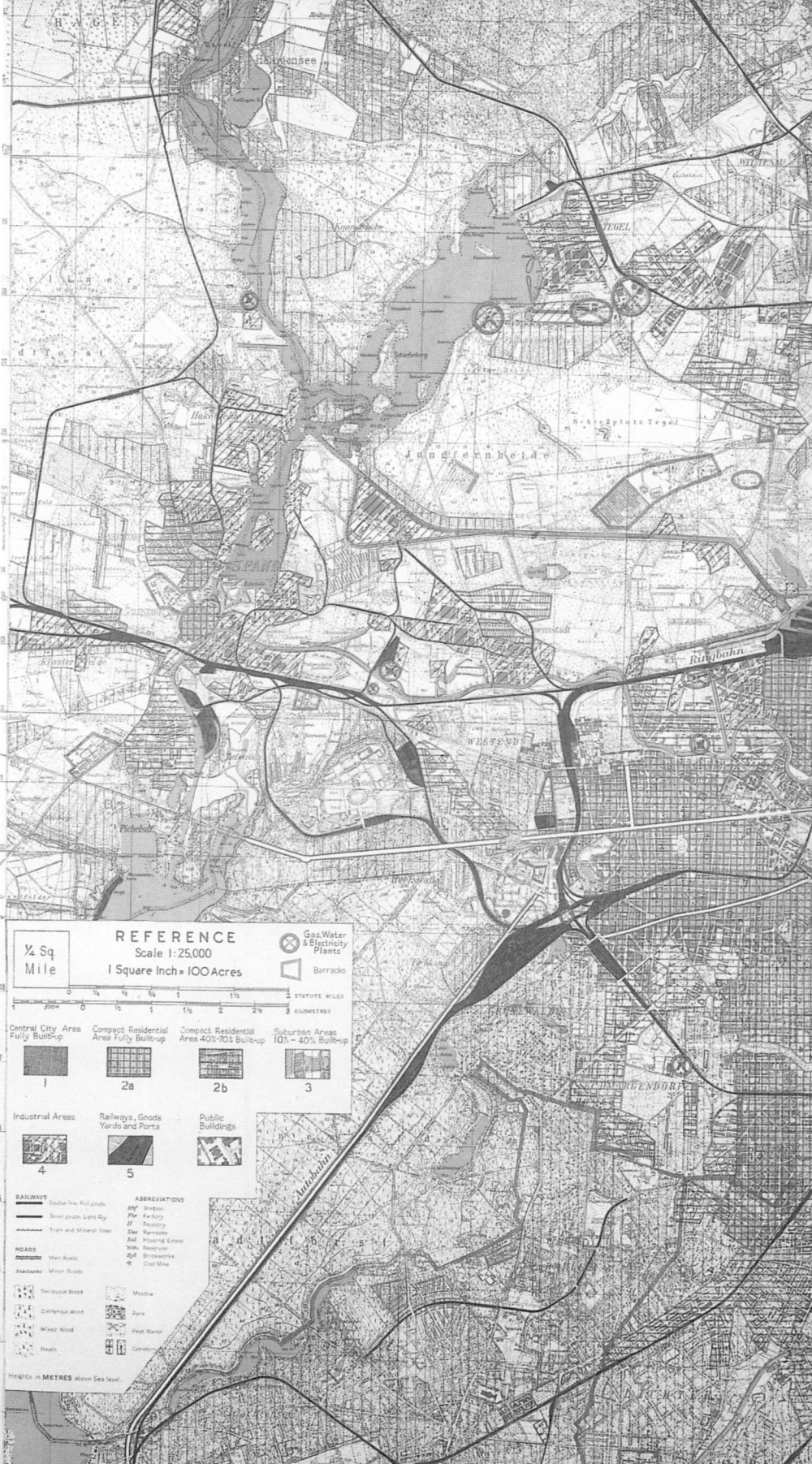

PEENEMÜNDE, 1944

RIGHT AND FAR RIGHT: Illustrations showing the German rocket testing and production site at Peenemünde on the Baltic coast, and a detailed diagram of the storage and launching procedure for the V-2 rockets that were built there. Allied intelligence officers first became aware that Germany was producing a pilotless missile, the jet-powered V-1, at Peenemünde in mid-1943, leading to a diversion of forces from the Strategic Bombing Offensive for Operation 'Crossbow'. Launched in August, this targeted both the production facilities and the launch sites on the French Channel coast. September 1944 saw the first attacks on London by V-2 liquid-fuel powered ballistic rockets, some 5,000 of which had been launched by the end of March 1945, when production at Peenemünde ended. AIR 34/632

STORAGE & LAUNCHING OF A.4. ROCKET PROJECTILE.
(BASED ON AVAILABLE INFORMATION)

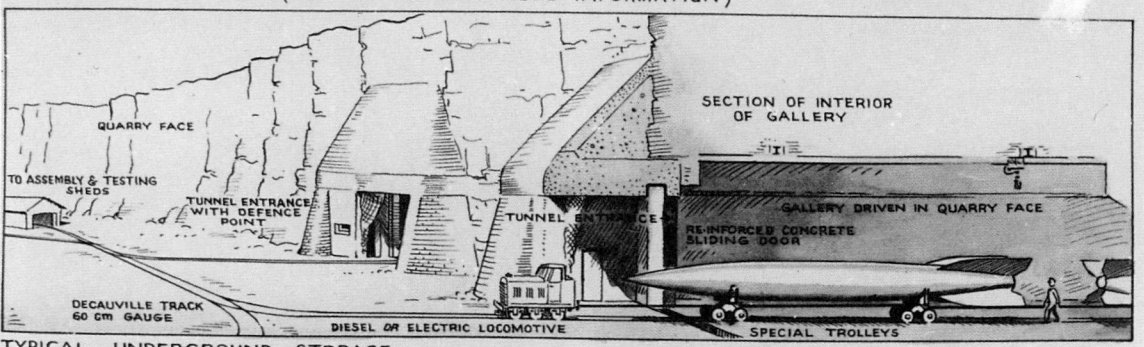

TYPICAL UNDERGROUND STORAGE.

TYPICAL DISPERSED SURFACE STORAGE.

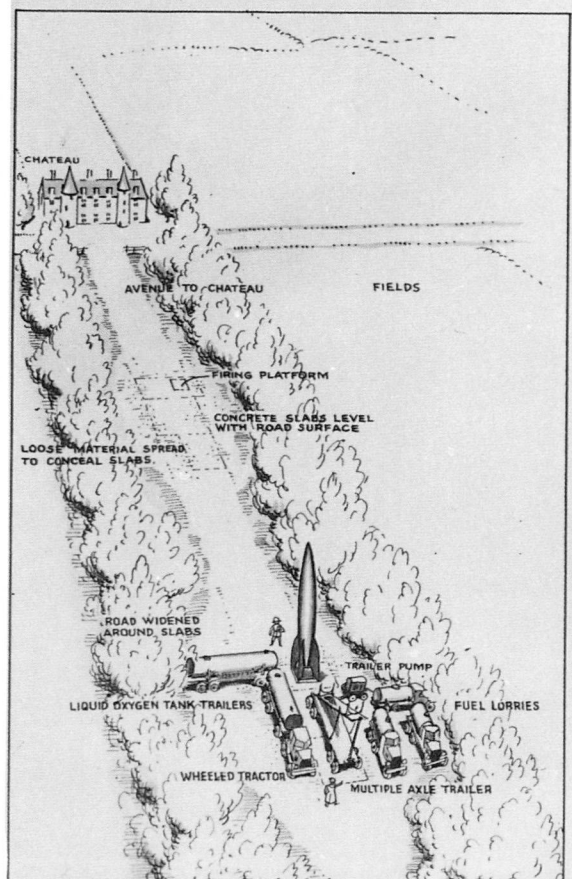

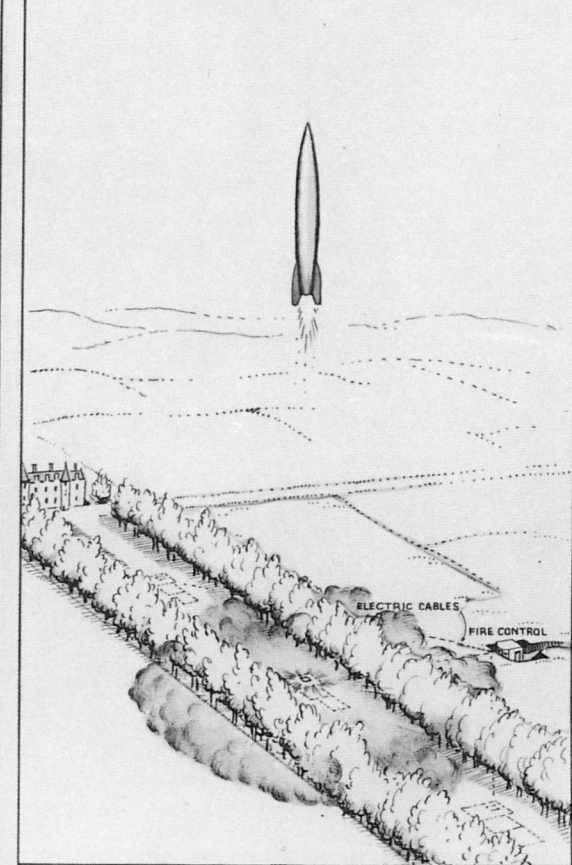

TYPICAL LAUNCHING SITE.

A.I.2.G. N°X/I4I.(8.44)

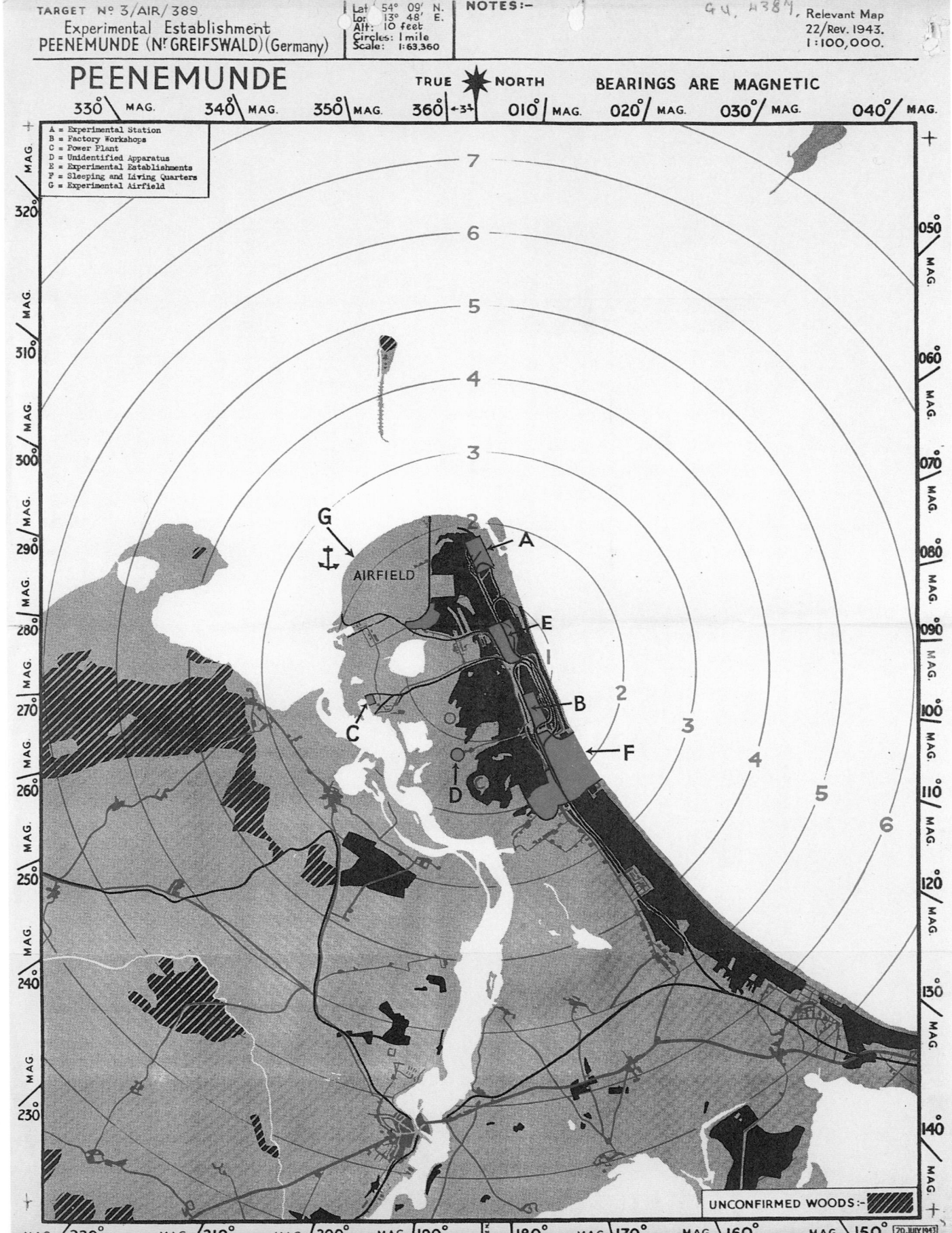

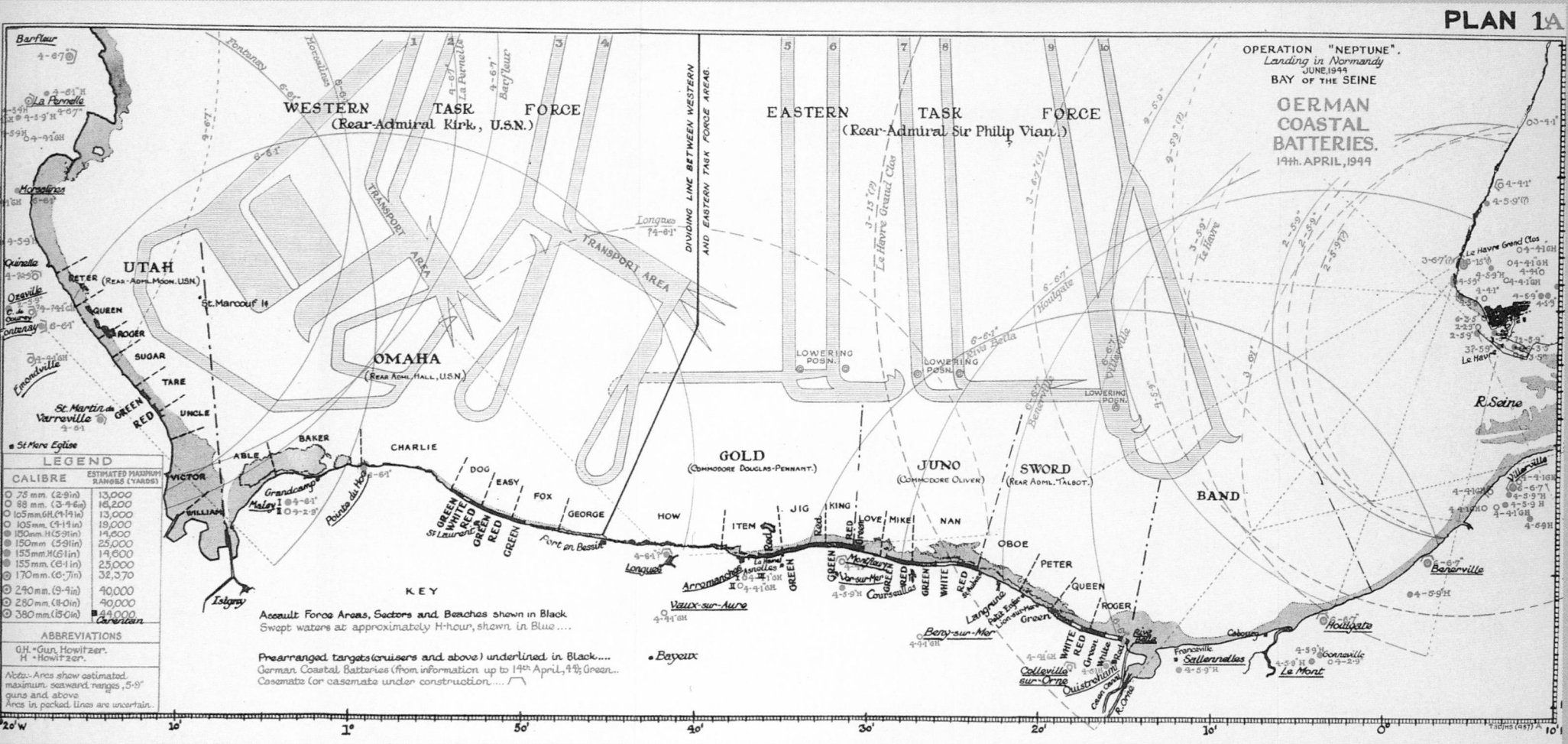

PLAN 1A

OPERATION "NEPTUNE".
Landing in Normandy
JUNE, 1944
BAY OF THE SEINE

GERMAN COASTAL BATTERIES.
19th. APRIL, 1944

D-DAY: GERMAN COASTAL BATTERIES, 19 APRIL 1944

One of a series of maps of the Normandy beaches prepared for Operation 'Neptune' — the cross-Channel assault phase of 'Overlord' (see also following pages) — this details the German coastal defence batteries. ADM 234/366

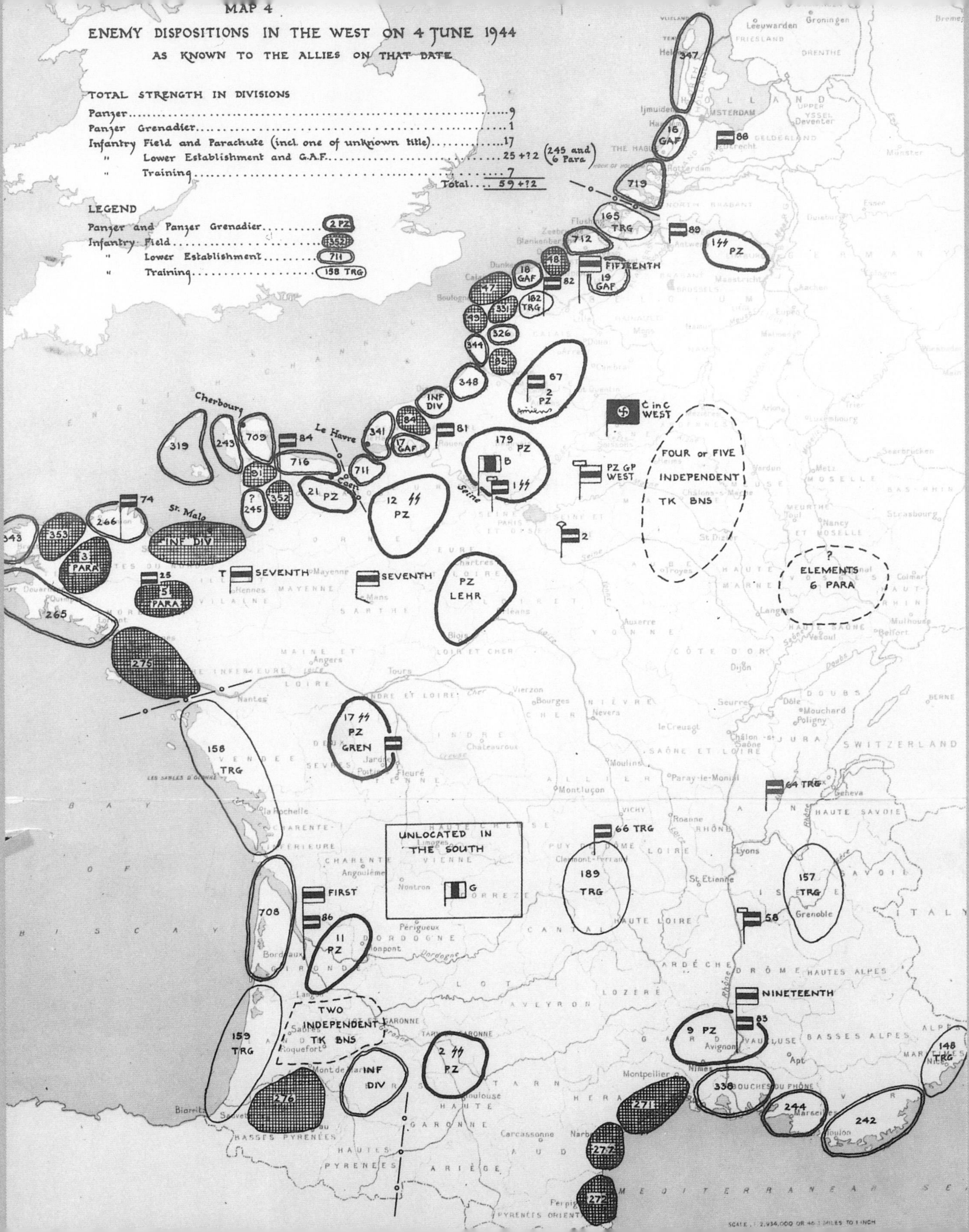

MAP 4
ENEMY DISPOSITIONS IN THE WEST ON 4 JUNE 1944
AS KNOWN TO THE ALLIES ON THAT DATE
TOTAL STRENGTH IN DIVISIONS
Panzer..........9
Panzer Grenadier..........1
Infantry Field and Parachute (incl. one of unknown title)..........17
" Lower Establishment and G.A.F..........25 +?2 (245 and 6 Para)
" Training..........7
Total..... 59 +?2
LEGEND
Panzer and Panzer Grenadier.......... 2 PZ
Infantry Field.......... 352
" Lower Establishment.......... 711
" Training.......... 158 TRG
C in C WEST
PZ GP WEST
FIFTEENTH
SEVENTH
FIRST
NINETEENTH
FOUR or FIVE INDEPENDENT TK BNS
TWO INDEPENDENT TK BNS
ELEMENTS 6 PARA
UNLOCATED IN THE SOUTH
PZ LEHR
12 SS PZ
21 PZ
17 SS PZ GREN
2 SS PZ
9 PZ
11 PZ
Cherbourg
Le Havre
St. Malo
SWITZERLAND
ITALY

D-DAY: GERMAN POSITIONS IN FRANCE, 1944

This overview shows the estimated dispositions of Axis forces in France on 4 June 1944. Most of von Rundstedt's Army Group West, which in June 1944 comprised some 50 divisions, are concentrated in the Pas de Calais region, where the Germans fully expected the attack to come. Their confusion was compounded by an elaborate and highly successful set of deception plans code-named 'Bodyguard', the major objective of which was to conceal the intentions of the Allies to invade northern and southern France. CAB 44/242

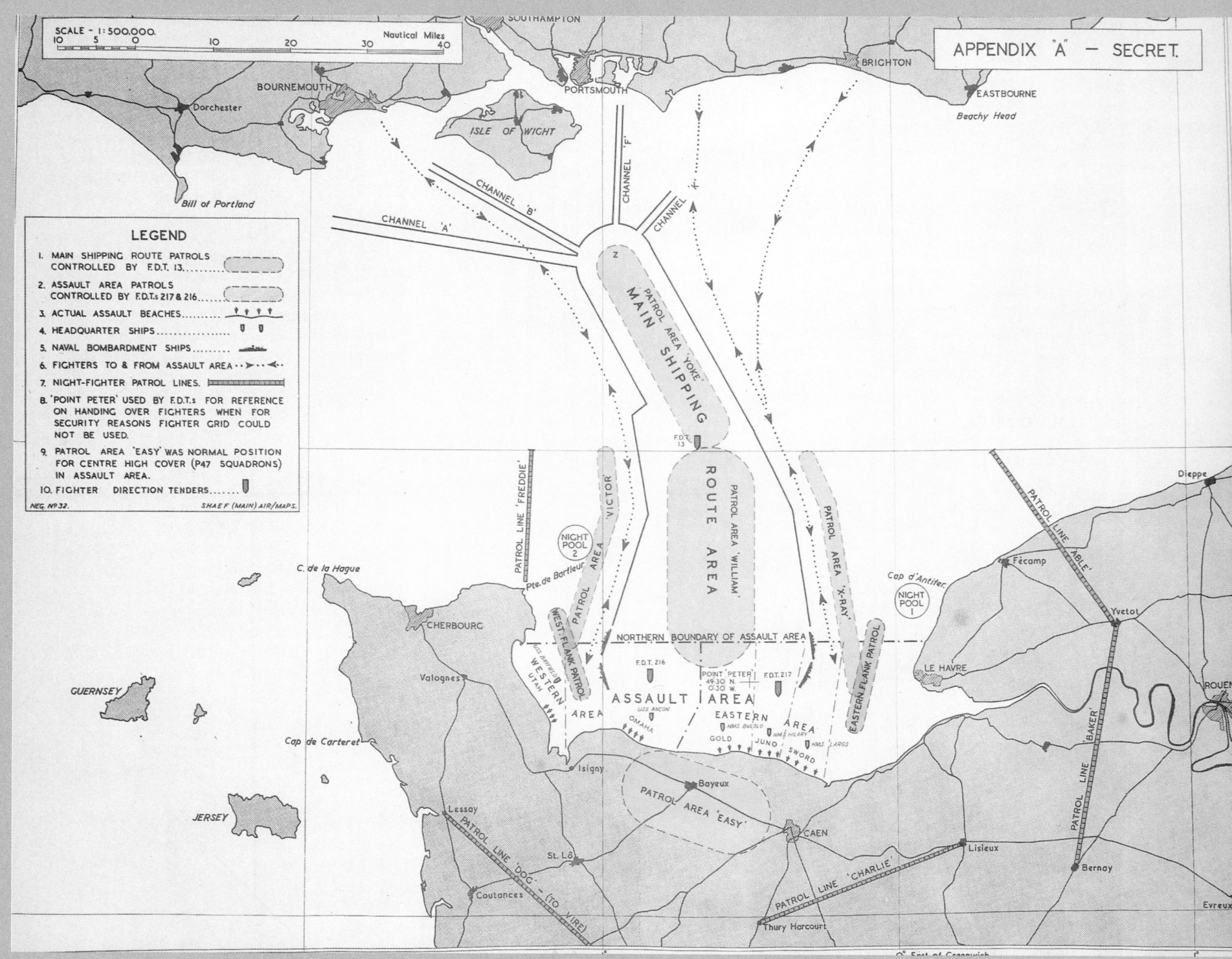

SCALE — 1:500,000.
10 5 0   10   20   30   Nautical Miles   40

LEGEND

1. MAIN SHIPPING ROUTE PATROLS CONTROLLED BY F.D.T. 13 ....
2. ASSAULT AREA PATROLS CONTROLLED BY F.D.T.s 217 & 216 ....
3. ACTUAL ASSAULT BEACHES ....
4. HEADQUARTER SHIPS ....
5. NAVAL BOMBARDMENT SHIPS ....
6. FIGHTERS TO & FROM ASSAULT AREA ▸·▸·◂·◂
7. NIGHT-FIGHTER PATROL LINES ....
8. 'POINT PETER' USED BY F.D.T.s FOR REFERENCE ON HANDING OVER FIGHTERS WHEN FOR SECURITY REASONS FIGHTER GRID COULD NOT BE USED.
9. PATROL AREA 'EASY' WAS NORMAL POSITION FOR CENTRE HIGH COVER (P47 SQUADRONS) IN ASSAULT AREA.
10. FIGHTER DIRECTION TENDERS ....

NEG. Nº 32.   SHAEF (MAIN) AIR/MAPS.

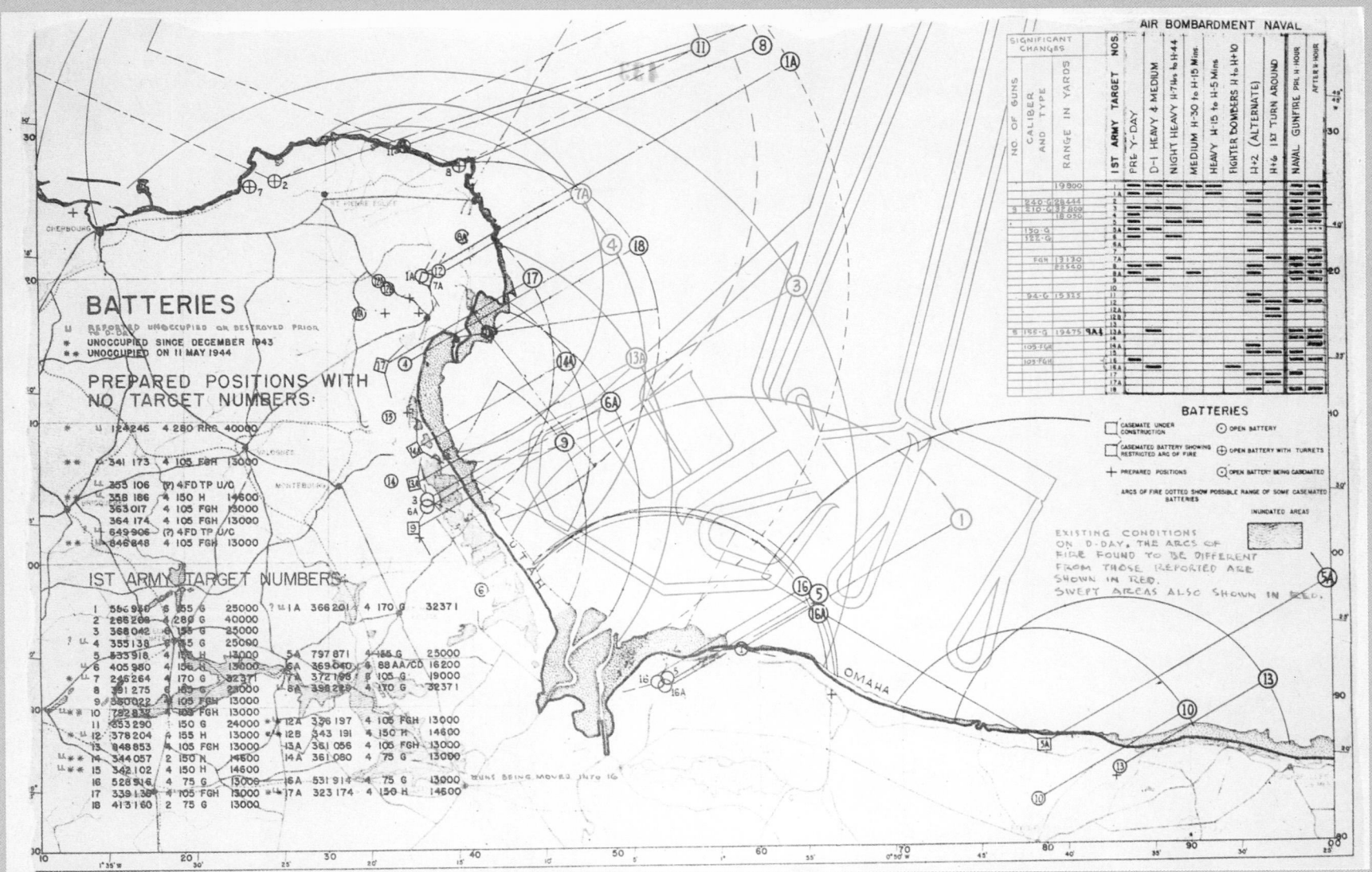

D-DAY: ALLIED AIR OPERATIONS, 6 JUNE 1944

LEFT: This map illustrates the main area of operation for Allied fighter aircraft tasked with providing cover for the invasion convoys (the naval element of 'Overlord' was codenamed 'Neptune') shuttling between the British southern ports and the Normandy beach-heads. The fighter cover was coordinated by Eisenhower's deputy, Air Chief Marshal Tedder, and the C-in-C of Air Forces, Leigh-Mallory, and was a vital element in an air task force that included over 13,000 American aircraft alone. MPI 450 (1)

D-DAY: U.S. NAVY BOMBARDMENT PLAN, 6 JUNE 1944

ABOVE: In the hours before the first waves of troops from the U.S. First Army came ashore on 'Utah' and 'Omaha' beaches, the U.S. Navy laid down a massive barrage on the German defensive positions in their path. The status and position of the German shore batteries are identified by grid references in the lower left hand table, and their arcs of fire are described by the overlapping arcs. The irregular geometric shapes marked in red are the paths of inbound ships. MPI 450 (2)

D-DAY: 'OMAHA' BEACH, 6 JUNE 1944

RIGHT: Plan for the landings on 'Omaha' Beach, showing the assault zones and phased objectives for the American troops. The planners could not have known that the U.S. assault force would meet the stiffest German resistance at Omaha, and suffer by far the heaviest casualties in achieving their objectives. DEFE 2/436

D-DAY: OPERATION 'NEPTUNE', 6 JUNE 1944

BELOW, OPPOSITE, AND ABOVE: Three maps of the Normandy beaches prepared for Operation 'Neptune', detailing the planned bombardment prior to the assault (**opposite, above**), and the fire support for the landings themselves (**opposite, below**). Also given is a detailed diagram of the assault force at 'Juno' Beach (**right**), showing the composition of the fire support force. The landings, hugely complex and involving vast numbers of men and supporting matériel, required an unprecedented scale of planning. 7,000 vessels of all kinds were required, and this put an enormous strain on Allied naval capacity for organisation and supply. First in were the minesweepers, clearing a path for the huge phalanx of transports; then a force of 138 warships bombarded the German defences while destroyers, sloops, frigates, corvettes and trawlers escorted the convoys from southern England. Total landing craft strength was over 4,000. ADM 234/366

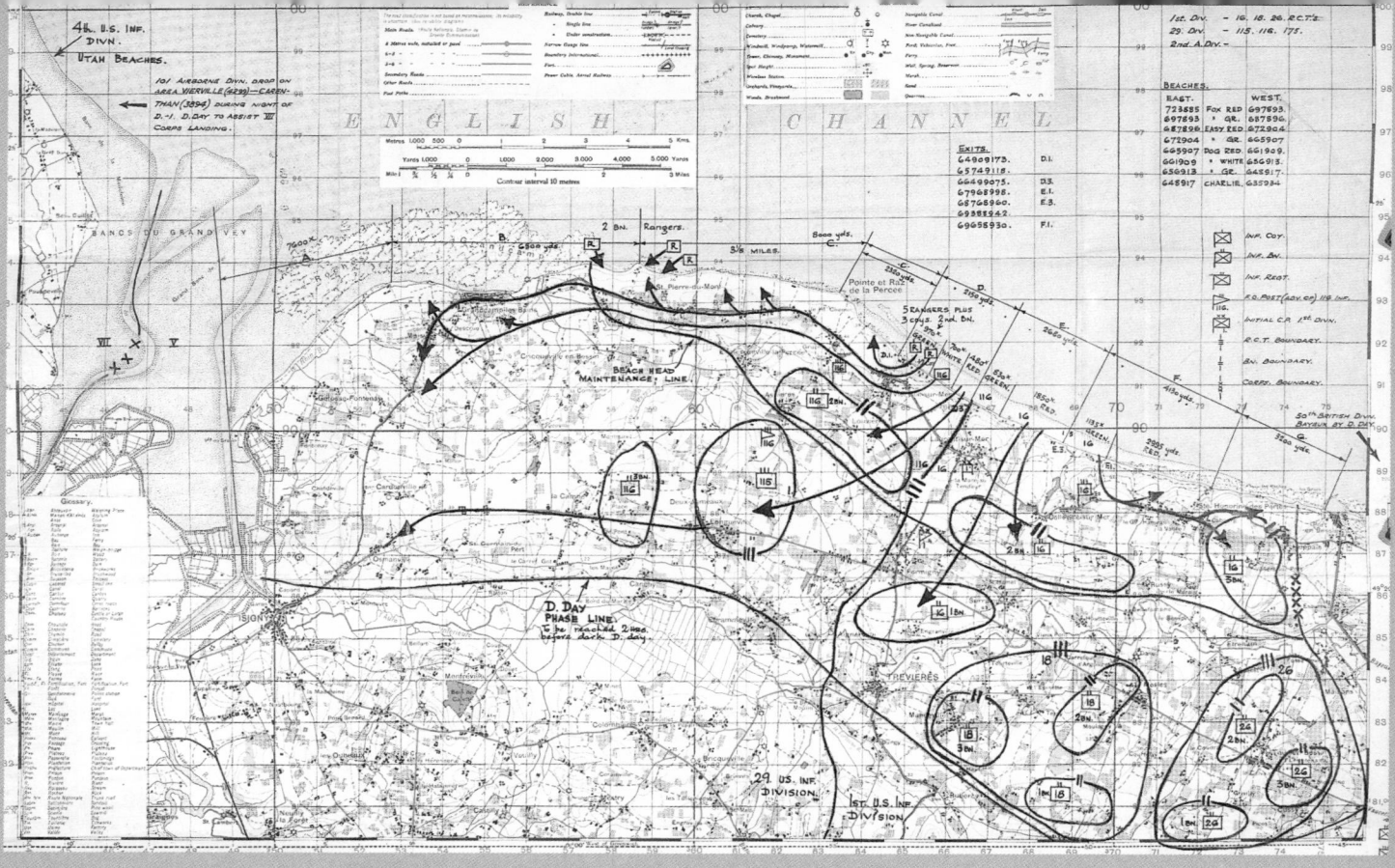

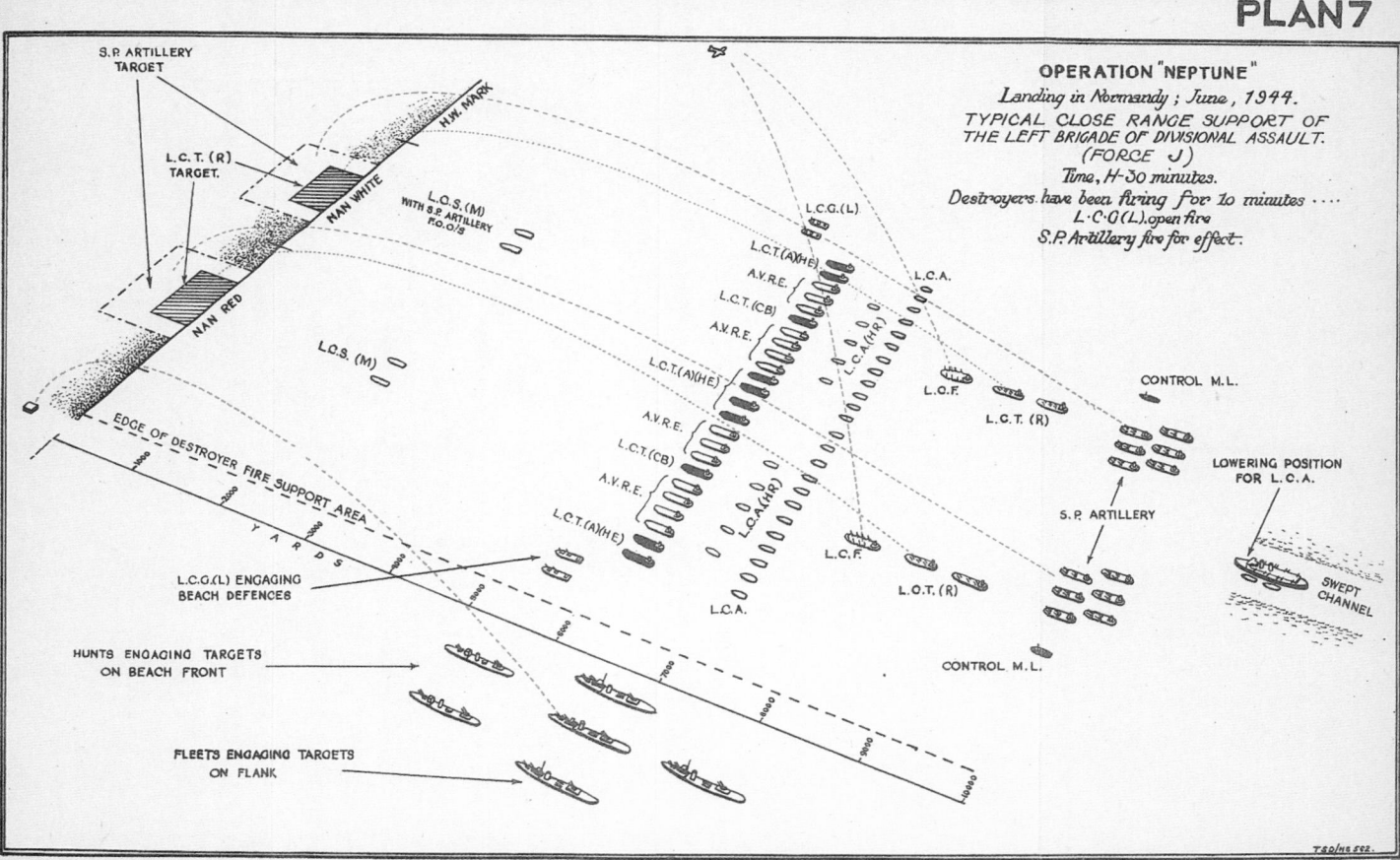

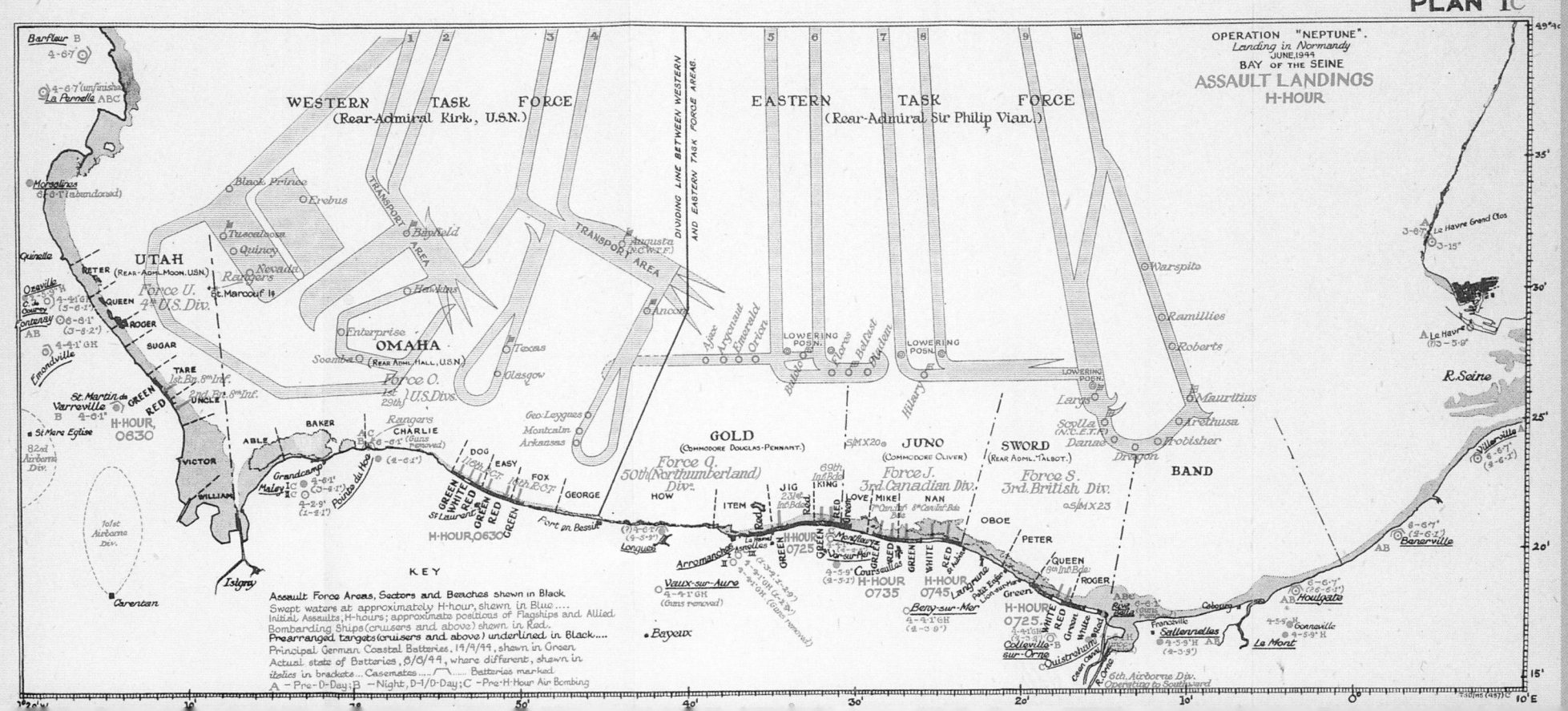

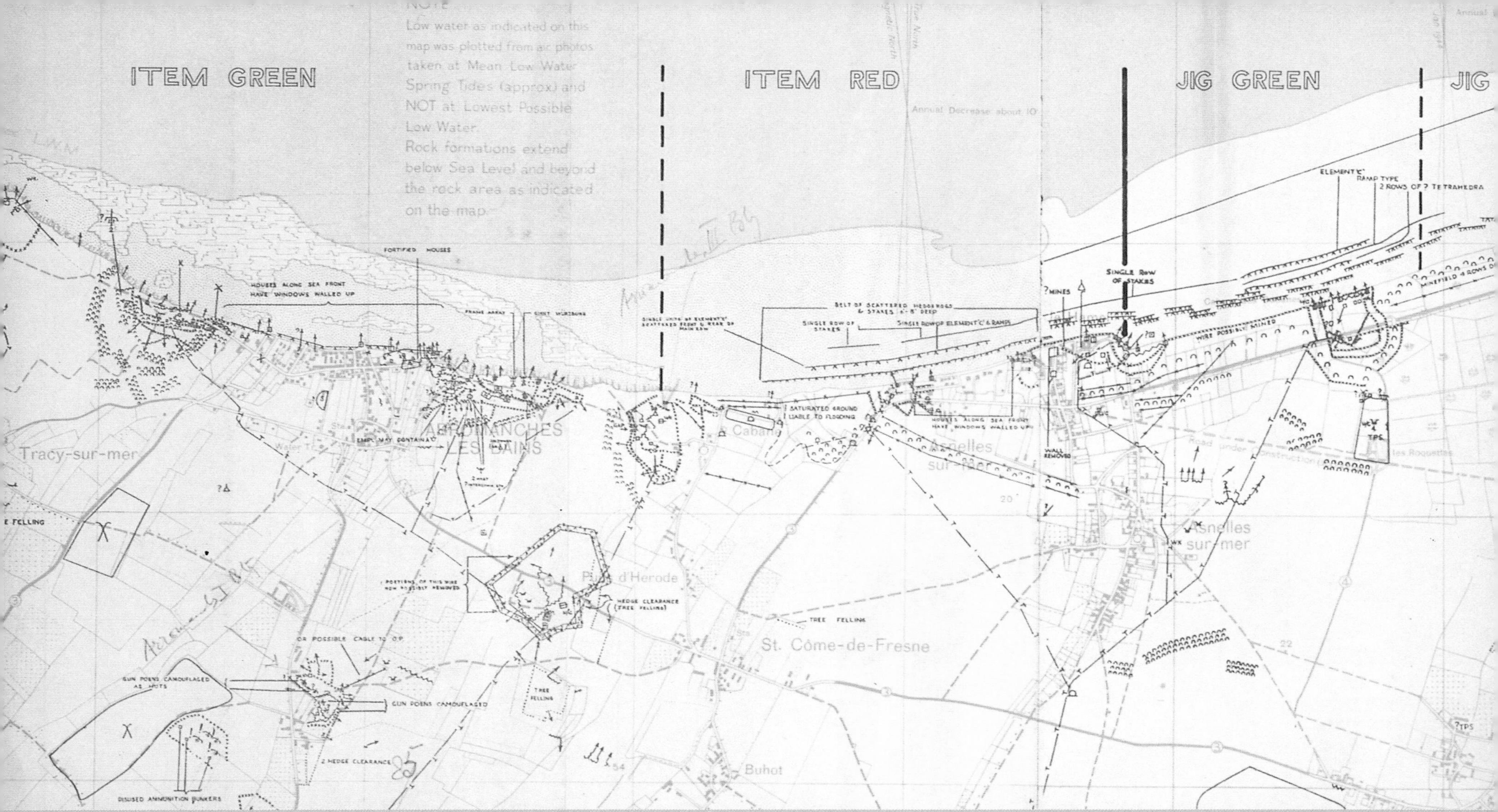

D-DAY: 'GOLD' AND 'JUNO' BEACH DEFENCES, 6 JUNE 1944

Reconnaissance of the Normandy beaches by Allied aircraft and frogmen of the Special Boat Service formed a vital part of the preparations for the Normandy landings, allowing cartographers to construct detailed maps showing the positions of underwater and beach defences. These two maps show the defences at 'Gold' Beach **(above)** at Arromanches-les-Bains and 'Juno' Beach **(right)** at Courseulles sur Mer, where elements of the British XXX and I Corps were landed. Note the annotation showing the positions of 'Hedgehog' and 'Tetraheda' obstacles. These pieces of angled iron were designed to rip the bottoms out of landing craft and impede amphibious tanks from advancing across the beaches. CAB 44/243 CAB 44/244

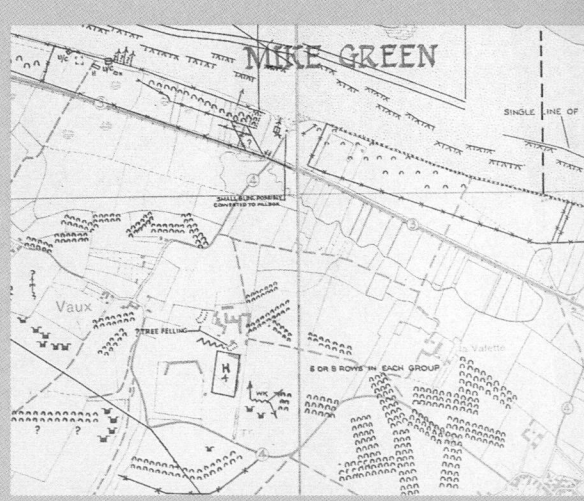

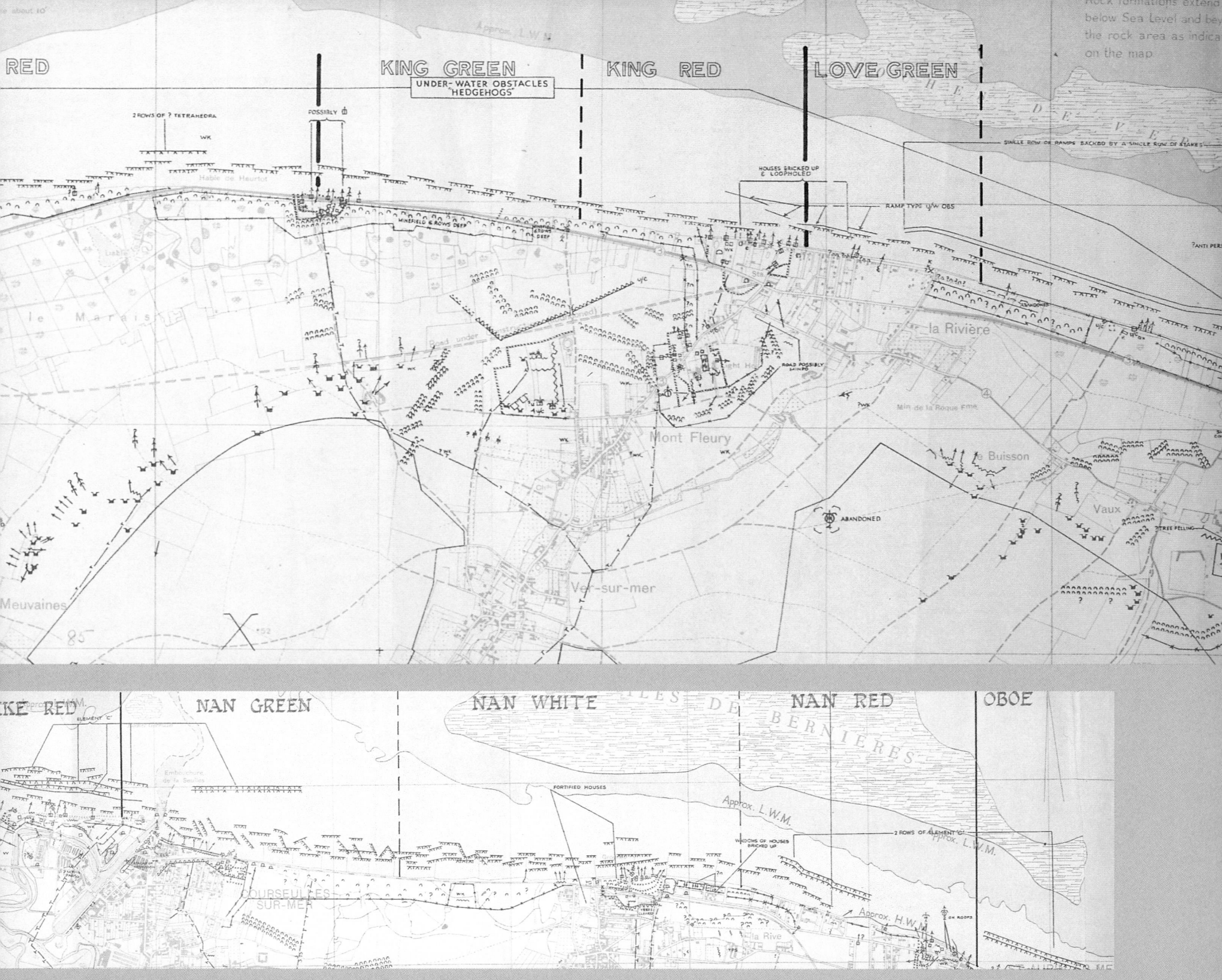

RED　KING GREEN　KING RED　LOVE GREEN

UNDER-WATER OBSTACLES "HEDGEHOGS"

2 ROWS OF ? TETRAHEDRA

POSSIBLY

Hâble de Heurtot

SINGLE ROW OF RAMPS BACKED BY A SINGLE ROW OF STAKES

HOUSES BRICKED UP & LOOPHOLED

RAMP TYPE U/W OBS

MINEFIELD 6 ROWS DEEP

le Marais

la Rivière

Mont Fleury

Mîn de la Roque Fme

le Buisson

ABANDONED

Vaux

Ver-sur-mer

Meuvaines

85

KE RED　NAN GREEN　NAN WHITE　NAN RED　OBOE

ÎLES DE BERNIÈRES

Embouchure de la Seulles

Approx. L.W.M.

FORTIFIED HOUSES

2 ROWS OF ELEMENT 'C'

WINDOWS OF HOUSES BRICKED UP

COURSEULLES-SUR-MER

Approx. H.W.M.

la Rive

D-DAY: 'SWORD' BEACH, 1944

These maps show 'Sword' Beach, the area of French coastline between Lion-sur-Mer and Ouistreham attacked by the remainder of the British Ist Corps. The first **(right)** shows the planned layout of supply dumps, headquarters units, bivouac areas and burial grounds after the landings; the second **(far right)** shows in detail the elaborate beach defences and minefields to the rear. CAB 44/247 CAB 44/244

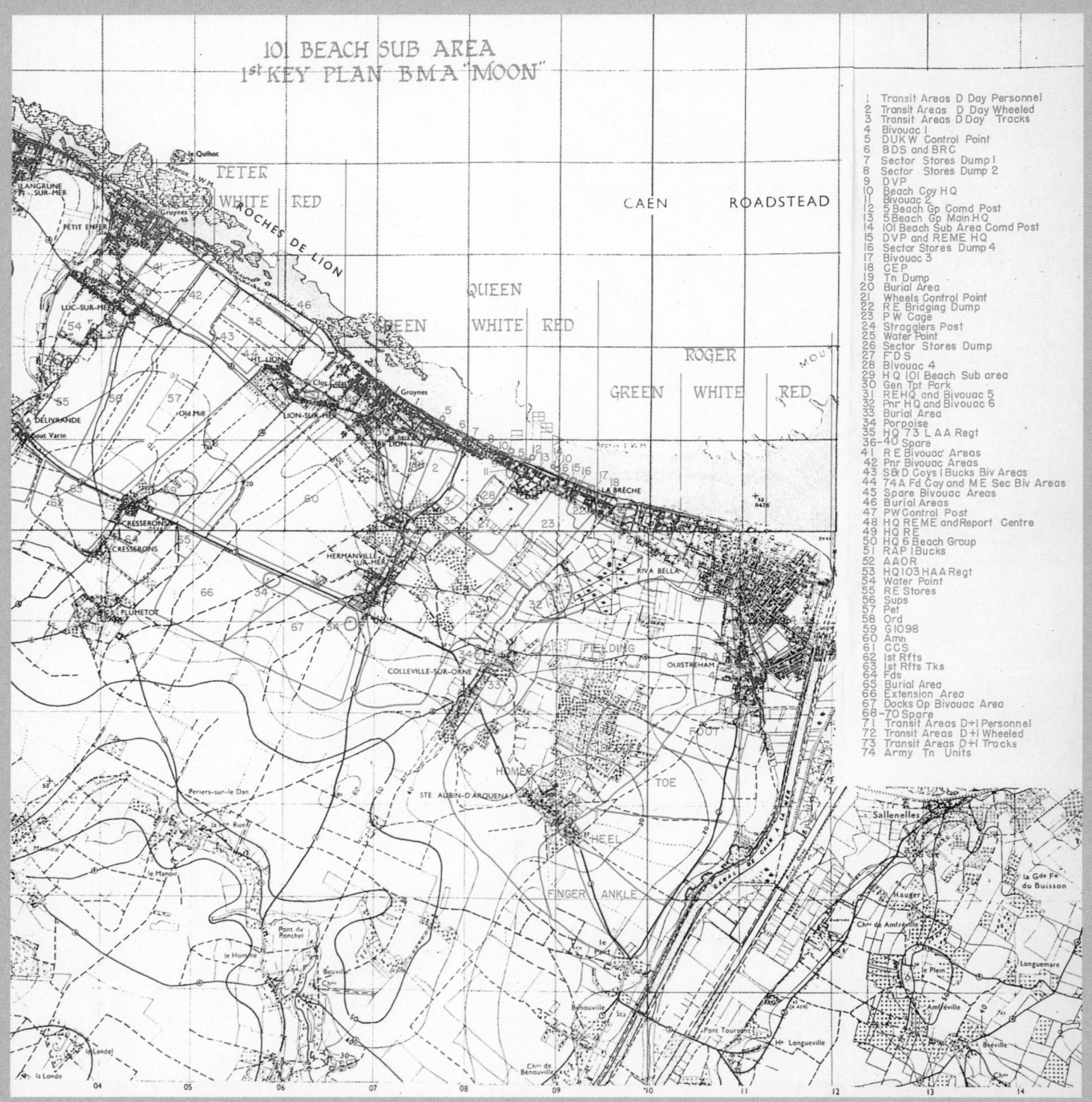

101 BEACH SUB AREA
1st KEY PLAN BMA "MOON"

1 Transit Areas D Day Personnel
2 Transit Areas D Day Wheeled
3 Transit Areas D Day Tracks
4 Bivouac I
5 DUKW Control Point
6 BDS and BRC
7 Sector Stores Dump I
8 Sector Stores Dump 2
9 DVP
10 Beach Coy HQ
11 Bivouac 2
12 S Beach Gp Comd Post
13 S Beach Gp Main HQ
14 101 Beach Sub Area Comd Post
15 DVP and REME HQ
16 Sector Stores Dump 4
17 Bivouac 3
18 CEP
19 Tn Dump
20 Burial Area
21 Wheels Control Point
22 RE Bridging Dump
23 PW Cage
24 Stragglers Post
25 Water Point
26 Sector Stores Dump
27 FDS
28 Bivouac 4
29 HQ 101 Beach Sub area
30 Gen Tpt Park
31 REHQ and Bivouac 5
32 Pnr HQ and Bivouac 6
33 Burial Area
34 Porpoise
35 HQ 73 LAA Regt
36-40 Spare
41 RE Bivouac Areas
42 Pnr Bivouac Areas
43 S&D Coys I Bucks Biv Areas
44 74A Fd Coy and ME Sec Biv Areas
45 Spare Bivouac Areas
46 Burial Areas
47 PW Control Post
48 HQ REME and Report Centre
49 HQ RE
50 HQ 6 Beach Group
51 RAP I Bucks
52 AAOR
53 HQ 103 HAA Regt
54 Water Point
55 RE Stores
56 Sios
57 Pet
58 Ord
59 G1098
60 Amn
61 CGS
62 Ist Rfts
63 Ist Rfts Tks
64 Fds
65 Burial Area
66 Extension Area
67 Docks Op Bivouac Area
68-70 Spare
71 Transit Areas D+I Personnel
72 Transit Areas D+I Wheeled
73 Transit Areas D+I Tracks
74 Army Tn Units

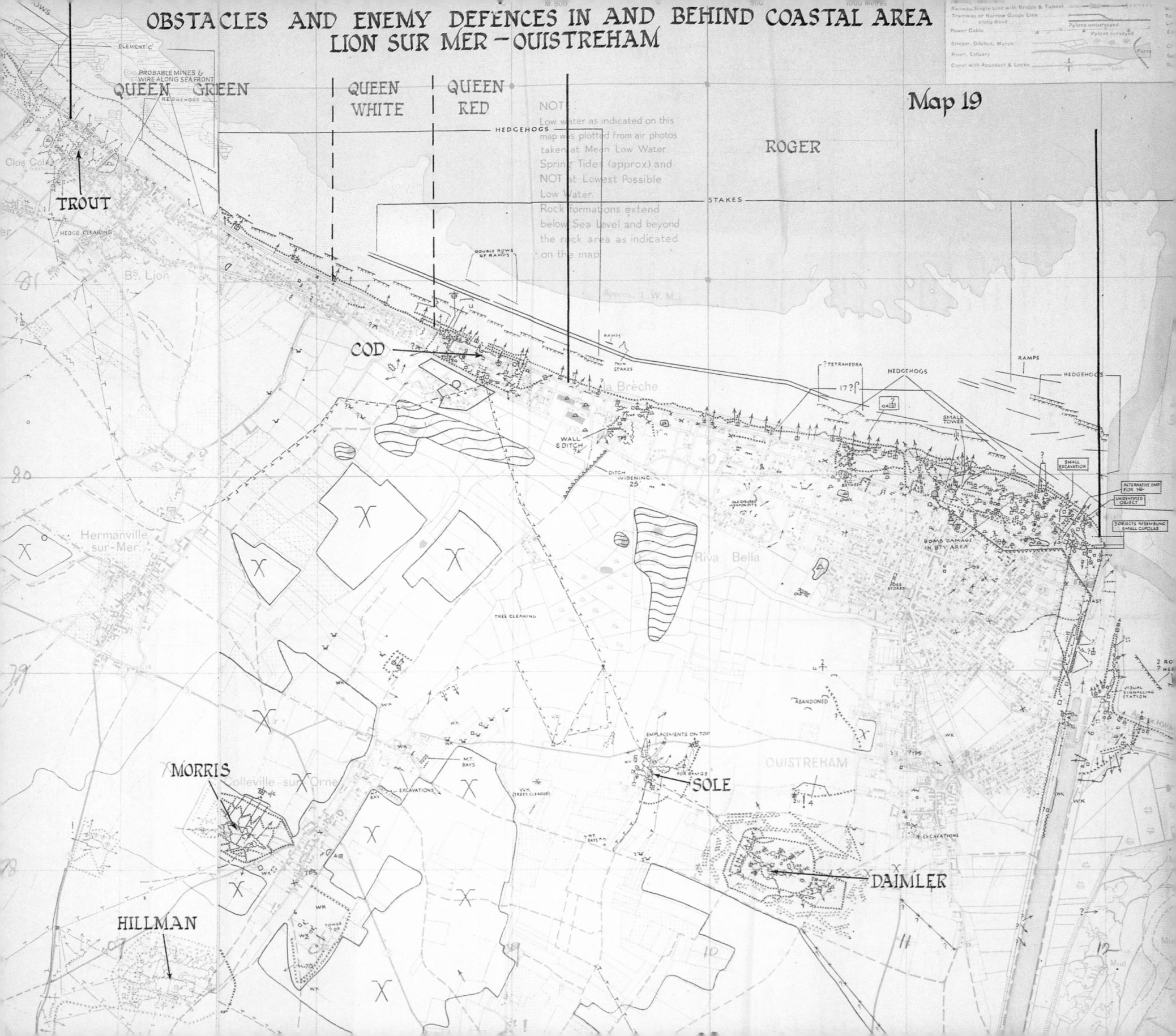

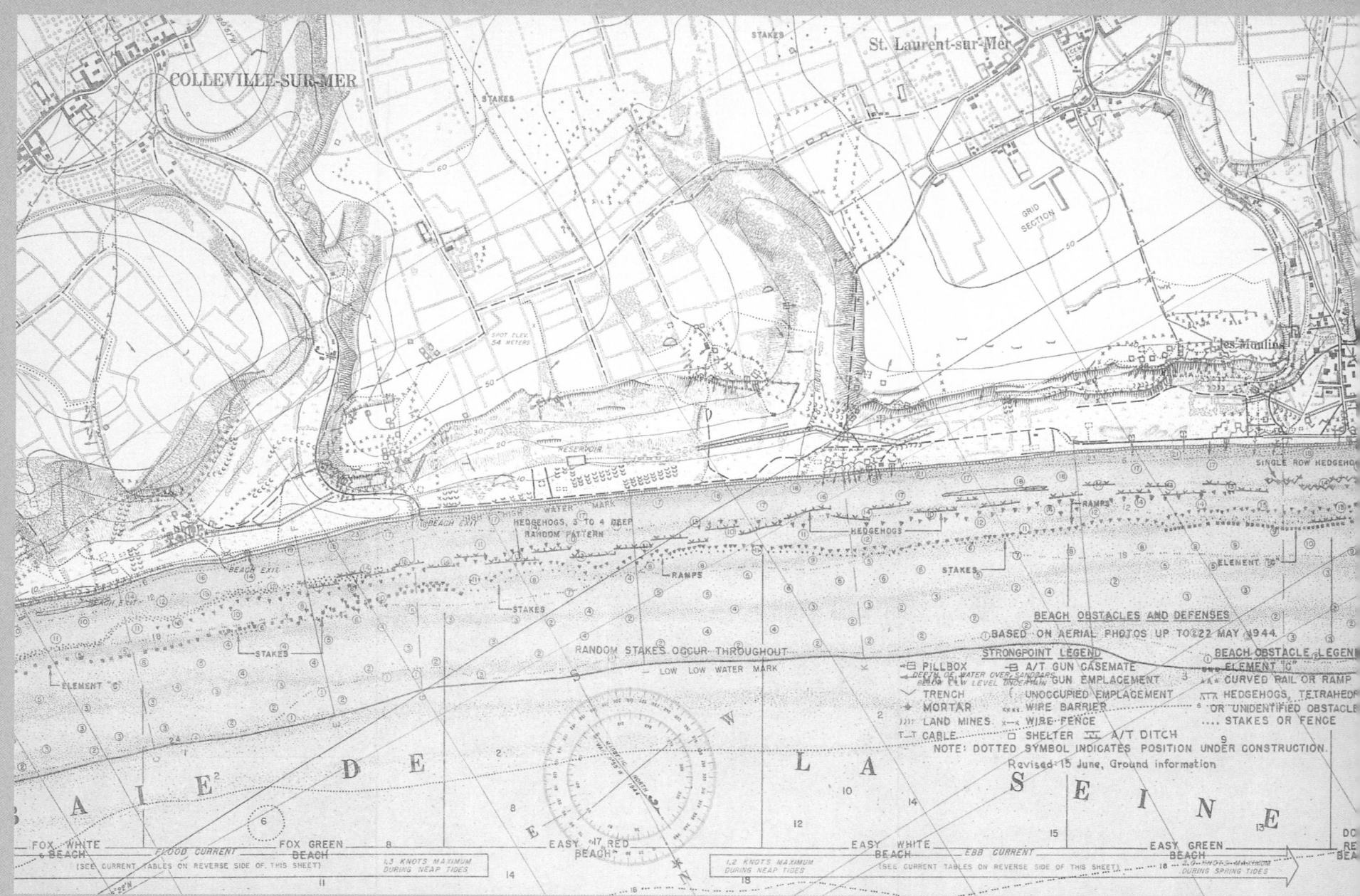

D-DAY: GERMAN DEFENCES ON 'OMAHA' BEACH, 6 JUNE 1944

A detailed plan of the beach and underwater defences guarding the section of Normandy coastline designated 'Omaha' during planning for Operation 'Overlord'. On 6 June 1944 'Omaha' Beach was assaulted by elements of the U.S. First Army. As may be discerned from the accompanying maps showing both eastern and western sectors, the beach was bounded by steep cliffs that favoured the defenders; the Americans lost some 2,500 men in the operation to capture 'Omaha', and a vast quantity of equipment. MPI 450 (3) MPI 450 (4)

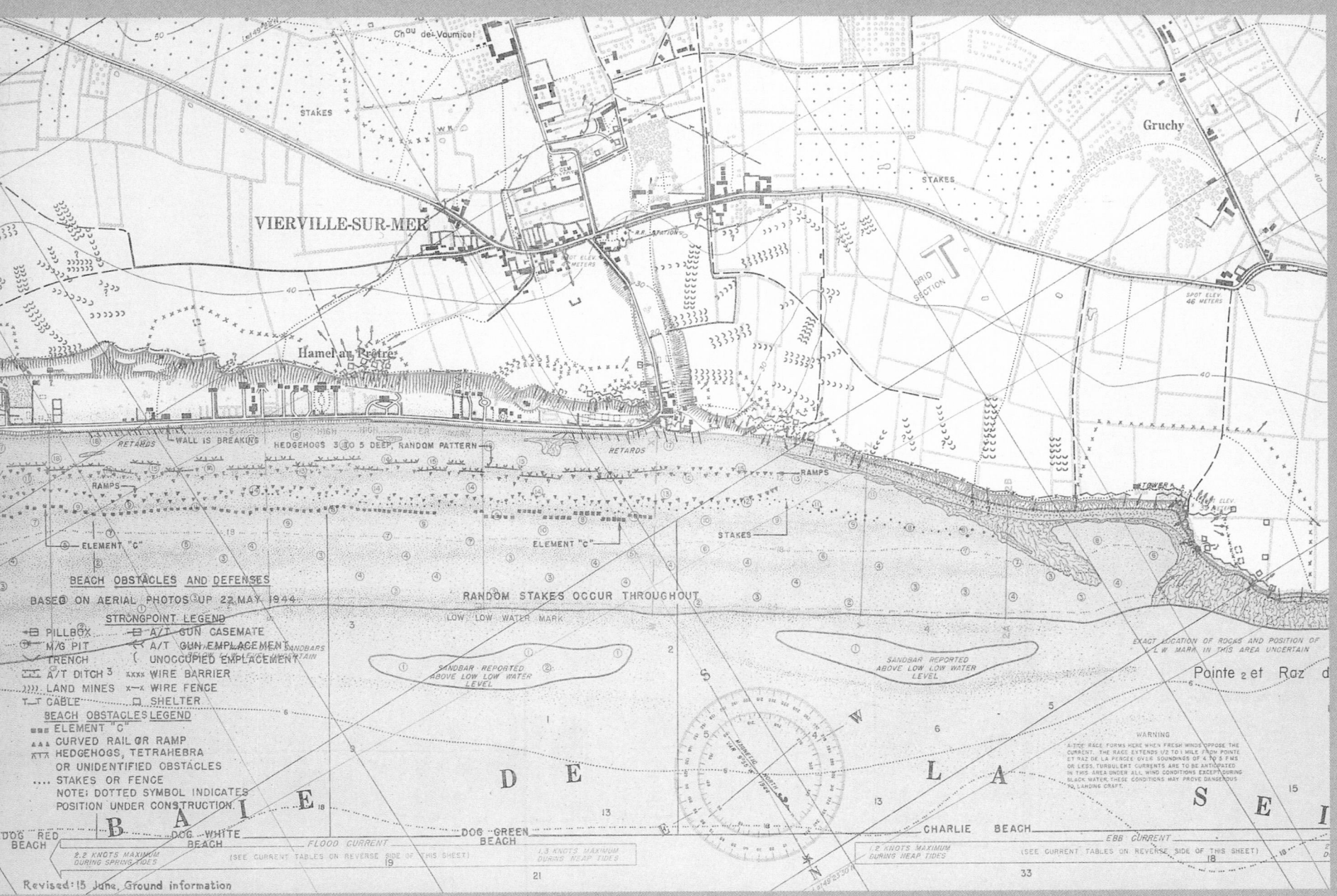

Gruchy

VIERVILLE-SUR-MER

Hamel au Prêtre

WALL IS BREAKING   HEDGEHOGS 3 TO 5 DEEP, RANDOM PATTERN

RETARDS

RAMPS

RAMPS

ELEMENT "C"

ELEMENT "C"

STAKES

BEACH OBSTACLES AND DEFENSES
BASED ON AERIAL PHOTOS UP 22 MAY 1944

RANDOM STAKES OCCUR THROUGHOUT

STRONGPOINT LEGEND

⊟ PILLBOX   ⊟ A/T GUN CASEMATE
⊏ M/G PIT   A/T GUN EMPLACEMENT
TRENCH   (UNOCCUPIED EMPLACEMENT
A/T DITCH   xxxx WIRE BARRIER
LAND MINES   x—x WIRE FENCE
CABLE   ⊡ SHELTER

BEACH OBSTACLES LEGEND

ELEMENT "C"
CURVED RAIL OR RAMP
HEDGEHOGS, TETRAHEBRA
OR UNIDENTIFIED OBSTACLES
STAKES OR FENCE
NOTE: DOTTED SYMBOL INDICATES
POSITION UNDER CONSTRUCTION.

LOW LOW WATER MARK

SANDBAR REPORTED
ABOVE LOW LOW WATER
LEVEL

SANDBAR REPORTED
ABOVE LOW LOW WATER
LEVEL

EXACT LOCATION OF ROCKS AND POSITION OF
L W MARK IN THIS AREA UNCERTAIN

Pointe et Raz d

WARNING

A TIDE RACE FORMS HERE WHEN FRESH WINDS OPPOSE THE
CURRENT. THE RACE EXTENDS 1/2 TO 1 MILE FROM POINTE
ET RAZ DE LA PERCEE OVER SOUNDINGS OF 4 TO 5 FMS
OR LESS. TURBULENT CURRENTS ARE TO BE ANTICIPATED
IN THIS AREA UNDER ALL WIND CONDITIONS EXCEPT DURING
BLACK WATER. THESE CONDITIONS MAY PROVE DANGEROUS
TO LANDING CRAFT.

BAIE   DE   LA   SEI

DOG RED
BEACH   DOG WHITE
BEACH   DOG GREEN
BEACH   CHARLIE BEACH

FLOOD CURRENT
2.2 KNOTS MAXIMUM
DURING SPRING TIDES
(SEE CURRENT TABLES ON REVERSE SIDE OF THIS SHEET)

1.3 KNOTS MAXIMUM
DURING NEAP TIDES

EBB CURRENT
1.2 KNOTS MAXIMUM
DURING NEAP TIDES
(SEE CURRENT TABLES ON REVERSE SIDE OF THIS SHEET)

Revised: 15 June, Ground information

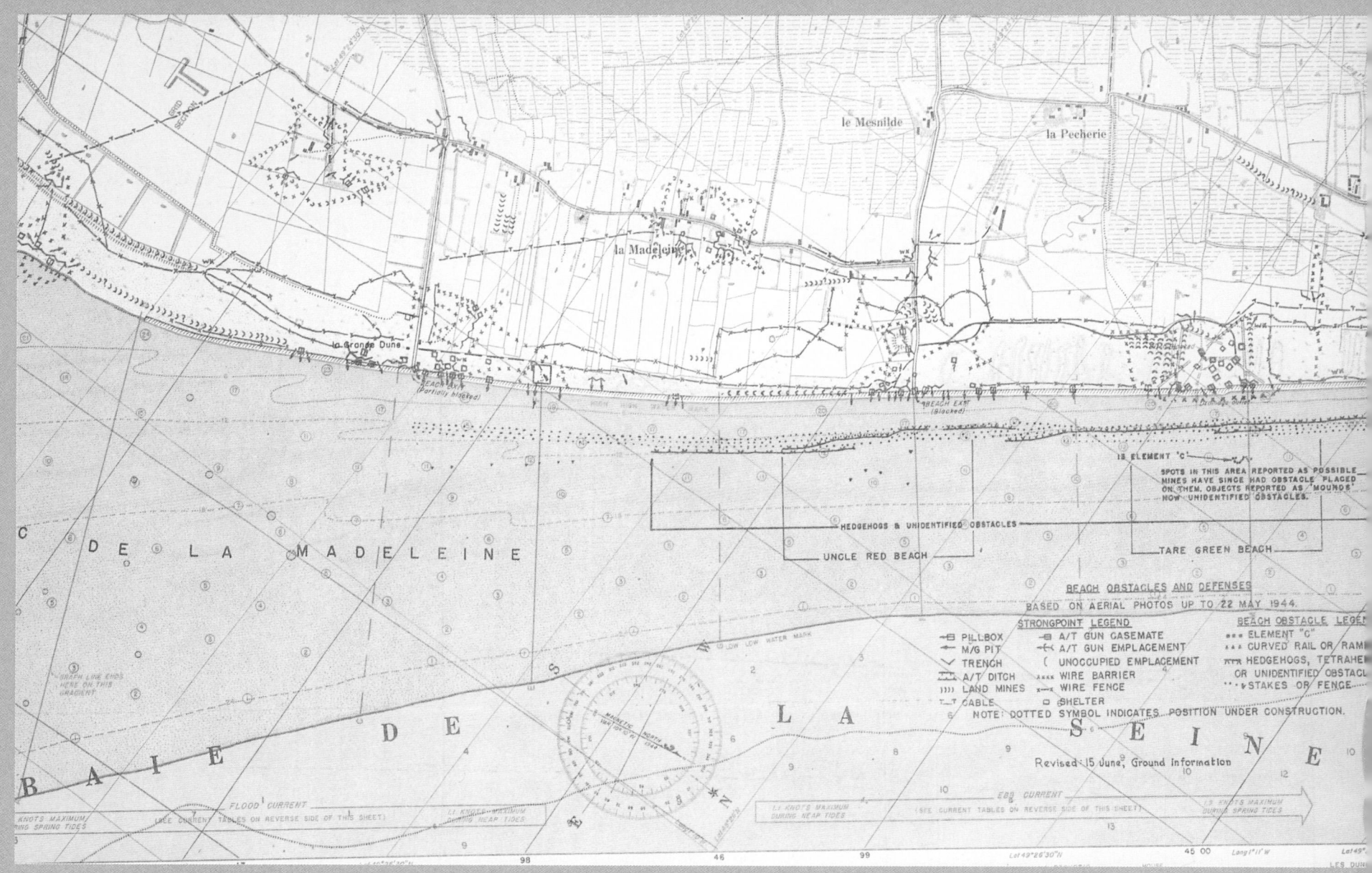

D-DAY: GERMAN DEFENCES ON 'UTAH' BEACH, 6 JUNE 1944

Plan of the western and eastern stretches of the beach and sea wall at 'Utah', the code-name for the area south of Les Dunes de Vatreville on the right flank of the Allied line, which was also allocated to the American assault forces. Assault Force U, supported by 12 convoys of 856 vessels, met with much more favourable conditions than their colleagues at 'Omaha'. Losses to the 4th Infantry Division, which put its men onto the 'Utah' beaches first, amounted to only 12 men. By noon on the 6th, Force U had cleared the beach and was moving to the secure the northern and southern flanks. MPI 450 (5) (6)

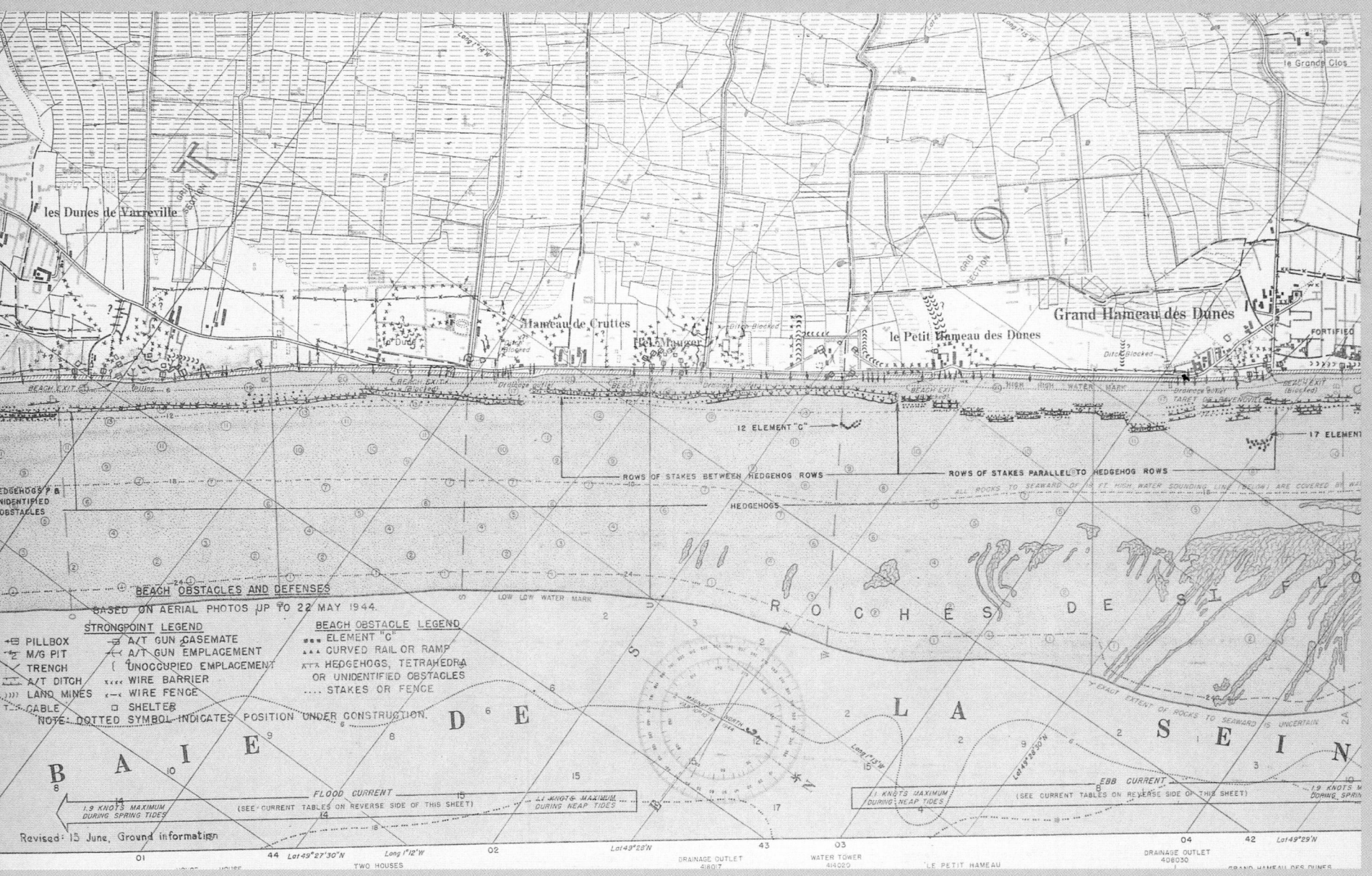

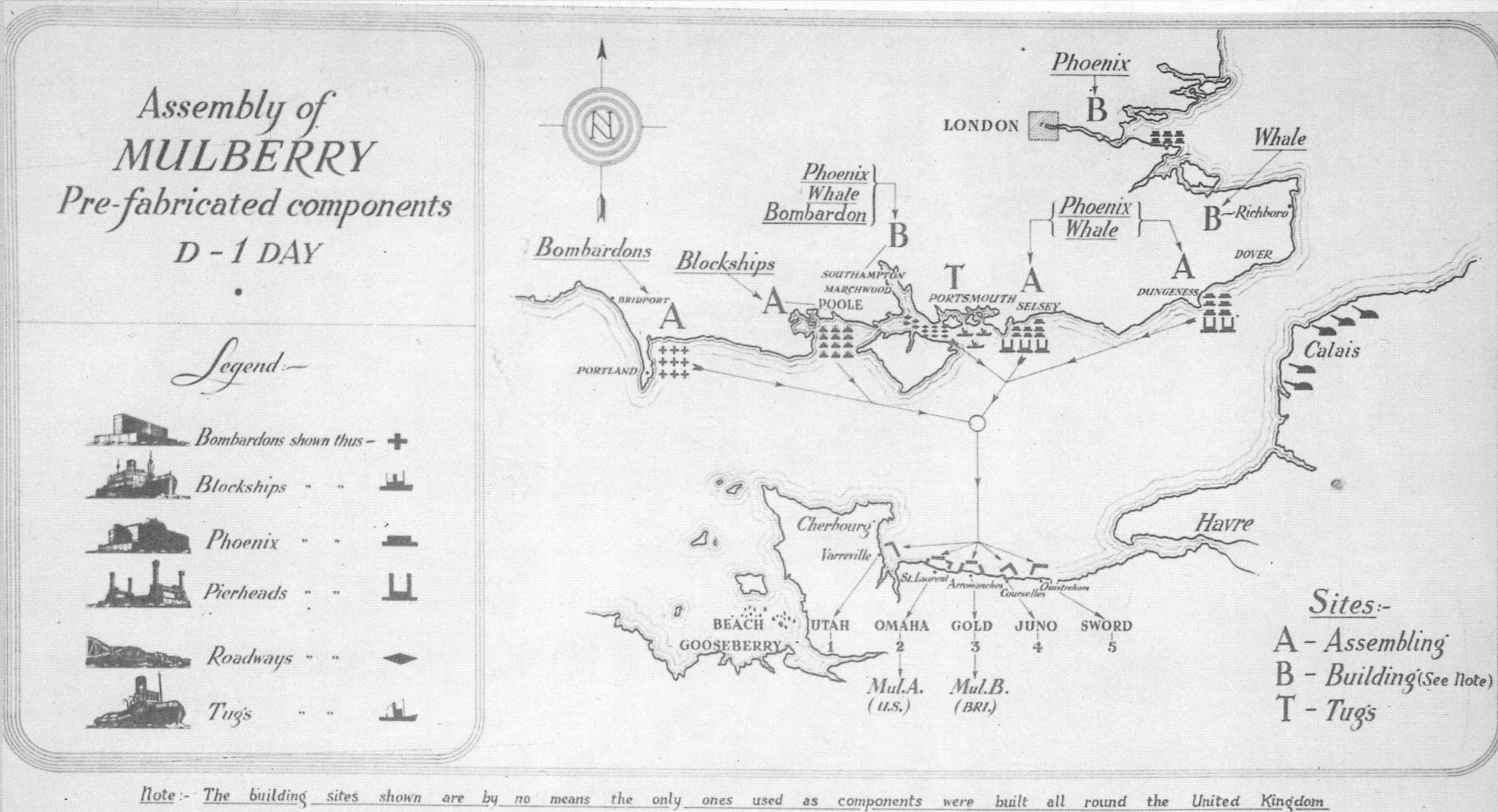

Assembly of MULBERRY Pre-fabricated components D – 1 DAY

Legend:—

Bombardons shown thus —
Blockships
Phoenix
Pierheads
Roadways
Tug's

Sites:—
A – Assembling
B – Building (See Note)
T – Tug's

Note:— The building sites shown are by no means the only ones used as components were built all round the United Kingdom

D-DAY: MULBERRY HARBOURS, 6 JUNE 1944

ABOVE AND RIGHT: Another of the tasks of Operation 'Neptune' was the transportation across the Channel of the 138 separate components of the Mulberry artificial harbours, which were erected off the beaches to facilitate the unloading of the huge volume of material required by the invasion armies. The blockships and bombardons were used to create a 200ft long, two-mile wide breakwater, within which a complex of pontoons and causeways provided mooring facilities. Two of these Mulberries were built, one off Arromanches and the other off St. Laurent beach, using some two million tons of concrete and iron. The one at Arromanches — still visible to this day — worked brilliantly, but the American one at St. Laurent was destroyed by storms on 19 June. DEFE 2/499

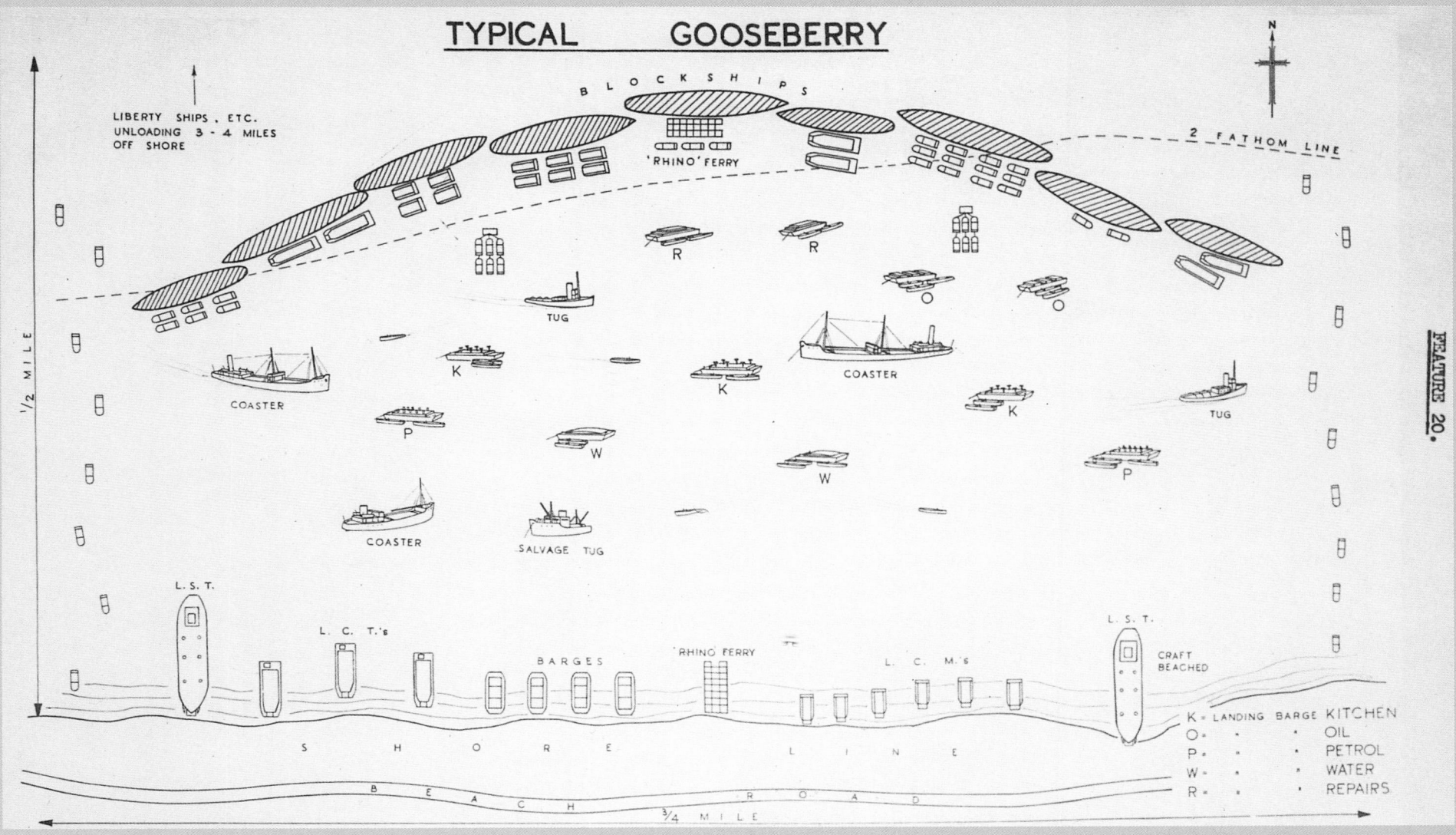

TYPICAL GOOSEBERRY

LIBERTY SHIPS, ETC.
UNLOADING 3 - 4 MILES
OFF SHORE

½ MILE

BLOCKSHIPS

'RHINO' FERRY

2 FATHOM LINE

N

FEATURE 20.

R   R

O   O

TUG

K   K   K   TUG

COASTER   COASTER

P   P

W   W

COASTER   SALVAGE TUG

L.S.T.

L.C.T.'s

BARGES   'RHINO' FERRY   L.C.M.'s   L.S.T.   CRAFT BEACHED

S H O R E   L I N E

B E A C H   R O A D

¾ MILE

K = LANDING BARGE KITCHEN
O = " " " OIL
P = " " " PETROL
W = " " " WATER
R = " " " REPAIRS

FRENCH RESISTANCE, APRIL 1942

RIGHT: Throughout the war the special operations wing of the Royal Air Force dropped supplies of arms and explosives to the various resistance movements operating in France. This map, dated for the month of April 1942, shows the main area of operations for these disparate groups. The Giraudist groups mentioned in the legend were supporters of the General Giraud, the French leader in North Africa, who was seen by both the British and U.S. as a more acceptable leader of French forces than de Gaulle. HS 6/597

NOTE

All areas to have standard loads, except

Maquis area shown, which will have Maquis

loads.

SOE ARMS' DROPS TO MAQUIS, 1944

LEFT: Special Operations Executive map of France showing, by area, the order of priority for supply drops to the French resistance movements. Not surprisingly, the highest priority is the northwest, which had the highest concentration of Axis troops and was the most likely location for Allied invasion forces. The Maquis was just one of a number of resistance movements operating in France during the war and as well as its task of infiltrating and exfiltrating agents into enemy territory, the SOE tried to coordinate these various groups into a cohesive resistance. MFQ 362 (2)

PRIORITY 1

PRIORITY 2

PRIORITY 3

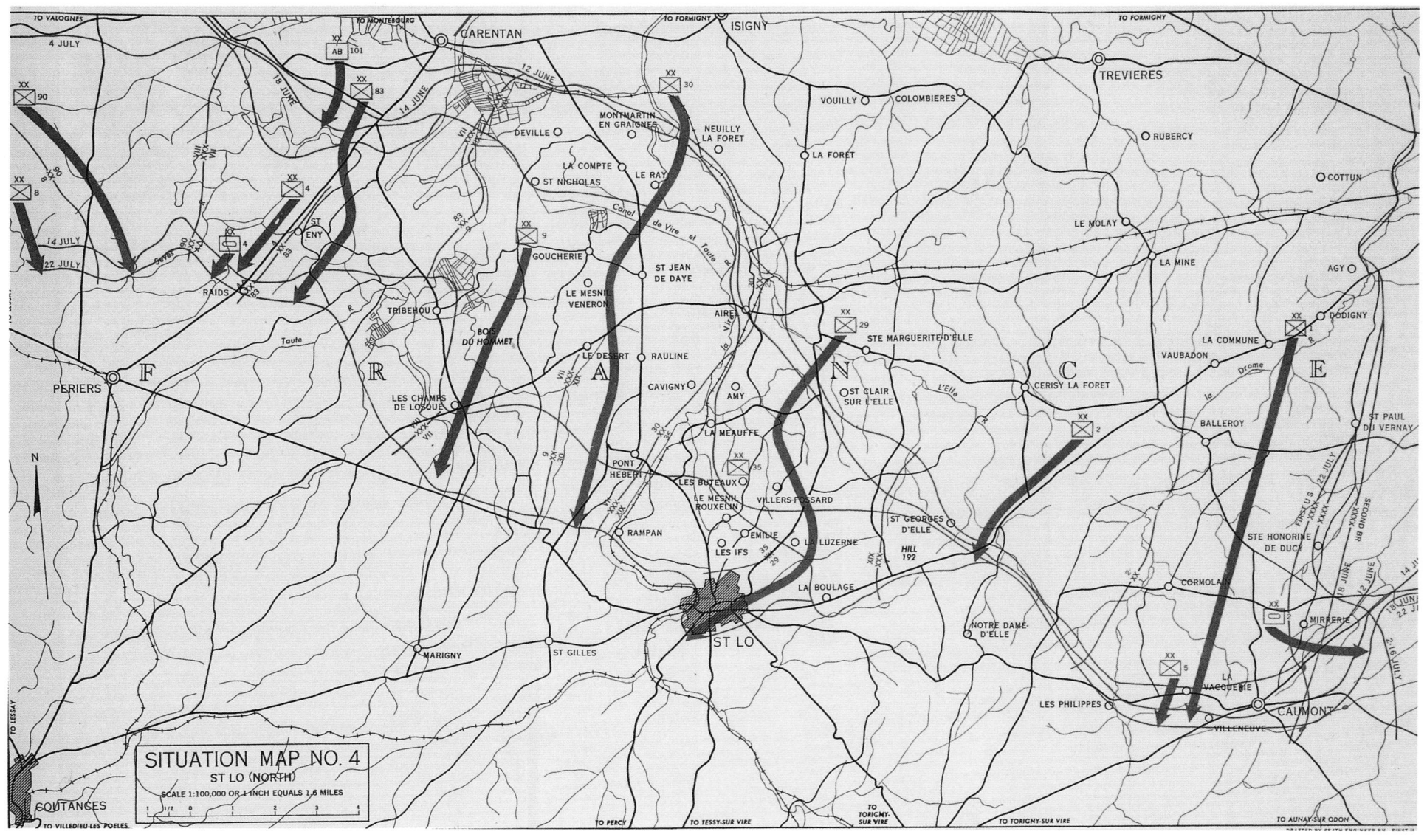

SITUATION MAP NO. 4
ST LO (NORTH)
SCALE 1:100,000 OR 1 INCH EQUALS 1.6 MILES

NORMANDY: U.S. FIRST ARMY BREAKOUT AT ST LÔ, JULY 1944

ABOVE AND RIGHT: While the British and Canadians kept the German forces occupied around Caen, the U.S. First Army launched attacks to cut off the port of Cherbourg and to break out of the western sector of the bridgehead south of St. Lô. But although they had amassed a wealth of information about the landing beaches, the Allies had failed to adequately reconnoitre the terrain behind them. In the case of the U.S. forces advancing from the bloodbath of 'Omaha' Beach, this was bocage country; broken ground, low ridges and narrow valleys, marshy depressions, sluggish streams and drainage ditches, all natural features which encouraged defensive warfare. Intensifying the problem was the endless bocage, half dirt and half hedge features, 3 to 15 feet high, which were designed to protect cattle and crops from ocean winds and offered perfect natural

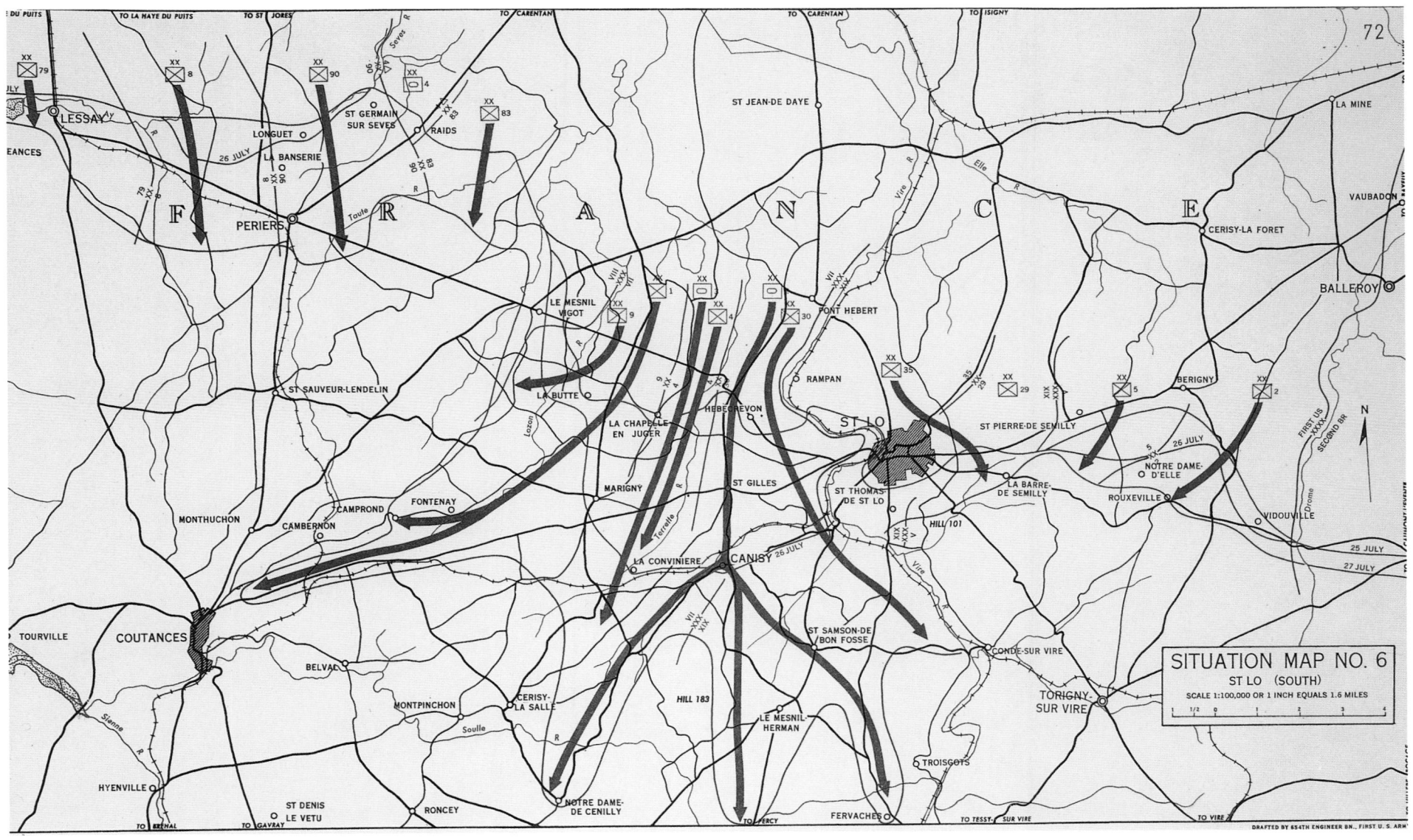

SITUATION MAP NO. 6
ST LO (SOUTH)
SCALE 1:100,000 OR 1 INCH EQUALS 1.6 MILES

defences for the Germans. Advancing through this country was tortuously slow and cost-ly both in men and materiel. Hitler ordered the defenders to stand fast along a line Lessay–St Lô–Caumont, convinced that his terror weapons could still bring Britain to its knees. The capture of St. Lô was an essential element of the breakout form Normandy, as it controlled a number of vital roads.. Defending St Lô was the German IInd Fallschirmjäger (Parachute) Corps, part of Dollman's Seventh Army, which held the town until 18 July. On 24 July the U.S. VIIth Corps pushed south and west towards Coutances, and by the end of the month was ready to start its eastward drive toward the Seine. CAB 106/1004 (4) (6)

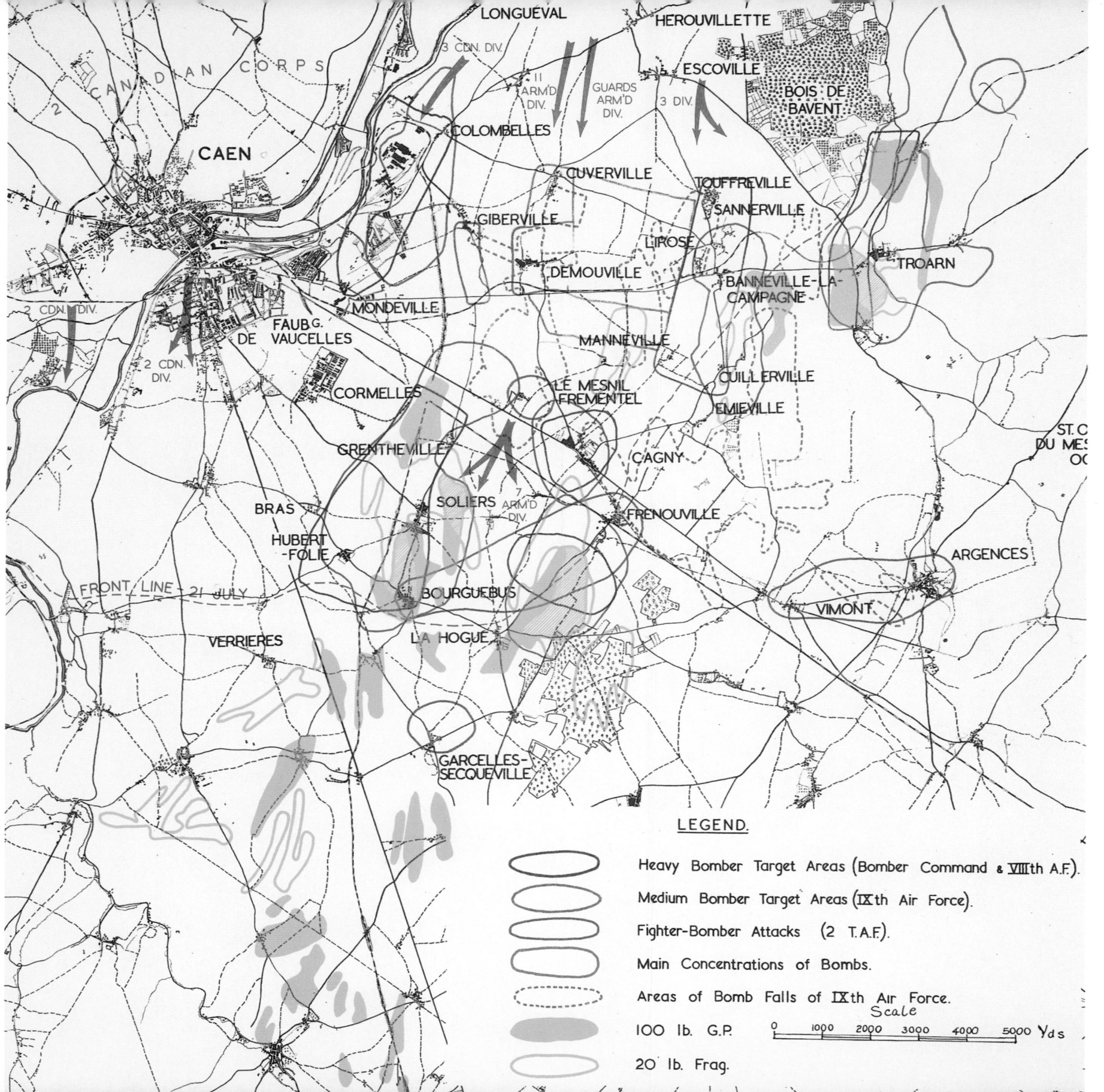

LEGEND.

Heavy Bomber Target Areas (Bomber Command & VIIIth A.F.).

Medium Bomber Target Areas (IXth Air Force).

Fighter-Bomber Attacks (2 T.A.F.).

Main Concentrations of Bombs.

Areas of Bomb Falls of IXth Air Force.

100 lb. G.P.

20 lb. Frag.

Scale

0   1000   2000   3000   4000   5000 Yds

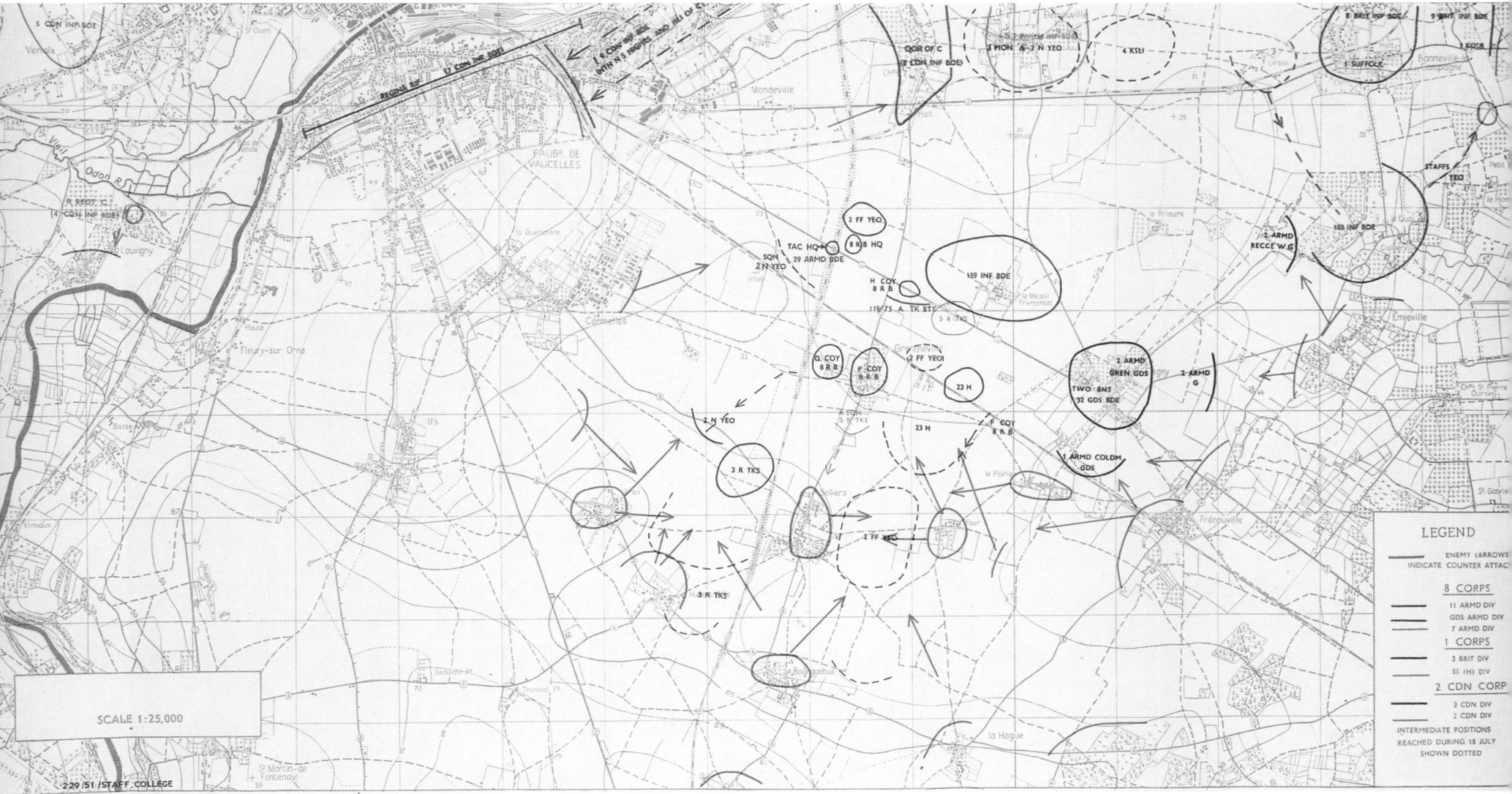

SCALE 1:25,000

229/51/STAFF COLLEGE

LEGEND

	ENEMY (ARROWS INDICATE COUNTER ATTACK)
8 CORPS	
	11 ARMD DIV
	GDS ARMD DIV
	7 ARMD DIV
1 CORPS	
	3 BRIT DIV
	51 (H) DIV
2 CDN CORPS	
	3 CDN DIV
	2 CDN DIV
INTERMEDIATE POSITIONS REACHED DURING 18 JULY SHOWN DOTTED	

OPERATION 'GOODWOOD', 18 JULY 1944

The town of Caen (the southwest corner of the town can be seen at top left on the map above) was one of the primary objectives for the British Second Army during planning for 'Overlord', for only by capturing it could the Allies push on towards Falaise. The British and Canadian attackers met with stiff resistance from six SS Panzer divisions (see page 109), and the streets of Caen saw some of the most intensive fighting of the whole war. On 26 June a major drive to the west of Caen, Operation 'Epsom', was halted after heavy losses. Operation 'Goodwood' was planned as a full-scale armoured offensive east of the city into the Falaise plain, to threaten a drive to Paris and reduce the German armour 'to

such an extent that it is of no further value', Montgomery suggested. At 0430hrs on 18 July the British VIIIth and the Canadian IInd Corps began their attack. Heavy bombers attacked Colombelles, Touffreville, Banneville and Emieville with 1,000lb bombs, while at the spearhead, fighter bomber aircraft dropped some 1,500 tons of fragmentation bombs to clear a path for the Allied armour **(left)**. CAB 44/249 (L) (G)

OPERATION 'GOODWOOD', 18 JULY 1944

LEFT: British and German dispositions at 1200hrs during the first day of the attack, 18 July. CAB 44/249 (K)

OPERATION 'SPRING', 31 JULY 1944

Map showing the disposition of German forces opposing the First Canadian Army south of Caen on 31 July 1944, after the advances of Operation 'Spring'. This was intended to maintain pressure on this sector of the line and thus allow the Americans to fully establish themselves along the Lessay/St.Lô/Caumont line. 'Spring' was launched on 25 July; its main objective to capture the ground commanding the Caen-Falaise Road. CAB 44/248 (K)

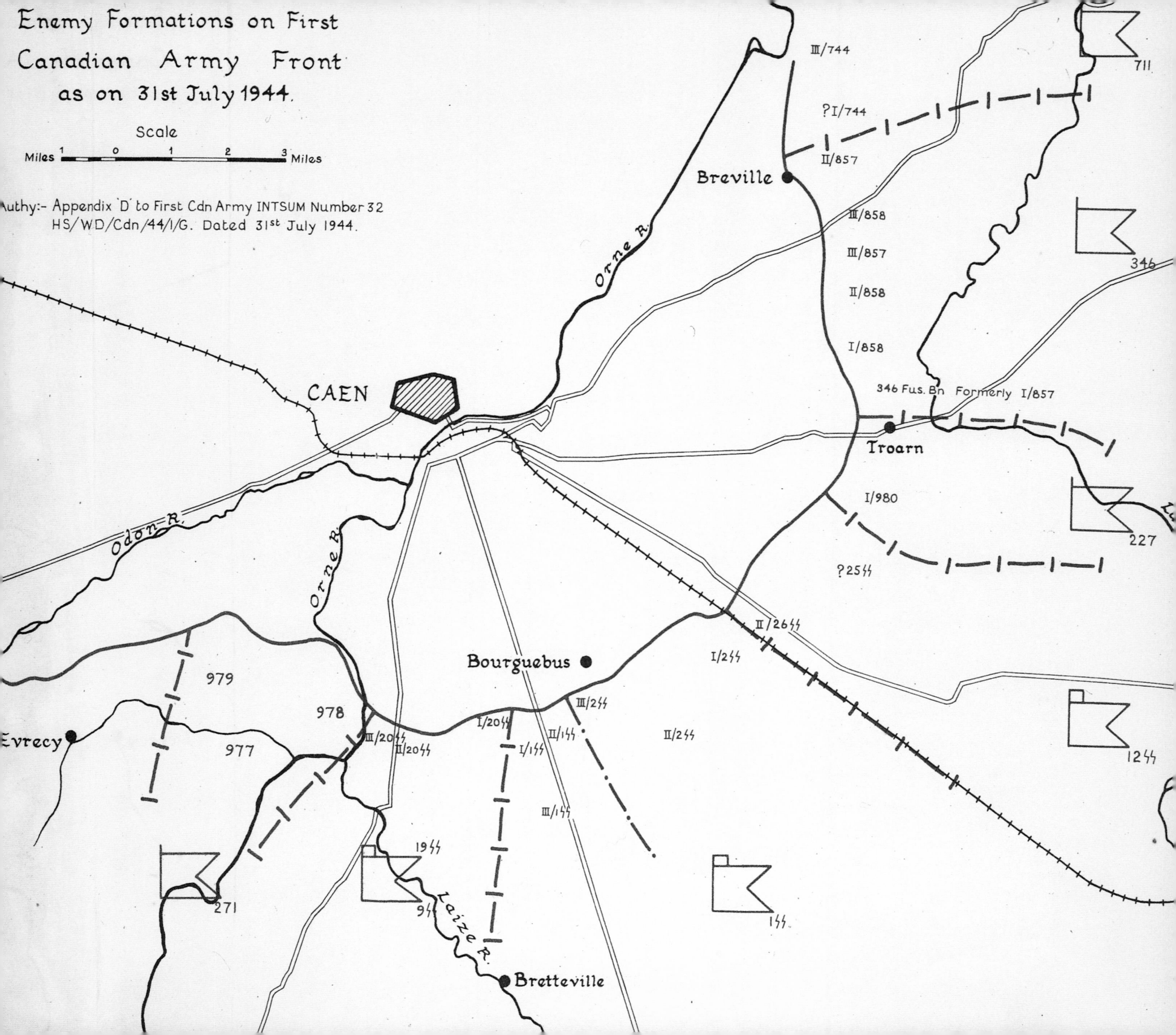

Enemy Formations on First Canadian Army Front as on 31st July 1944.

Scale

Miles 1 0 1 2 3 Miles

Authy:- Appendix 'D' to First Cdn Army INTSUM Number 32
HS/WD/Cdn/44/I/G. Dated 31st July 1944.

III/744
?I/744
II/857
711
Breville
III/858
III/857
II/858
I/858
346
Orne R.
CAEN
346 Fus. Bn. Formerly I/857
Troarn
Odon R.
I/980
227
?25§§
II/26§§
II/26§§
I/2§§
Bourguebus
979
III/2§§
978
I/20§§ III/2§§ II/2§§
III/20§§ II/20§§ II/1§§
Evrecy
977
I/1§§
I/155
12§§
III/1§§
271
19§§
9§§
Laize R.
§§
Bretteville

NORMANDY, OPERATION 'TOTALISE', AUGUST 1944

RIGHT: This map shows the drive along the main Caen-Falaise road by British and Canadian forces between 5 and 16 August 1944 (Operation 'Totalise'), showing the forward positions on successive days. On the 7th more than 1,000 Allied heavy bombers and fighter-bombers dropped more than 5,000 tons of bombs on the defences protecting the approaches to Falaise, while more than 720 artillery pieces delivered high explosive and lighted the terrain with flares. At this time the U.S. XVth Corps was driving from the south towards Argentan, to try to enclose the mouth of the Falaise Pocket. CAB 44/248 (C)

NORMANDY, FALAISE POCKET, 7 AUGUST 1944

FAR RIGHT: The first in a sequence of maps **(see pages 112 and 113)** showing the encirclement of German forces in the so-called 'Falaise Pocket' during two weeks in August 1944. Having successfully completed the capture of Caen (see preceding pages), Montgomery ended Operation 'Goodwood' on 21/22 July. The Supreme Commander, Eisenhower, had hoped that 'Goodwood' would 'break open' the campaign in Normandy and he urged Montgomery to keep driving forward. WO 205/1099

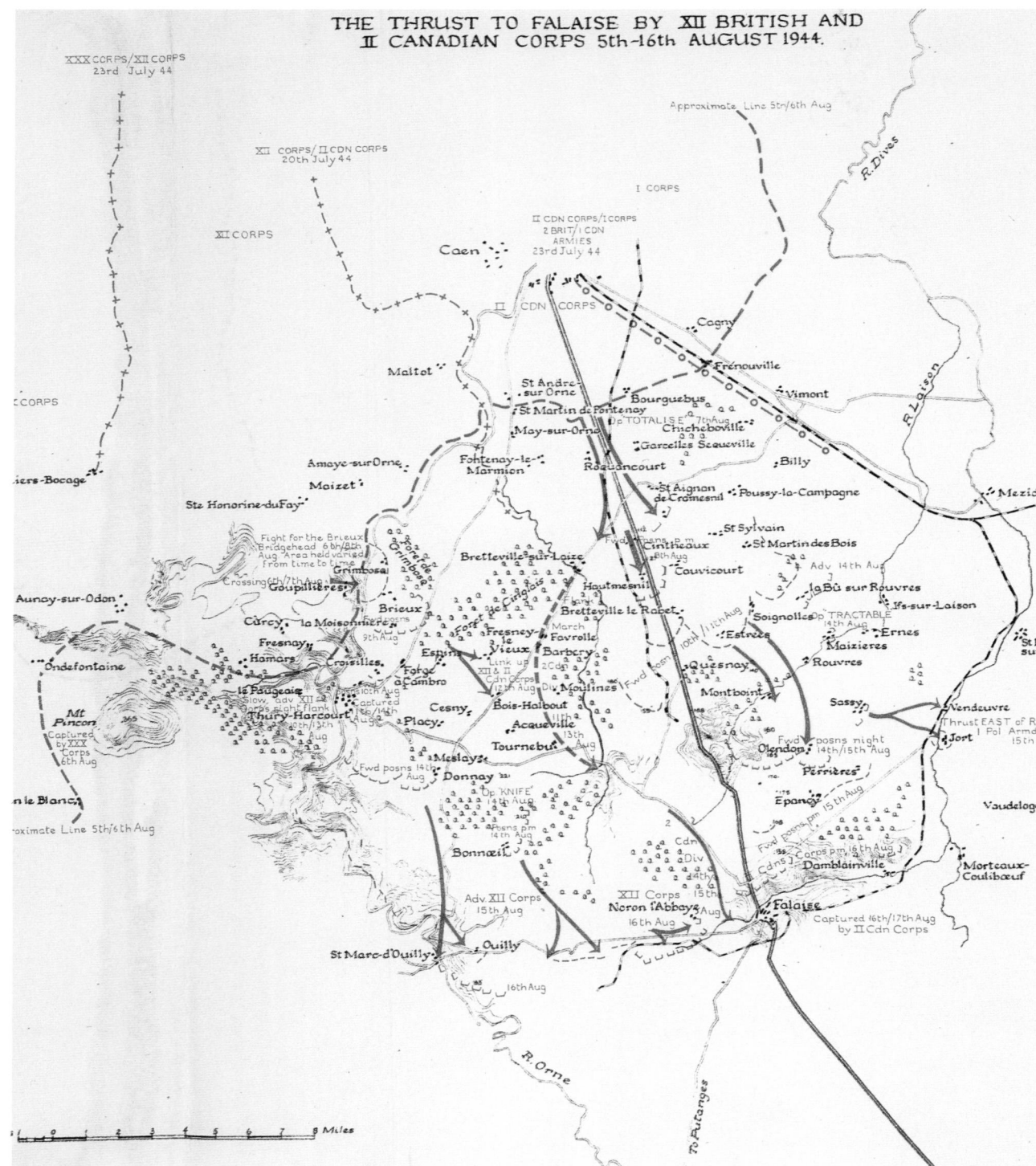

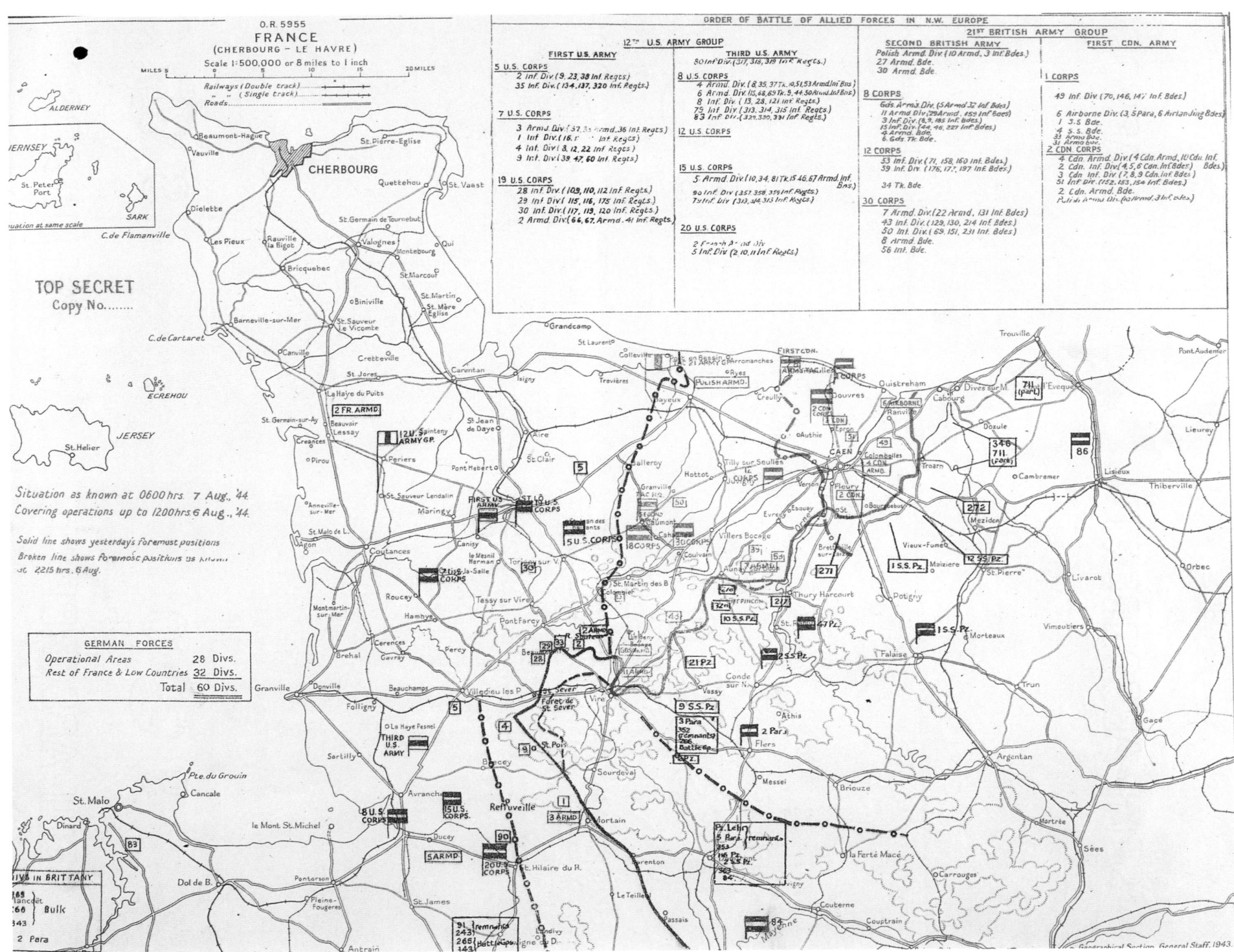

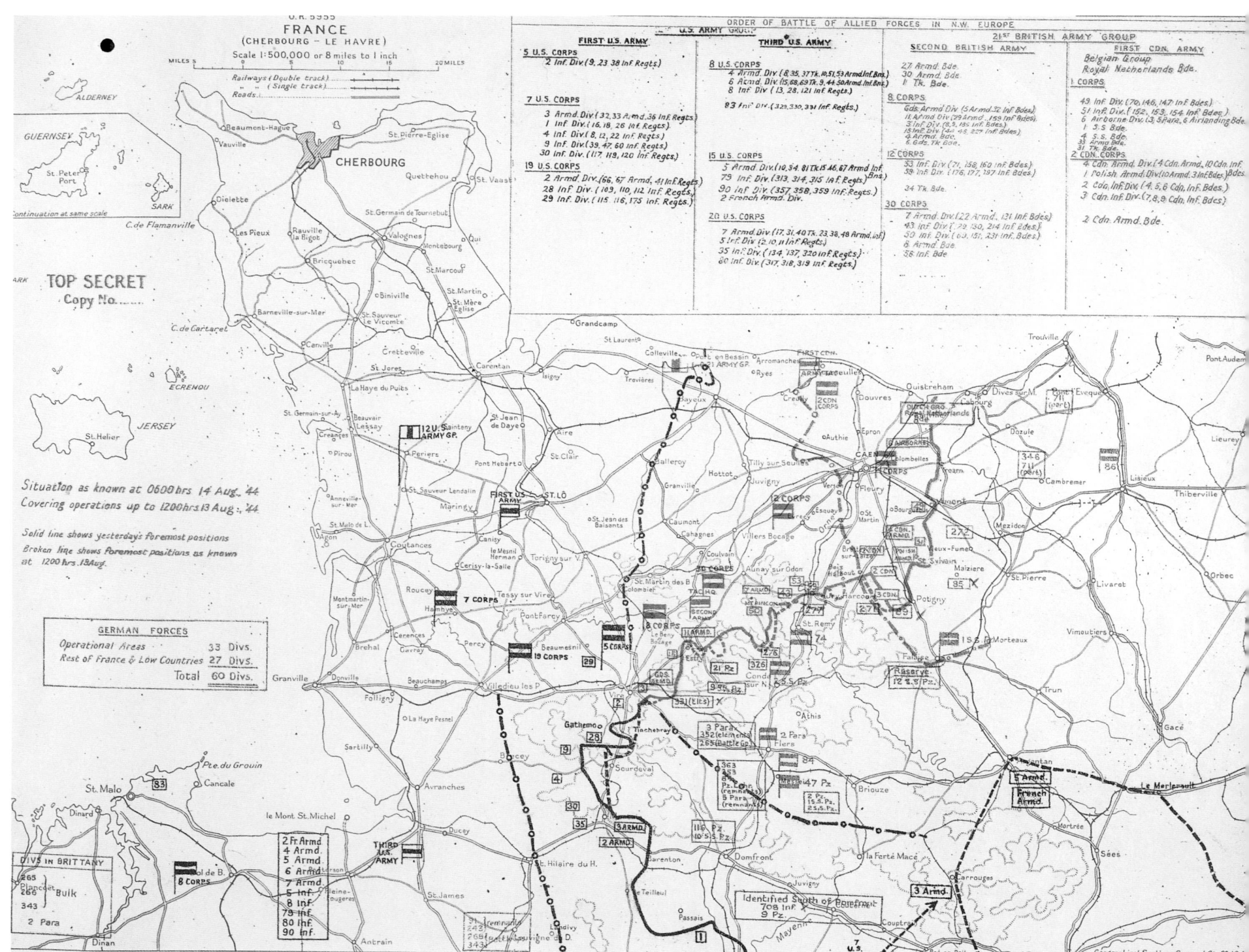

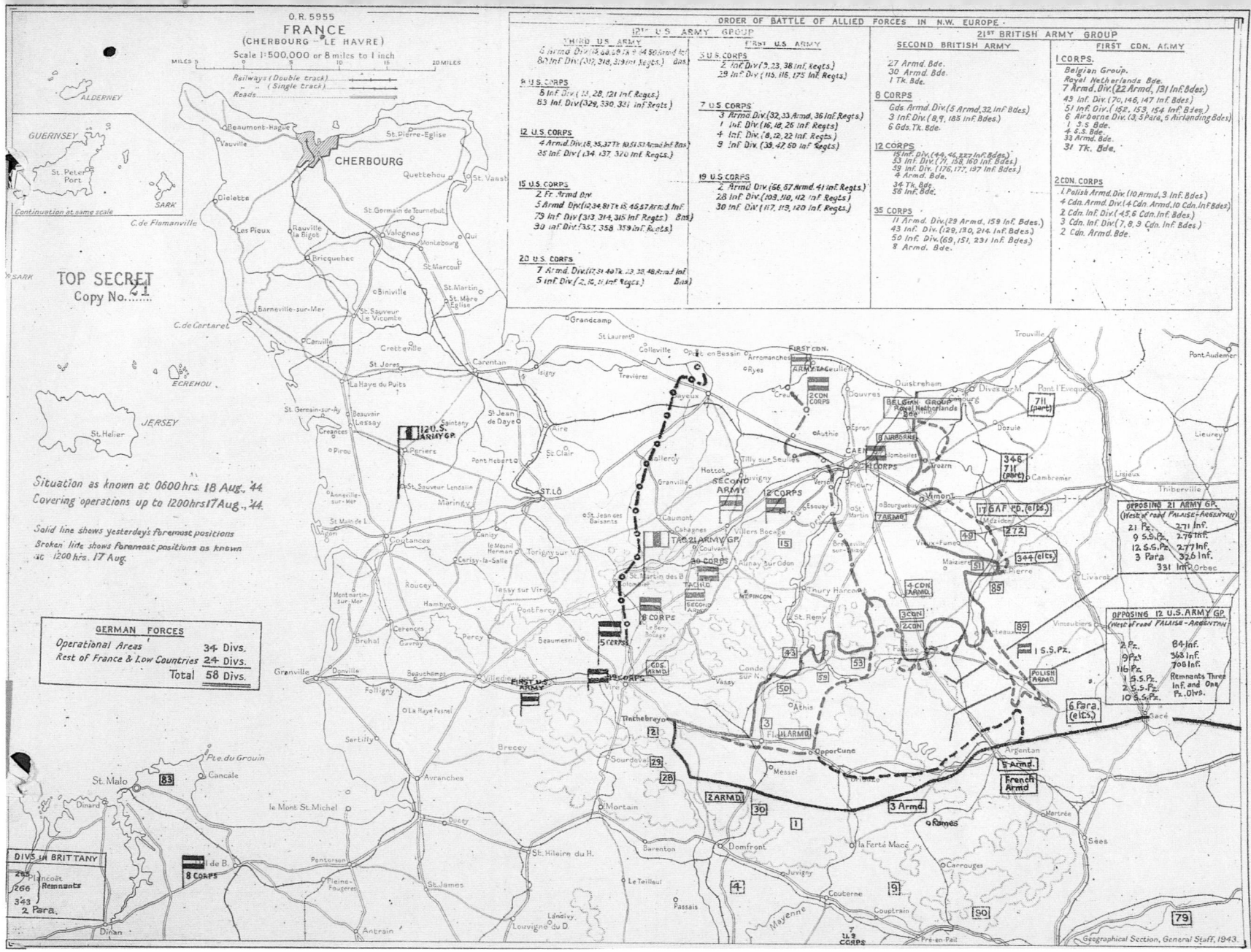

NORMANDY, FALAISE POCKET, AUGUST 1944

During the operations around the crucible of Caen, Bradley's First U.S. Army was engaged in tough fighting to cut off the port of Cherbourg and to extend the western sector south of St. Lô. With both of these objectives secured by the end of June, Bradley launched Operation 'Cobra', against Avranches on 24 July, — it fell on 30 July. As may be seen from the first map **(page 110)**, this presented an excellent opportunity to trap the Germans in Normandy. Bradley's First Army drove along the southern flank of the German Seventh Army (Hausser) and Panzergruppe Ehrbach, while the British Second

and Canadian First Armies pushed south. German forces in the pocket were pounded mercilessly by Allied fighter-bombers and artillery fire during the two-week campaign. On 16 August the remnants of their battered forces began to withdraw through a narrow mouth between the pincers. The Allies then concentrated efforts to seal the pocket, and this was achieved at St. Lambert on 20 August, when some 50,000 German troops were taken prisoner. These two maps show the position on 14 August **(left)** and 18 August **(above)**. WO 205/1099 (both)

BOULOGNE DEFENCES, 12 SEPTEMBER 1944

Map of the defensive works and emplacements surrounding Boulogne as at 12 September 1944. The Boulogne defences formed part of the 'Atlantic Wall', and their strength and depth is indicative of the fact that the German commanders had prepared for the Allies to launch the invasion force at this part of the coast. Although the attack came elsewhere, the rapid advance of the Allied armies through Northwestern France depended very much on capturing the Channel ports. Correspondingly, on 4 September 1944, in the face of the Allied advance, Hitler ordered that Le Havre, Boulogne, Calais, Dunkirk and Dieppe be held as fortresses. Le Havre fell on the 11th; Boulogne followed after much bloodshed on 22 September. MPI 453 (2)

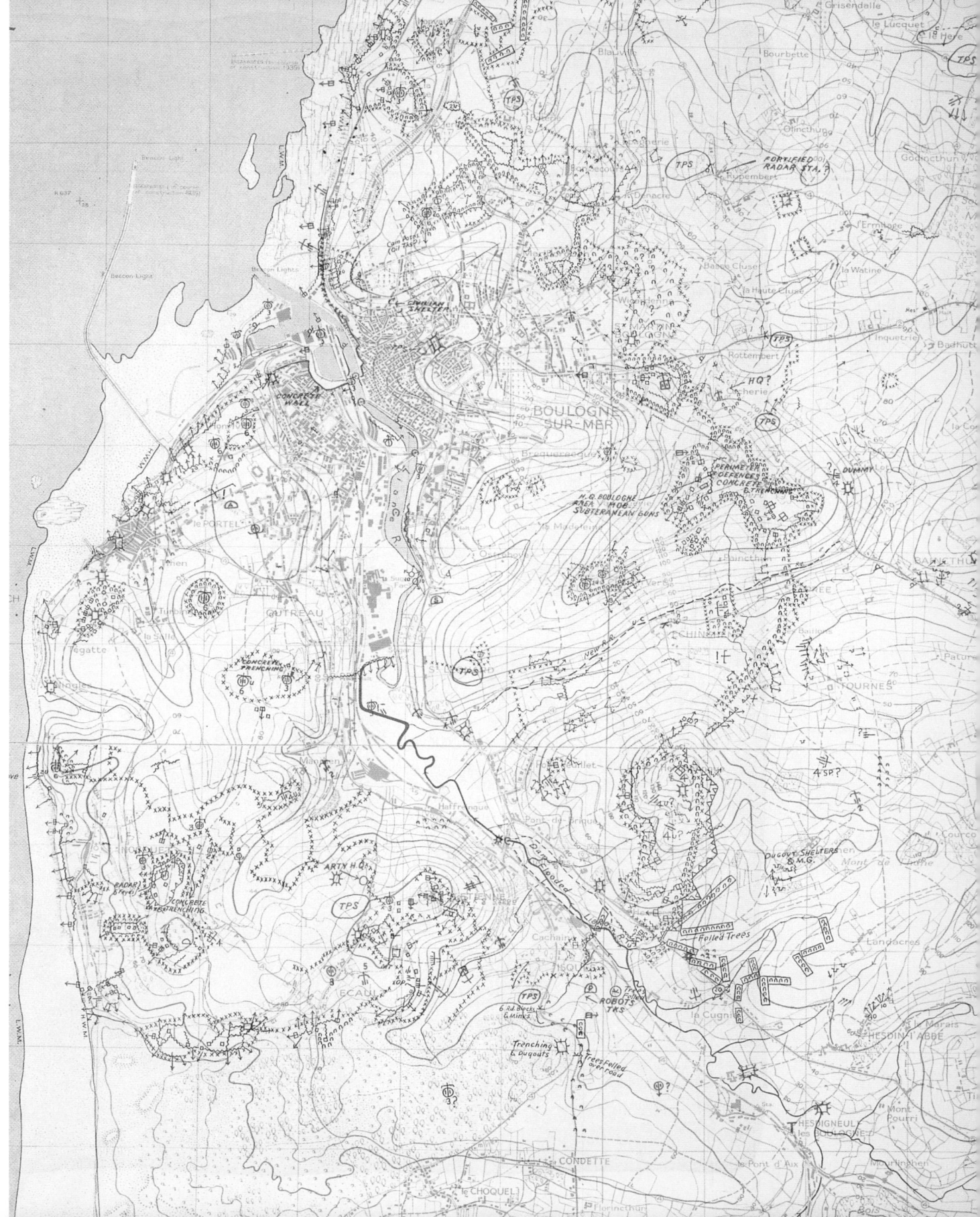

CALAIS DEFENCES, 12 SEPTEMBER 1944

Map of the defensive works and emplacements surrounding Calais as at 12 September 1944. After Boulogne had fallen, the Canadian 3rd Division began its attack on Calais, flanked by the great guns at Cap Gris Nez. As may be seen, the port was defended by a complex, interlocking system of minefields linking extensive inundations, but casualties to the assailants when Calais fell on the 30th amounted to only 300. MPI 453 (4)

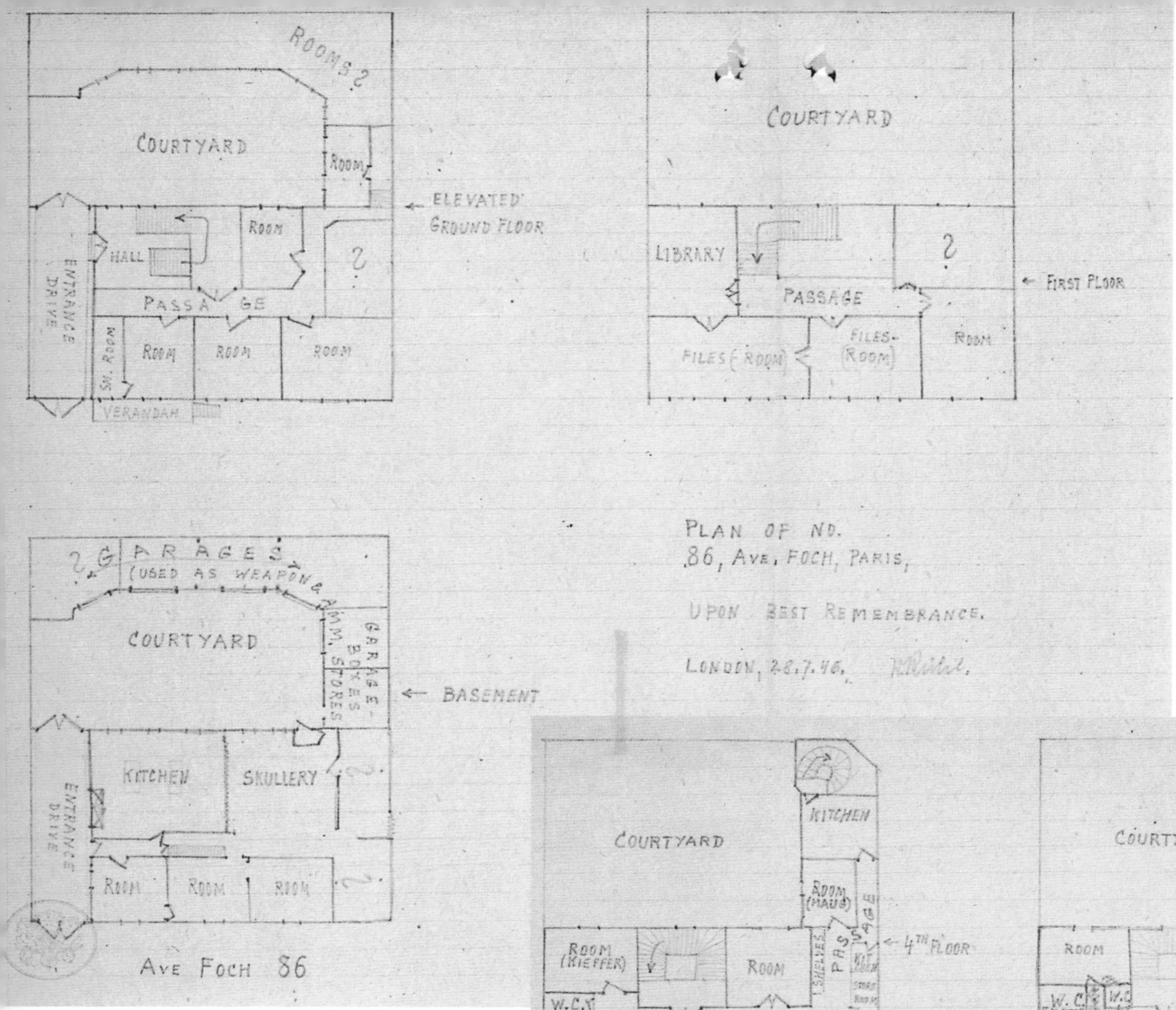

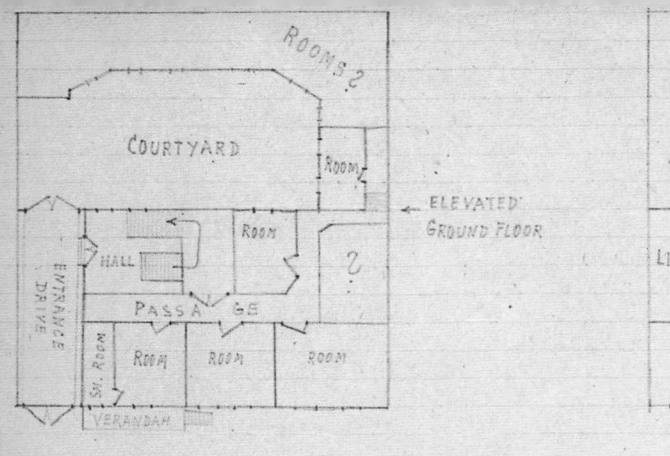

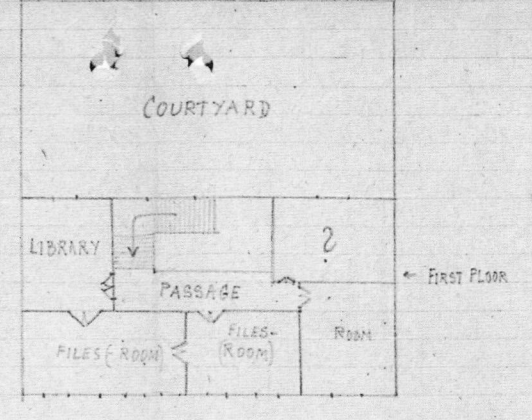

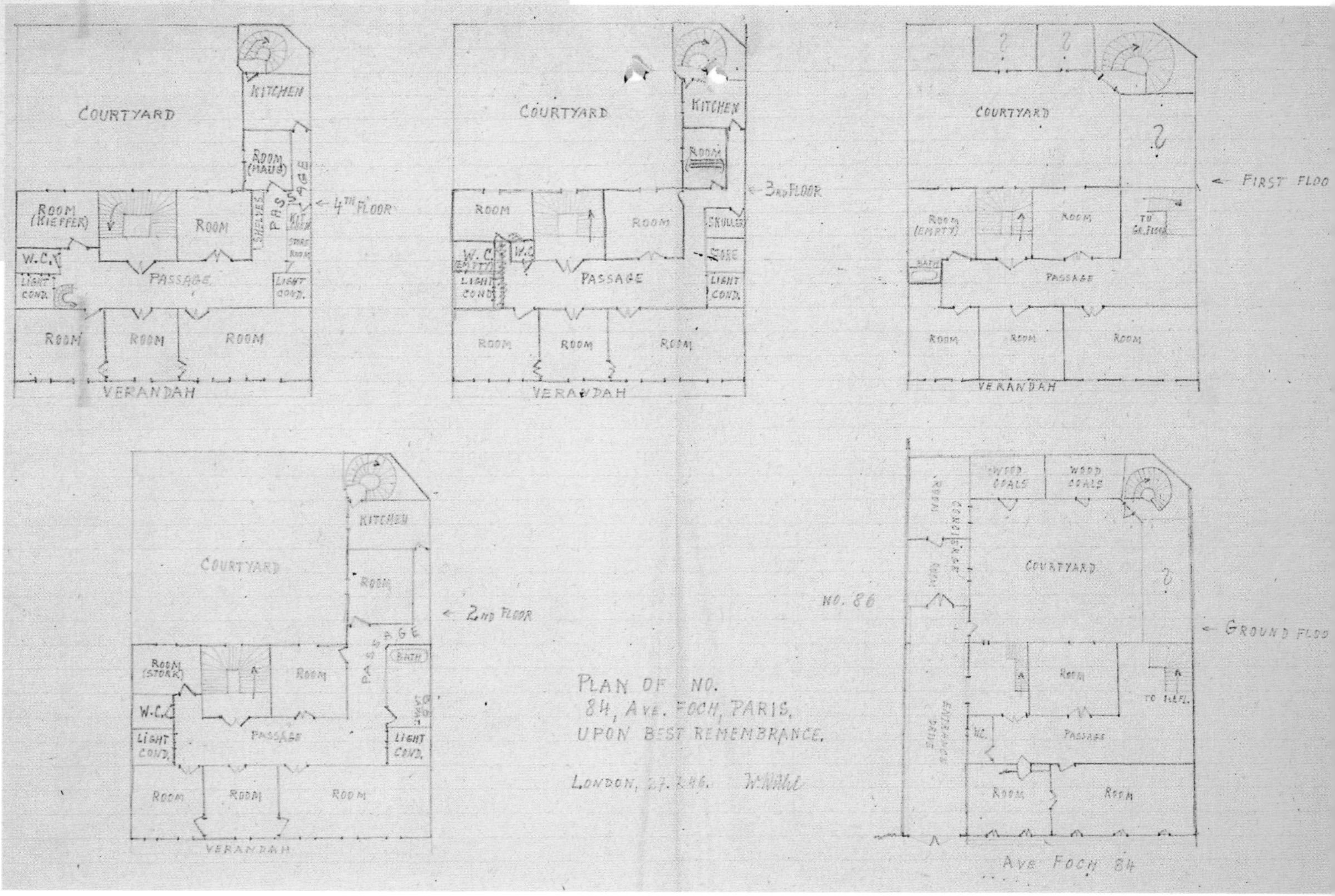

GESTAPO HQ PARIS, 1944

Sketch map of the Gestapo (Geheime Staatspolizei — German secret police) headquarters building at No. 84 Avenue Foch in Paris, drawn in 1946 presumably by a former (and sadly unidentifiable) inmate. From this building the Gestapo exerted its brutal authority over the population of Paris. Among the thousands of people who were tortured there were the SOE agents Violette Szabo ('Corinne') and Wing Commander Yeo-Thomas ('The White Rabbit'). Paris was liberated on 25 August 1944. WO 208/4679

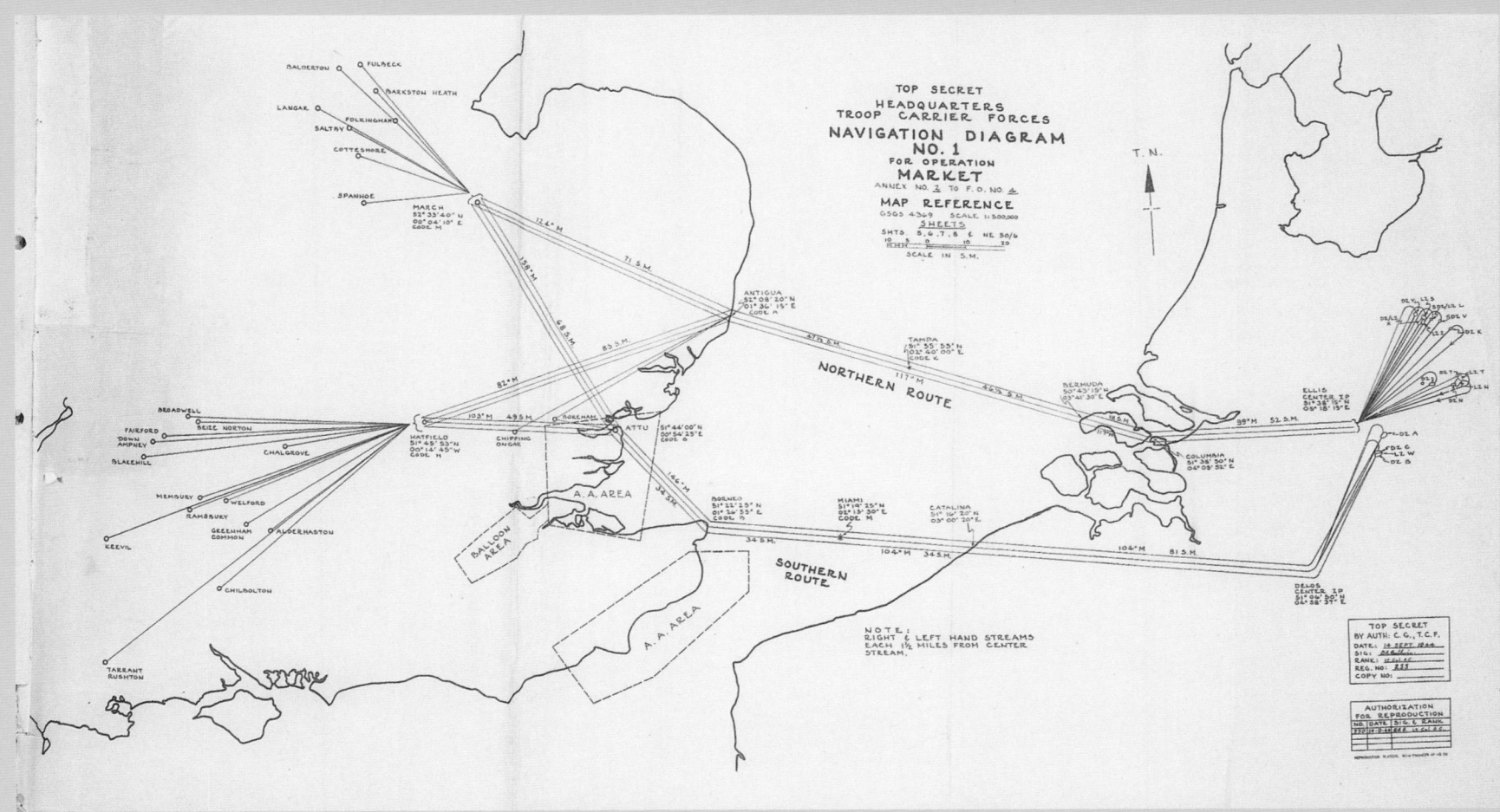

OPERATION 'MARKET',
17 SEPTEMBER 1944

This map constitutes the 'Market' of 'Market Garden' — the dropping of airborne troops. It shows the northerly and southerly routes for transport aircraft tasked with carrying airborne troops to drop zones during the operation. Note the code-named, grid-referenced waypoints that are located at the end of each stage length. AIR 25/705

OPERATION 'MARKET GARDEN', SEPTEMBER 1944

Large scale map of the Netherlands, showing the strategic concept of Operation 'Market Garden', launched on 17 September 1944. Field Marshal Montgomery, who devised the plan, believed a large airborne force could be dropped in the enemy rear at the points marked (see Legend) and by capturing crossing points over the large Dutch rivers, the Maas, Waal and Neder Rijn, the advance of his Second Army could be aided before winter halted operations. Three divisions of the Allied First Airborne Army were committed, the U.S. 101st and 82nd, and the British 1st. It was intended that they would set up defensive perimeters, also marked on the map, to await the arrival of XXX Corps. WO 205/872

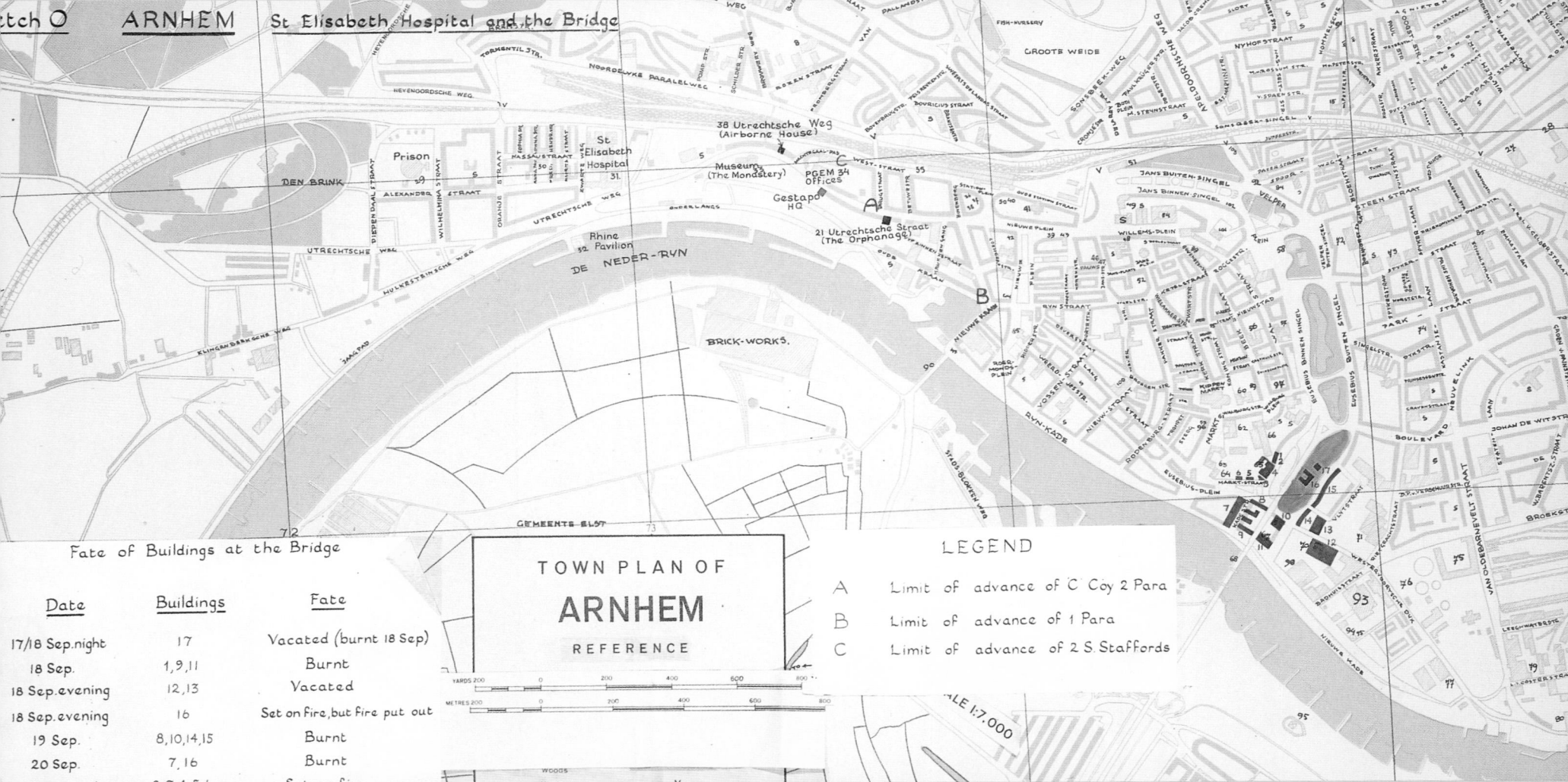

 tch O   ARNHEM   St Elisabeth Hospital and the Bridge

Fate of Buildings at the Bridge

Date	Buildings	Fate
17/18 Sep. night	17	Vacated (burnt 18 Sep)
18 Sep.	1,9,11	Burnt
18 Sep. evening	12,13	Vacated
18 Sep. evening	16	Set on fire, but fire put out
19 Sep.	8,10,14,15	Burnt
20 Sep.	7,16	Burnt

TOWN PLAN OF

ARNHEM

REFERENCE

LEGEND

A   Limit of advance of 'C' Coy 2 Para
B   Limit of advance of 1 Para
C   Limit of advance of 2 S. Staffords

SCALE 1:7,000

OPERATION 'MARKET GARDEN', SEPTEMBER 1944

Detailed map of the area surrounding the bridge over the Neder Rijn at Arnhem, one of the objectives of Operation 'Market Garden'. The Arnhem bridge was the most ambitious of the objectives (many considered it 'a bridge too far') and, contrary to intelligence briefings, heavily defended by German forces. The task of taking it fell to the British 1st Airborne Division under Major-General R. E. Urquhart, who was forced to select drop zones well outside the town because of the threat of flak. The advance into Arnhem was slow, giving time for the 9th and 10th SS Panzer Divisions to reinforce the bridge and cut off the relieving troops advancing north from Nijmegen (see previous and subsequent maps). Fighting through the town, only one British battalion was able to reach the bridge, and this was cut off. On 21 September these troops were overwhelmed, and the remainder formed a defensive perimeter to the west, prior to their evacuation on 25 September. CAB 44/254

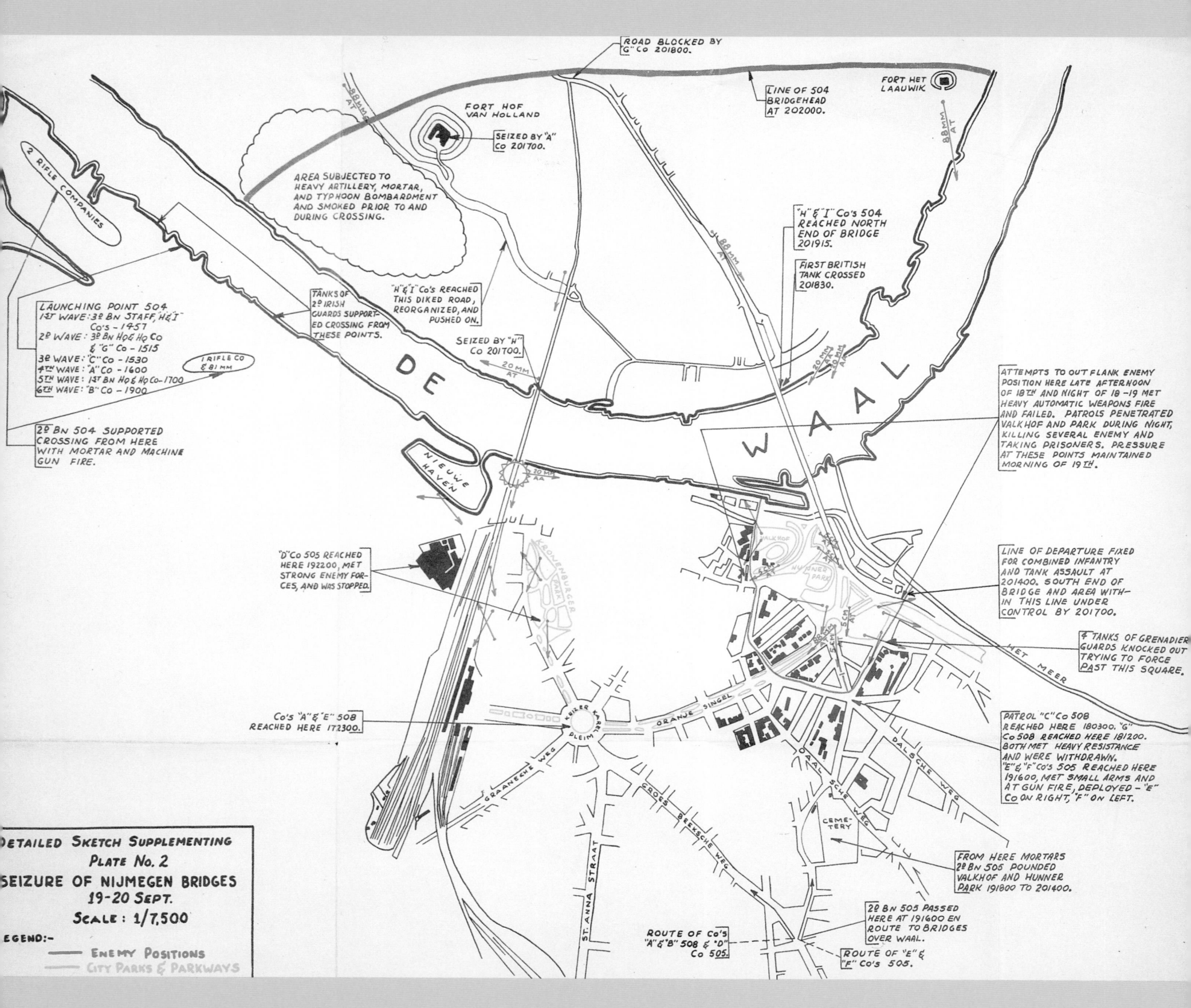

ROAD BLOCKED BY
"G" Co 201800.

FORT HET
LAAUWIK

LINE OF 504
BRIDGEHEAD
AT 202000.

FORT HOF
VAN HOLLAND

88MM AT

SEIZED BY "A"
Co 201700.

AREA SUBJECTED TO
HEAVY ARTILLERY, MORTAR,
AND TYPHOON BOMBARDMENT
AND SMOKED PRIOR TO AND
DURING CROSSING.

"H" & "I" Co's 504
REACHED NORTH
END OF BRIDGE
201915.

88 MM AT

FIRST BRITISH
TANK CROSSED
201830.

2 RIFLE COMPANIES

TANKS OF
2º IRISH
GUARDS SUPPORT-
ED CROSSING FROM
THESE POINTS.

"H" & "I" Co's REACHED
THIS DIKED ROAD,
REORGANIZED, AND
PUSHED ON.

LAUNCHING POINT 504
1ST WAVE: 3º BN STAFF, H & I
Co's - 1457
2º WAVE: 3º BN HQ & HQ Co
& "G" Co - 1515
3º WAVE: "C" Co - 1530
4TH WAVE: "A" Co - 1600
5TH WAVE: 1ST BN HQ & HQ Co - 1700
6TH WAVE: "B" Co - 1900

1 RIFLE CO
& 81 MM

SEIZED BY "H"
Co 201700.

20 MM AT

DE

WAAL

20 MM AA

20 MM AA

ATTEMPTS TO OUT FLANK ENEMY
POSITION HERE LATE AFTERNOON
OF 18TH AND NIGHT OF 18-19 MET
HEAVY AUTOMATIC WEAPONS FIRE
AND FAILED. PATROLS PENETRATED
VALKHOF AND PARK DURING NIGHT,
KILLING SEVERAL ENEMY AND
TAKING PRISONERS. PRESSURE
AT THESE POINTS MAINTAINED
MORNING OF 19TH.

2º BN 504 SUPPORTED
CROSSING FROM HERE
WITH MORTAR AND MACHINE
GUN FIRE.

NIEUWE
HAVEN

20 MM
AA

VALKHOF

HUNNER
PARK

"D" Co 505 REACHED
HERE 192200, MET
STRONG ENEMY FOR-
CES, AND WAS STOPPED.

KRONENBURGER
PARK

LINE OF DEPARTURE FIXED
FOR COMBINED INFANTRY
AND TANK ASSAULT AT
201400. SOUTH END OF
BRIDGE AND AREA WITH-
IN THIS LINE UNDER
CONTROL BY 201700.

HET MEER

4 TANKS OF GRENADIER
GUARDS KNOCKED OUT
TRYING TO FORCE
PAST THIS SQUARE.

Co's "A" & "E" 508
REACHED HERE 172300.

KEIZER
KAREL
PLEIN

ORANGE SINGEL

PATROL "C" Co 508
REACHED HERE 180300. "G"
Co 508 REACHED HERE 181200.
BOTH MET HEAVY RESISTANCE
AND WERE WITHDRAWN.
"E" & "F" Co's 505 REACHED HERE
191600, MET SMALL ARMS AND
AT GUN FIRE, DEPLOYED - "E"
Co ON RIGHT, "F" ON LEFT.

GRAAFSCHE WEG

ST. ANNA STRAAT

CROOS
BEEKSCHE WEG

WAAL
SCHE
WEG

DALSCHE
WEG

CEMETERY

FROM HERE MORTARS
2º BN 505 POUNDED
VALKHOF AND HUNNER
PARK 191800 TO 201400.

DETAILED SKETCH SUPPLEMENTING
PLATE No. 2
SEIZURE OF NIJMEGEN BRIDGES
19-20 SEPT.
SCALE: 1/7,500
LEGEND:-
———— ENEMY POSITIONS
———— CITY PARKS & PARKWAYS

ROUTE OF Co's
"A" & "B" 508 & "D"
Co 505.

2º BN 505 PASSED
HERE AT 191600 EN
ROUTE TO BRIDGES
OVER WAAL.

ROUTE OF "E" &
"F" Co's 505.

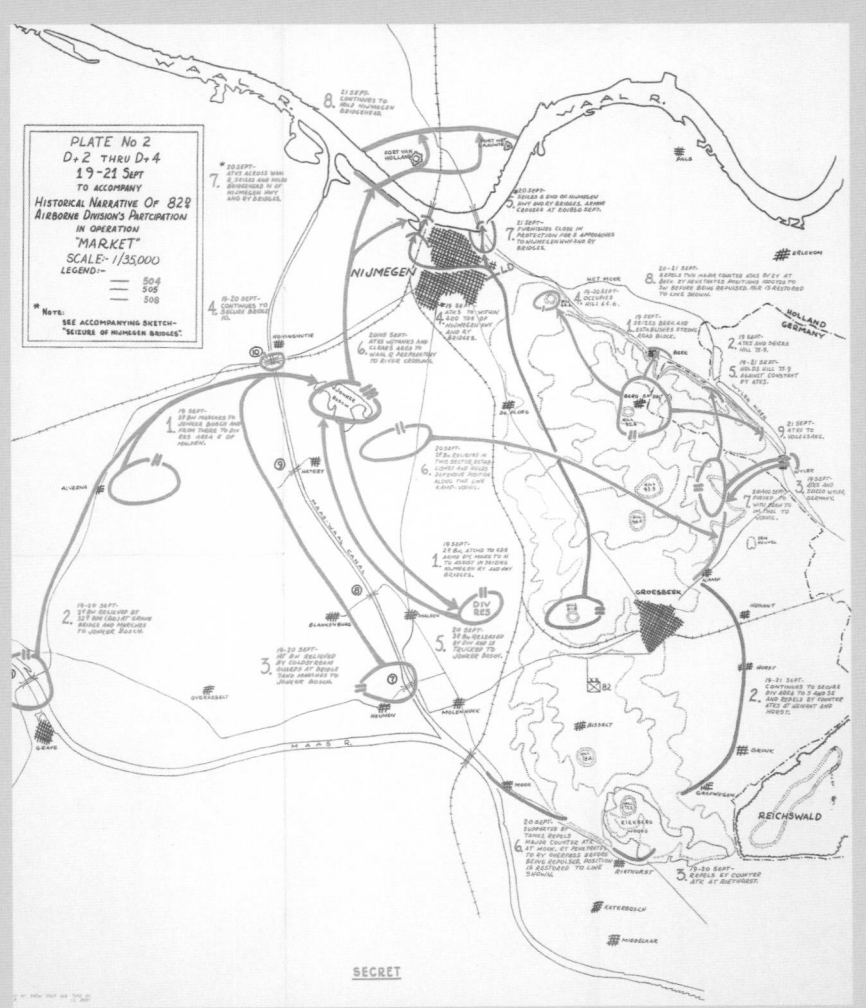

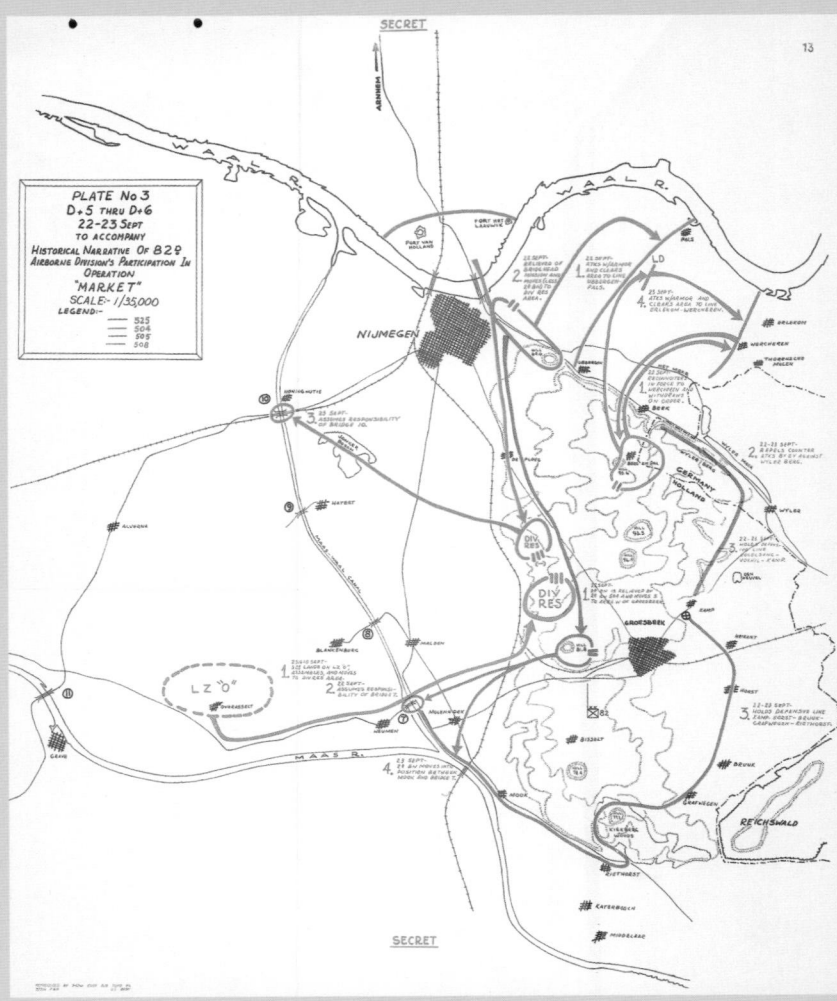

U.S. 82ND AIRBORNE DIVISION, NIJMEGEN, SEPTEMBER 1944

As its contribution to 'Market Garden' the U.S. 82nd Airborne Division was tasked with capturing the bridges over the River Maas at Grave and over the Waal at Nijmegen. These maps **(left and above left)**, produced as part of the operational post-mortem, show the movements and dispositions of the division between 19 and 21 September. It had landed without major opposition on the morning of the 17th and soon captured the bridges at Grave. At Nijmegen the 82nd met with much greater opposition. Before they could launch an assault on the bridge, the Germans launched a series of fierce counter-attacks from the east, tying up forces needed to attack the well-defended bridges. By late afternoon on the 20th, the railway bridge had fallen and finally that evening, the first

British tanks were able to cross the road bridge. The detailed map **(left)** shows enemy troop dispositions in Nijmegen, notably the position of anti-tank weapons. Dispositions and movements of the 82nd Airborne Division at Nijmegen on 22-23 September 1944 are shown separately **(above right)**. By this stage the 82nd had secured a bridgehead over the River Waal. However, the advance to link with the British 1st Airborne Division fighting to secure the bridge at Arnhem failed in the face of heavy German opposition. The British troops were evacuated to Nijmegen under concentrated fire on 25 September. CAB 106/1056 (2) (2a) (3)

OPERATION 'MARKET GARDEN', 17 SEPTEMBER 1944

RIGHT, FAR RIGHT AND PAGES 122, 123: Maps showing German defence (blue) against the British paras (red) moving along the Edo-Arnhem railway line towards Arnhem, and the outflanking of the defence to the south by 2 PARA (2nd Parachute Battalion) under Lt-Col J.D. Frost. The German troops are from SS Panzergrenadier Depot and Reserve Battalion 16, commanded by SS-Captain Sepp Krafft, who moved to block the advance from the British drop zones to the west of Arnhem in the aftermath of the airborne assault (Operation 'Market'). In these German maps Kp (Kompanie) = Company; Zug = Platoon. Späh = light. Allied intelligence officers had vastly underestimated the strength of the Germans in the area of Arnhem, despite information received from Dutch resistance workers. The German forces included IInd SS Panzer Corps (9th and 10th Panzer Divisions) comprising 8,500 men under General Wilhelm Bittrich. The British advance from the dropping zones was slow. Two of the three battalions of the 1st Parachute Brigade were blocked — 1 PARA, north of the railway line, by an SS battle group (Kampfgruppe Spindler) and 3 PARA as shown here. Frost's 2 PARA outflanked the defenders and reached Arnhem bridge late in the day on 17 September, capturing the northern end of the bridge but becoming cut off. The other Parachute battalions then became engaged in a desperate battle to break through to Frost but were decimated on 19 September and retreated to a defensive perimeter around Oosterbeek and were

only just able to hold on to them before the order to withdraw came. Frost's 2 PARA was overwhelmed on 21 September after bitter fighting.

WO 205/1124 (2) (4) (5) (7)

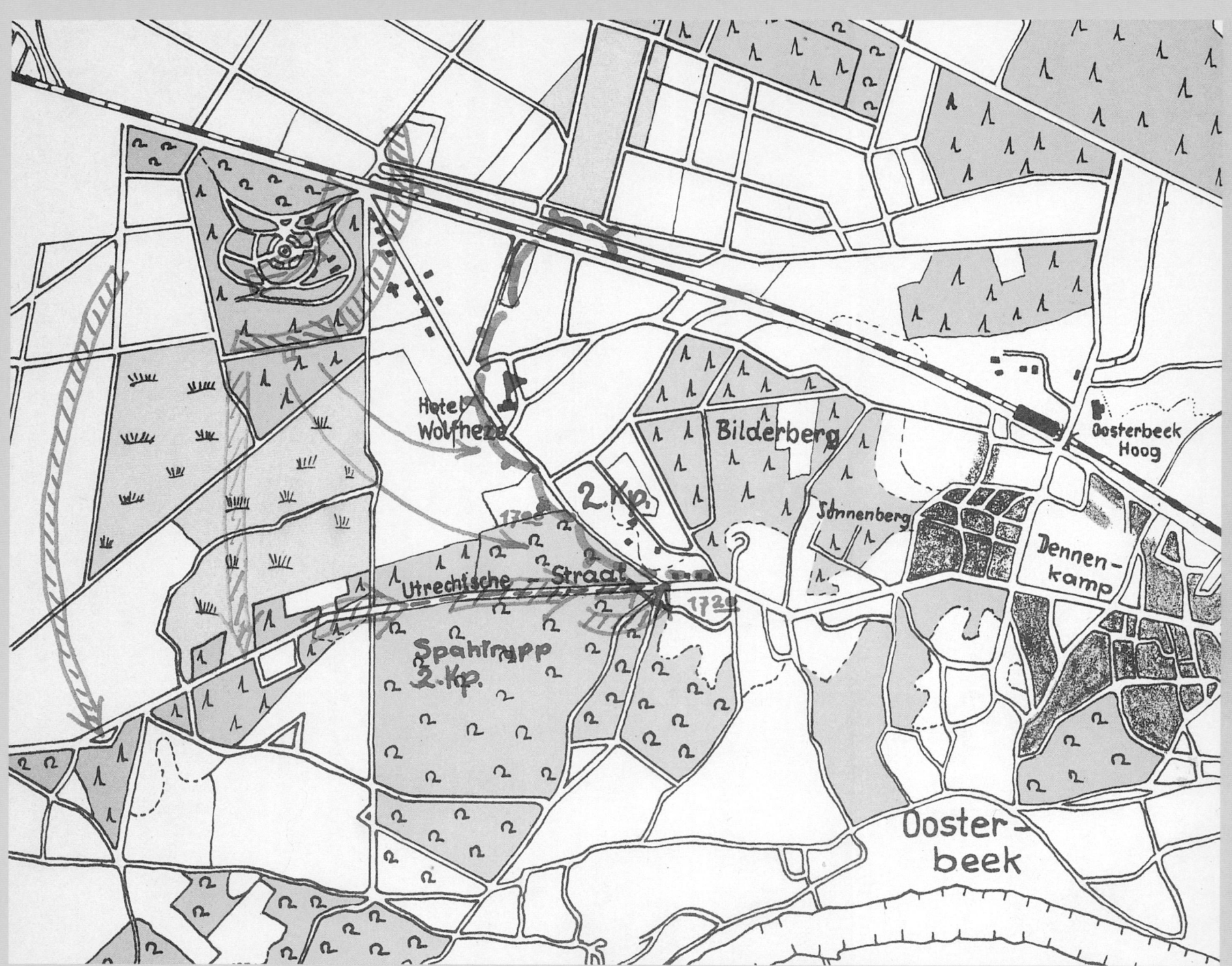

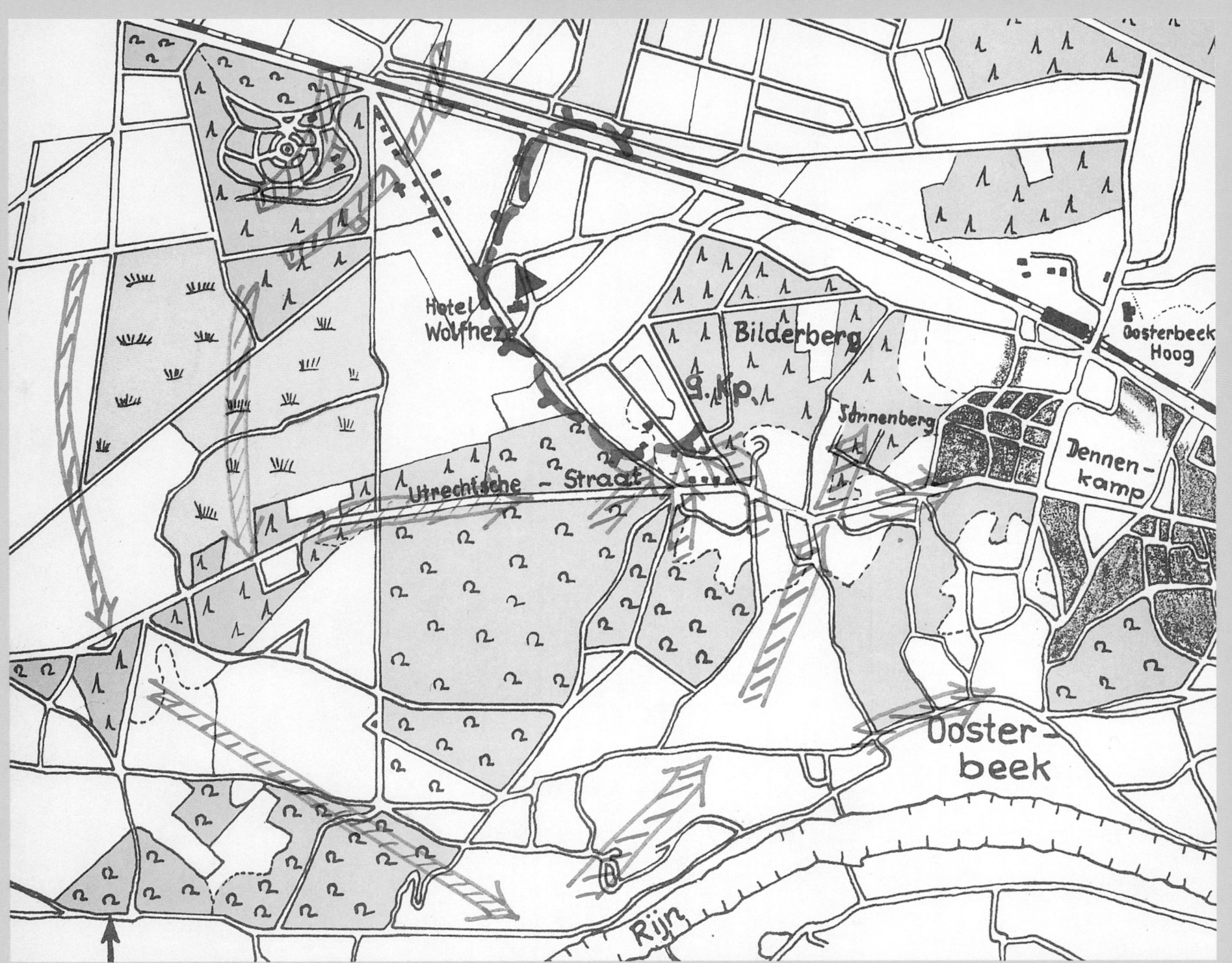

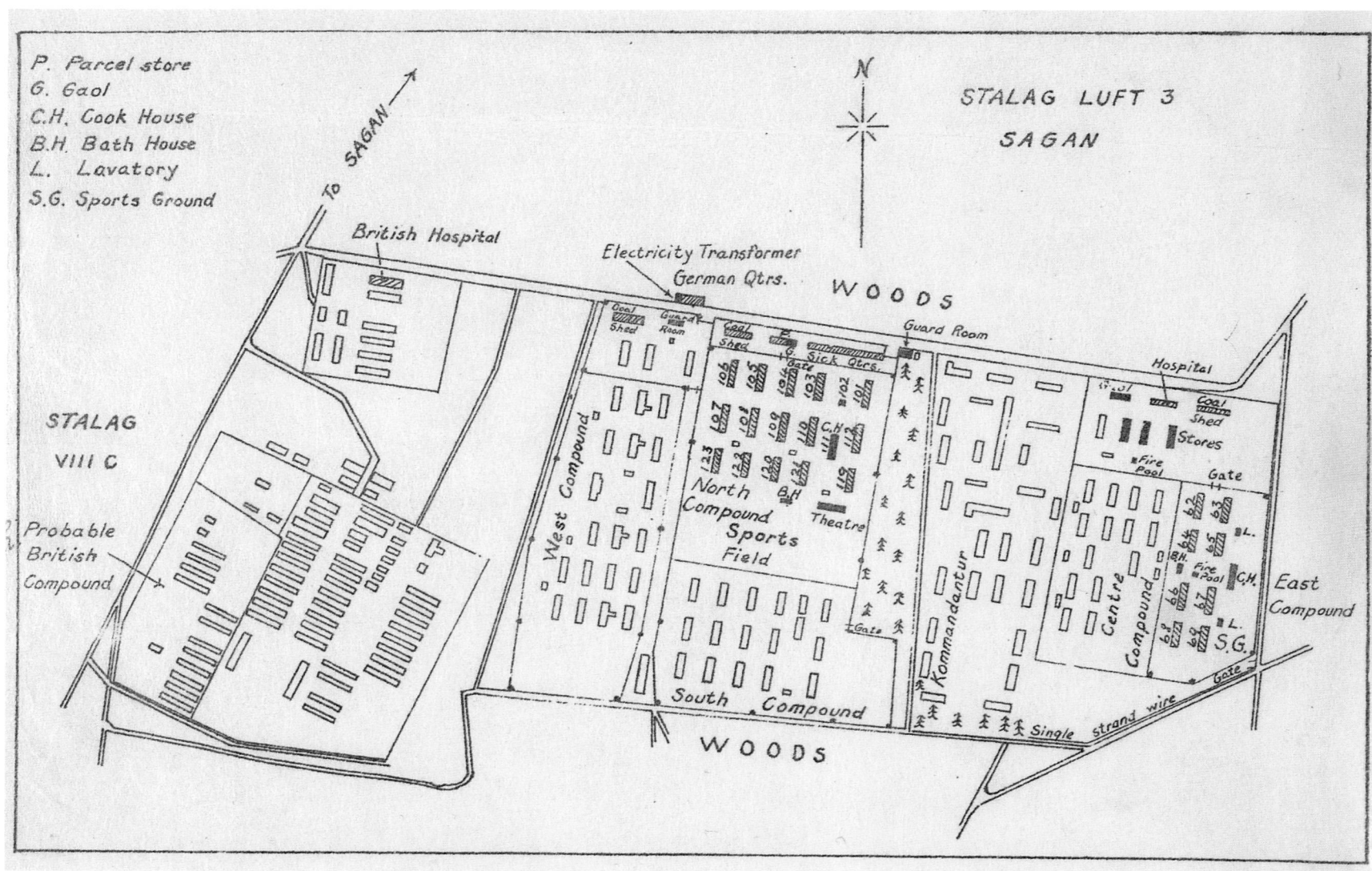

STALAG LUFT III, 1944

Sketch map of the POW camp Stalag Luft III at Sagan, Silesia, Germany, made famous by Hollywood. For this camp was the scene of 'The Great Escape', a famous massed escape by British, American and Polish servicemen who dug a tunnel from one of the huts, under the perimeter wire and to freedom. It emerged during the Nuremberg Trials that 50 of those who had escaped and were subsequently recaptured had been shot by the Gestapo. AIR 40/229

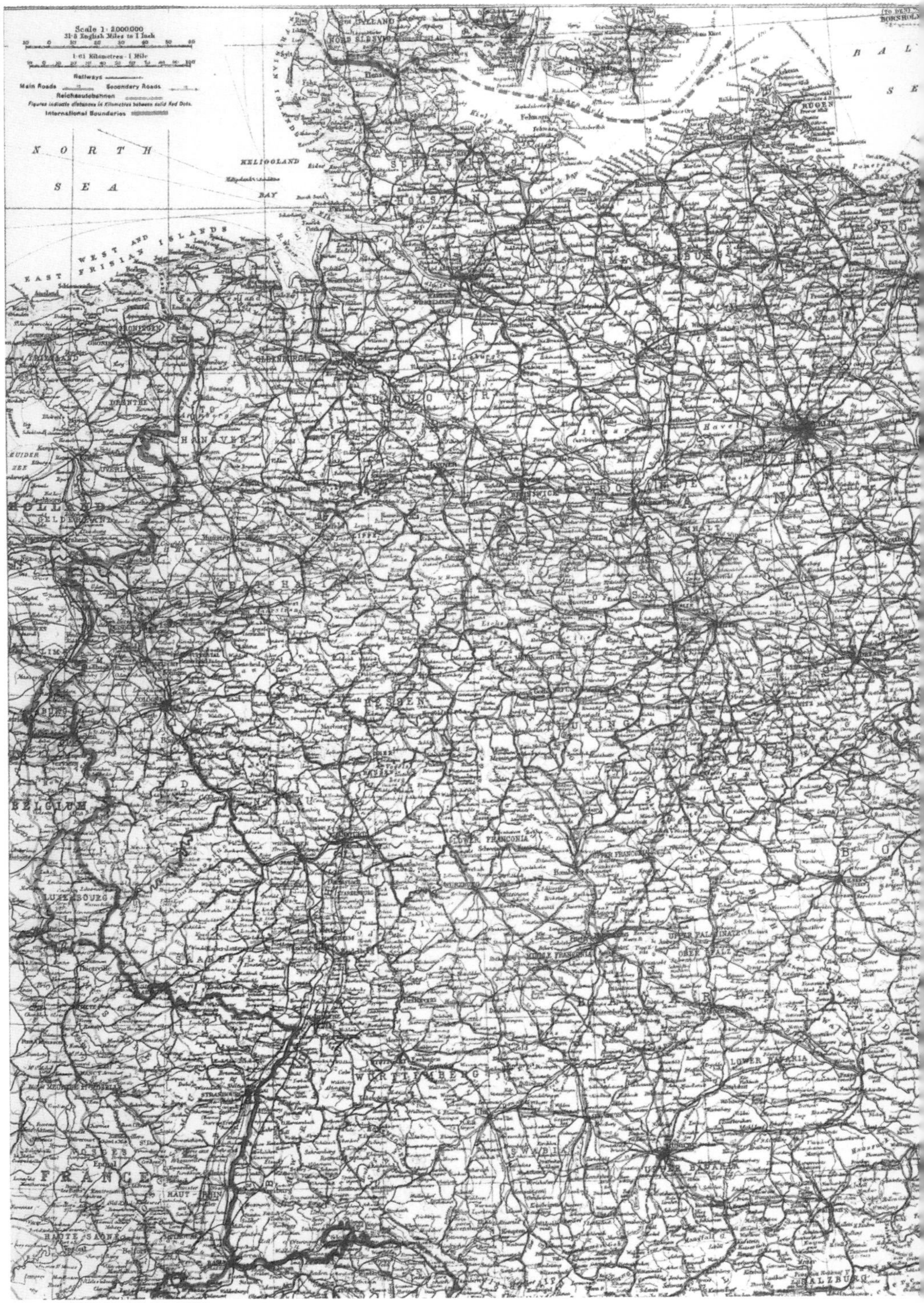

RAF ESCAPE MAP, 1944

To aid would-be escapers, maps of the Germany, France and the Low Countries were printed onto silk and sewn into the clothing of RAF flying crew. If they were shot down and captured in enemy territory, the maps could be recovered, and were often laboriously copied by internees. Maps were also smuggled into the POW camps sandwiched between the covers of books, games boards and playing cards. Among the numerous other ingenious devices developed for British servicemen were miniature compasses disguised as coat buttons; within the camps themselves, a whole escape industry grew up producing other ingenious escape aids. MF2 (1) (2)

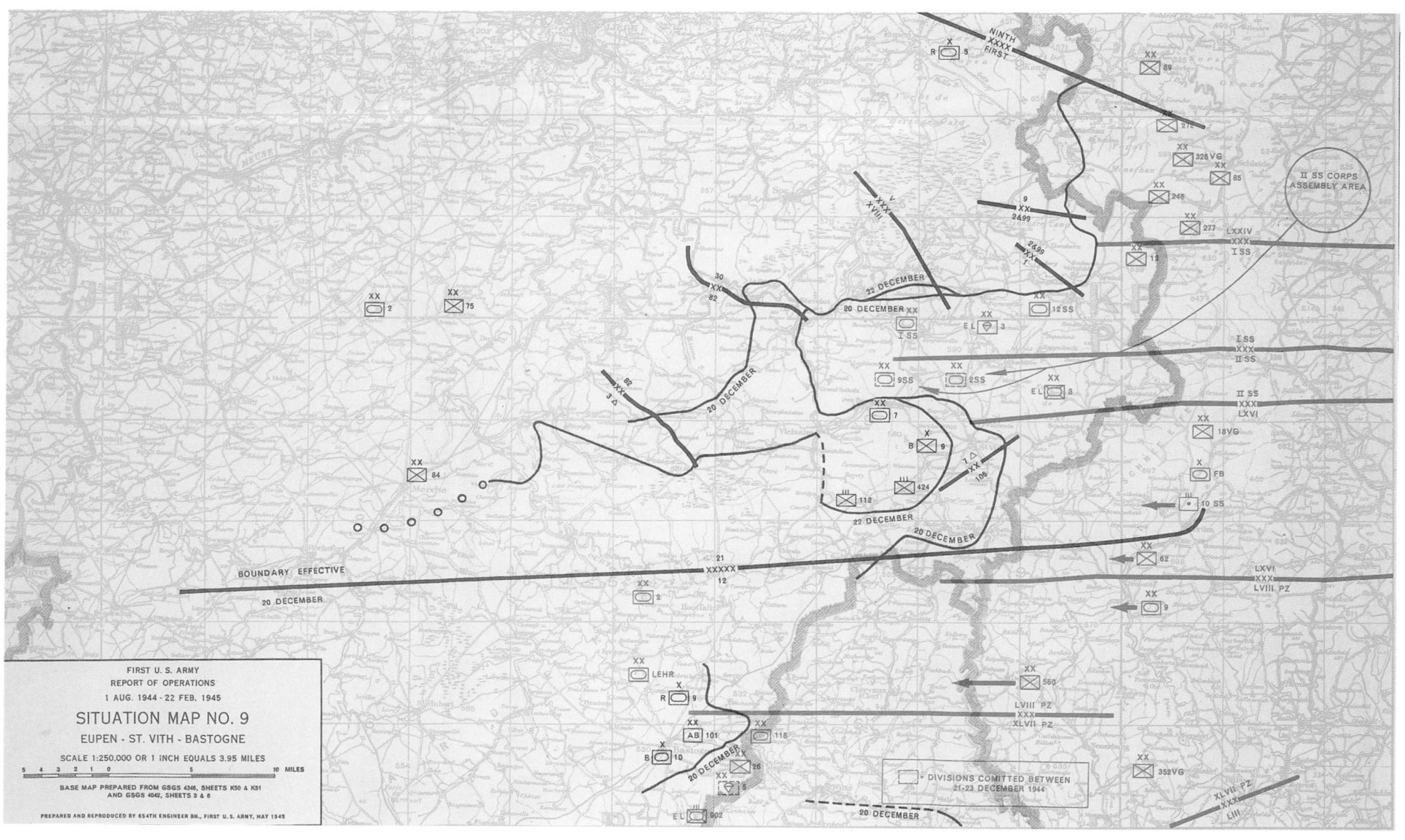

FIRST U. S. ARMY
REPORT OF OPERATIONS
1 AUG. 1944 - 22 FEB. 1945

SITUATION MAP NO. 9

EUPEN - ST. VITH - BASTOGNE

SCALE 1:250,000 OR 1 INCH EQUALS 3.95 MILES

5 4 3 2 1 0   5   10 MILES

BASE MAP PREPARED FROM GSGS 4346, SHEETS K50 & K51
AND GSGS 4042, SHEETS 3 & 8

PREPARED AND REPRODUCED BY 654TH ENGINEER BN., FIRST U.S. ARMY, MAY 1945

BATTLE OF THE BULGE,
DECEMBER 1944–FEBRUARY 1945

Part of a report detailing U.S. First Army operations from the Normandy break-out to February 1945, these two maps cover the area Eupen–St. Vith–Bastogne — the crucible in which the German's last great attack of the war came to grief. The maps show the advance and subsequent withdrawals of German forces through the U.S. VIIIth Corps positions strung out between Eupen, St.Vith and Bastogne during the German offensive, December 1944–February 1945. The Ardennes offensive, otherwise known as the 'Battle of the Bulge', was Hitler's last great gamble in the West. During the early autumn of 1944 he assembled a new army group on the Western Front, Army Group B (under Generalfeldmarschall Walther Model), which comprised the Sixth SS Panzer Army, Fifth

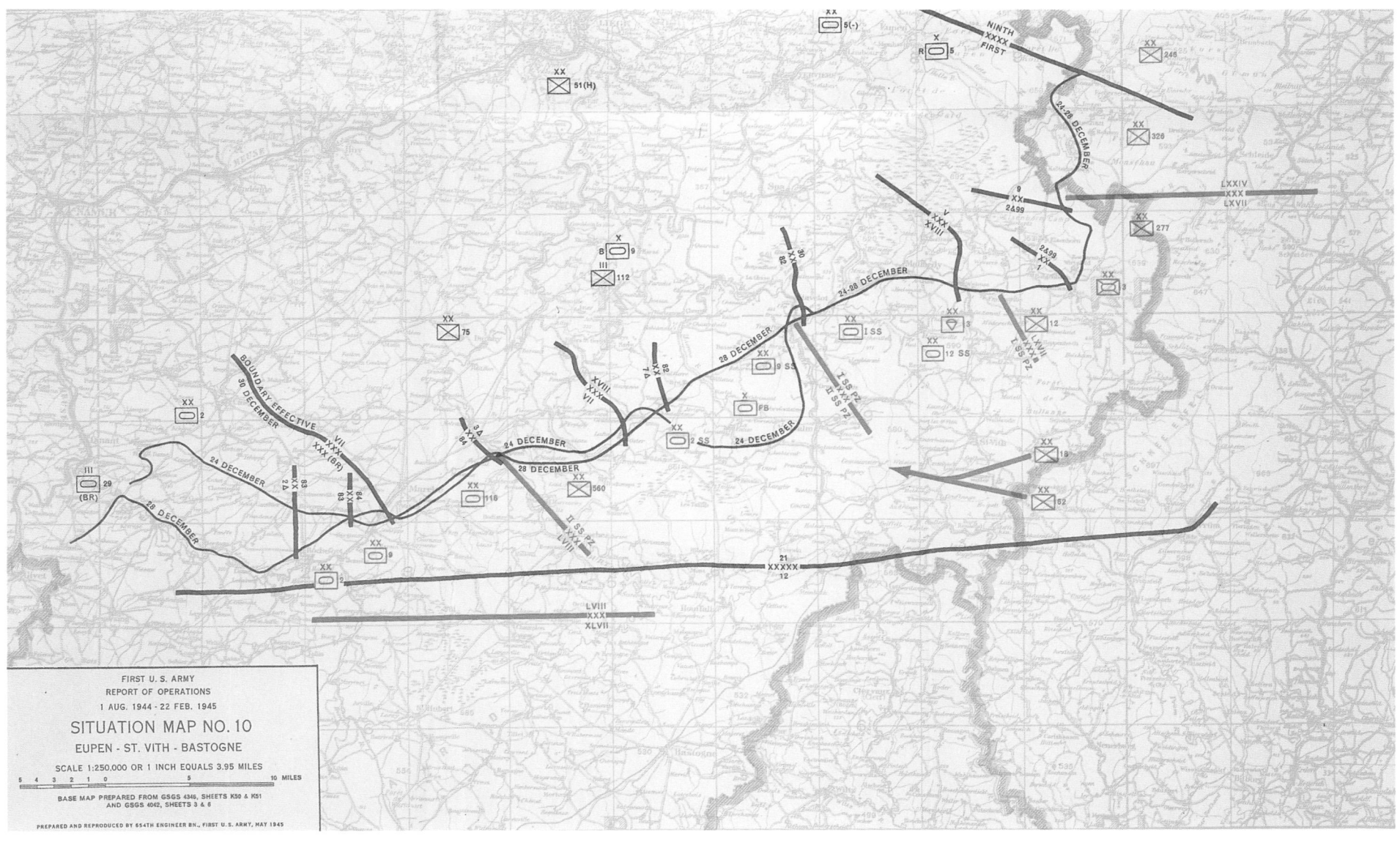

FIRST U. S. ARMY
REPORT OF OPERATIONS
1 AUG. 1944 - 22 FEB. 1945

SITUATION MAP NO. 10

EUPEN - ST. VITH - BASTOGNE

SCALE 1:250,000 OR 1 INCH EQUALS 3.95 MILES

BASE MAP PREPARED FROM GSGS 4346, SHEETS K50 & K51
AND GSGS 4042, SHEETS 3 & 6

PREPARED AND REPRODUCED BY 654TH ENGINEER BN., FIRST U.S. ARMY, MAY 1945

Panzer Army and Seventh Army. The plan was for a drive westward, as in 1940, through the Ardennes region to the Meuse and on to Antwerp and Brussels, so cutting off the northern (British) flank of the Allied armies, stabilising the Western Front and capturing vital supplies. The attack — by 25 divisions — was launched along a 60-mile front from Monschau in the north to Echternach in the south on 16 December and took the six American divisions completely by surprise. Only speedy troop reinforcement, German fuel shortages, which halted the advance short of the Meuse, heavy Allied fighter-bomber attacks after the weather had cleared on 23rd, and strong counter-attacks by the U.S. First and Third Army during late December and early January saw the situation stabilise and the German forces driven back. During the battle Bastogne was defended by 101st Airborne Division under Brig-Gen Anthony C. McAuliffe, who gave the famous reply 'Nuts!' when asked to surrender by the surrounding Germans. CAB 106/1010 (9) (10)

OPERATION 'VERITABLE', 8 FEBRUARY 1945

RIGHT AND FAR RIGHT: The Allied battle plan to seize the west bank of the Rhine was outlined in October 1944, but after the Ardennes offensive it underwent extensive modification. With most of the U.S. forces still embroiled in driving the Germans out of the Ardennes salient in the spring of 1945 and intent on projecting that same axis into Germany, it fell to Montgomery's 21st Army Group to take the initiative for the attack on the strategically vital Ruhr industrial region. The objective of Operation 'Veritable' was to overcome the committed German defenders that stood in the path of the advance to the Rhine between Nijmegen and Cologne. As may be seen from the maps of German defences, this part of the front was heavily defended by prepared positions. CAB 44/257 (O) (Q)

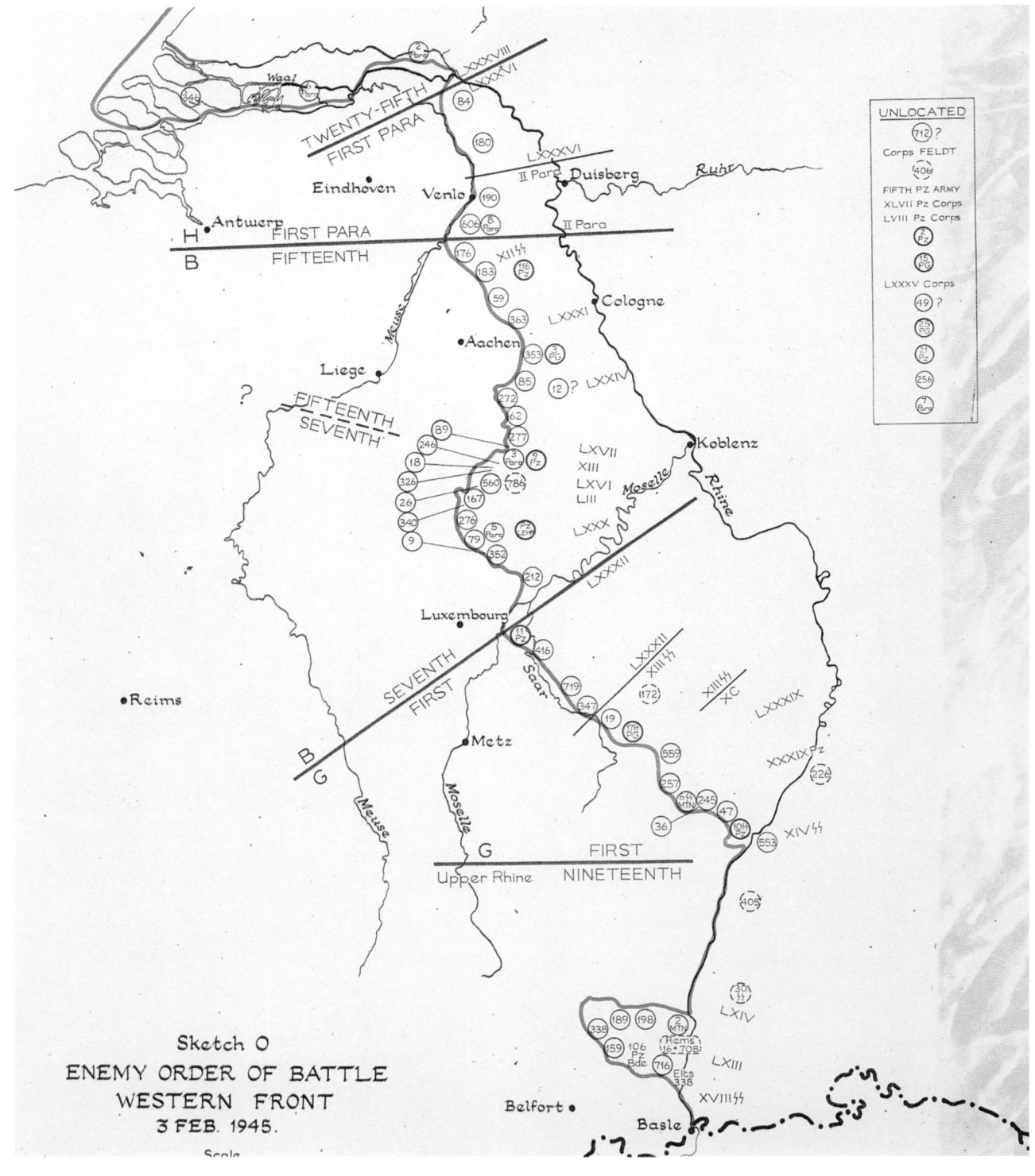

Sketch O
ENEMY ORDER OF BATTLE
WESTERN FRONT
3 FEB. 1945.

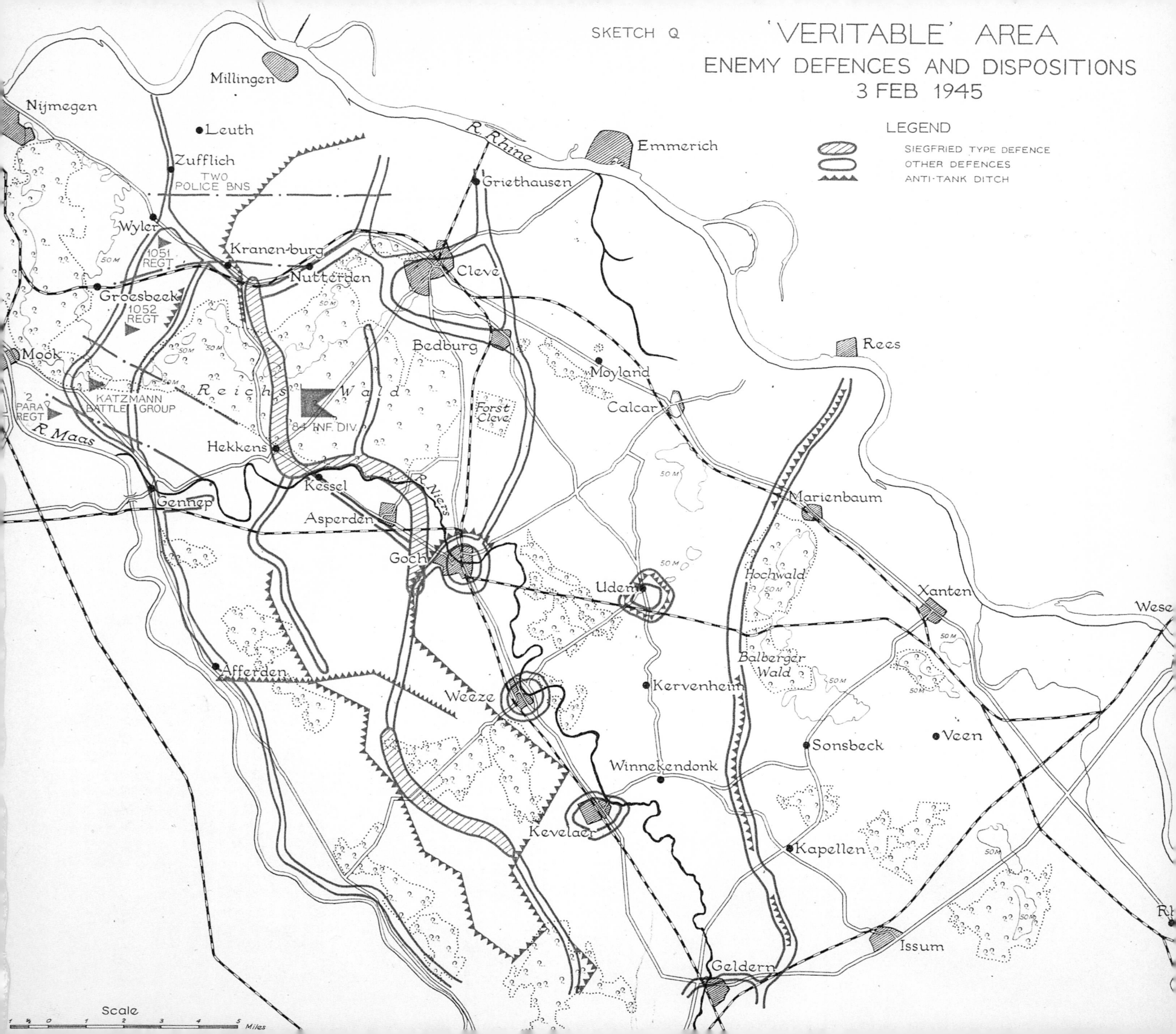

SKETCH Q

'VERITABLE' AREA
ENEMY DEFENCES AND DISPOSITIONS
3 FEB 1945

LEGEND

SIEGFRIED TYPE DEFENCE
OTHER DEFENCES
ANTI-TANK DITCH

Nijmegen

Millingen

Leuth

Zufflich

R. Rhine

Emmerich

Griethausen

TWO
POLICE BNS

Wyler

1051
REGT

Kranen-burg

Nutterden

Cleve

Groesbeek

1052
REGT

Bedburg

Moyland

Rees

Mook

R e i c h s

W a l d

Calcar

2 PARA
REGT

KATZMANN
BATTLE GROUP

Forst
Cleve

84 INF. DIV.

R. Maas

Hekkens

Marienbaum

Kessel

R. Niers

Asperden

Goch

Udem

Hochwald

Xanten

Wese

Gennep

Balberger
Wald

Afferden

Kervenheim

Weeze

Sonsbeck

Veen

Winnekendonk

Kevelaer

Kapellen

Issum

Geldern

Scale

Miles

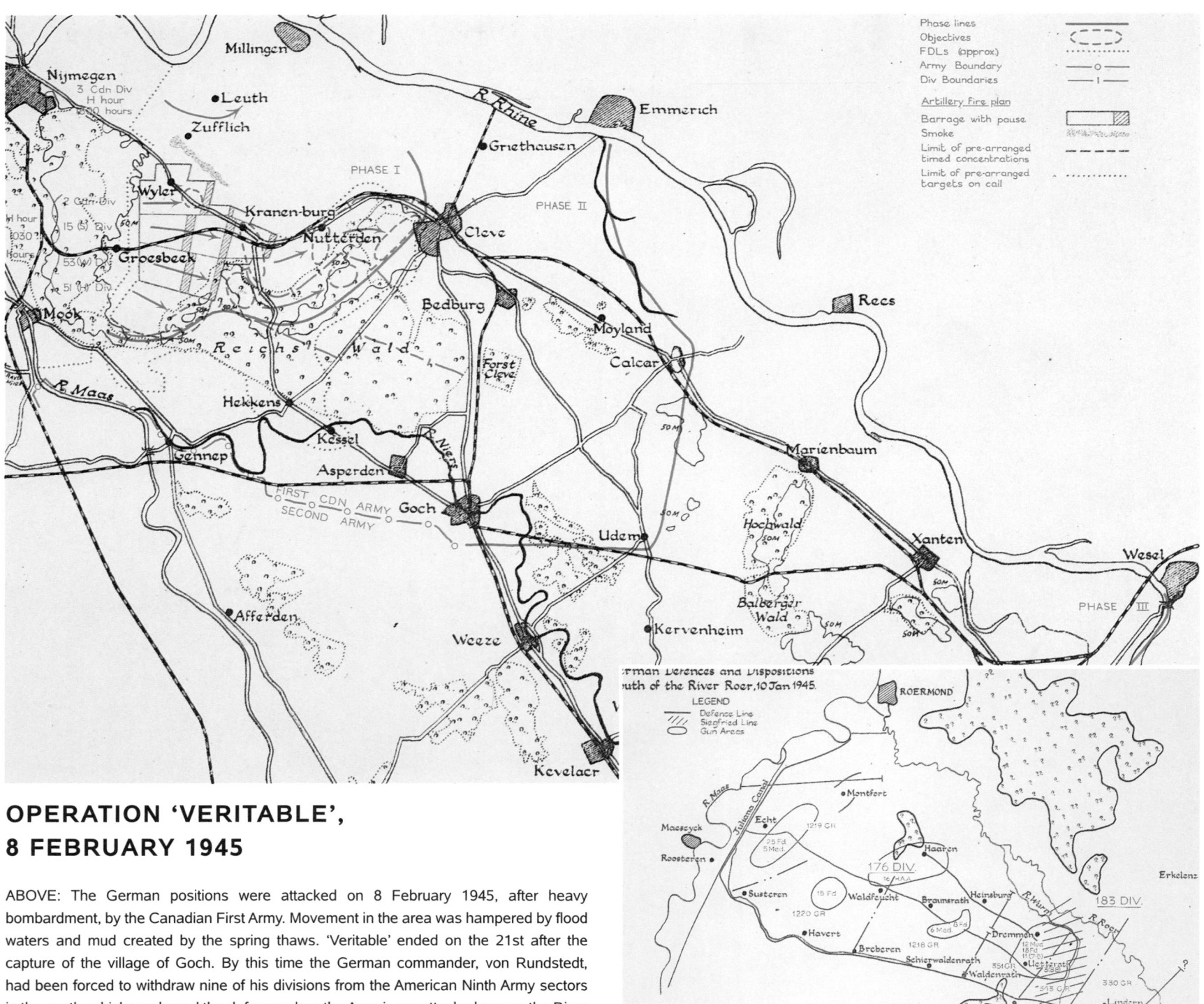

OPERATION 'VERITABLE',
8 FEBRUARY 1945

ABOVE: The German positions were attacked on 8 February 1945, after heavy bombardment, by the Canadian First Army. Movement in the area was hampered by flood waters and mud created by the spring thaws. 'Veritable' ended on the 21st after the capture of the village of Goch. By this time the German commander, von Rundstedt, had been forced to withdraw nine of his divisions from the American Ninth Army sectors in the south, which weakened the defence when the Americans attacked across the River Roer on the 24th. CAB 44/257 (S)

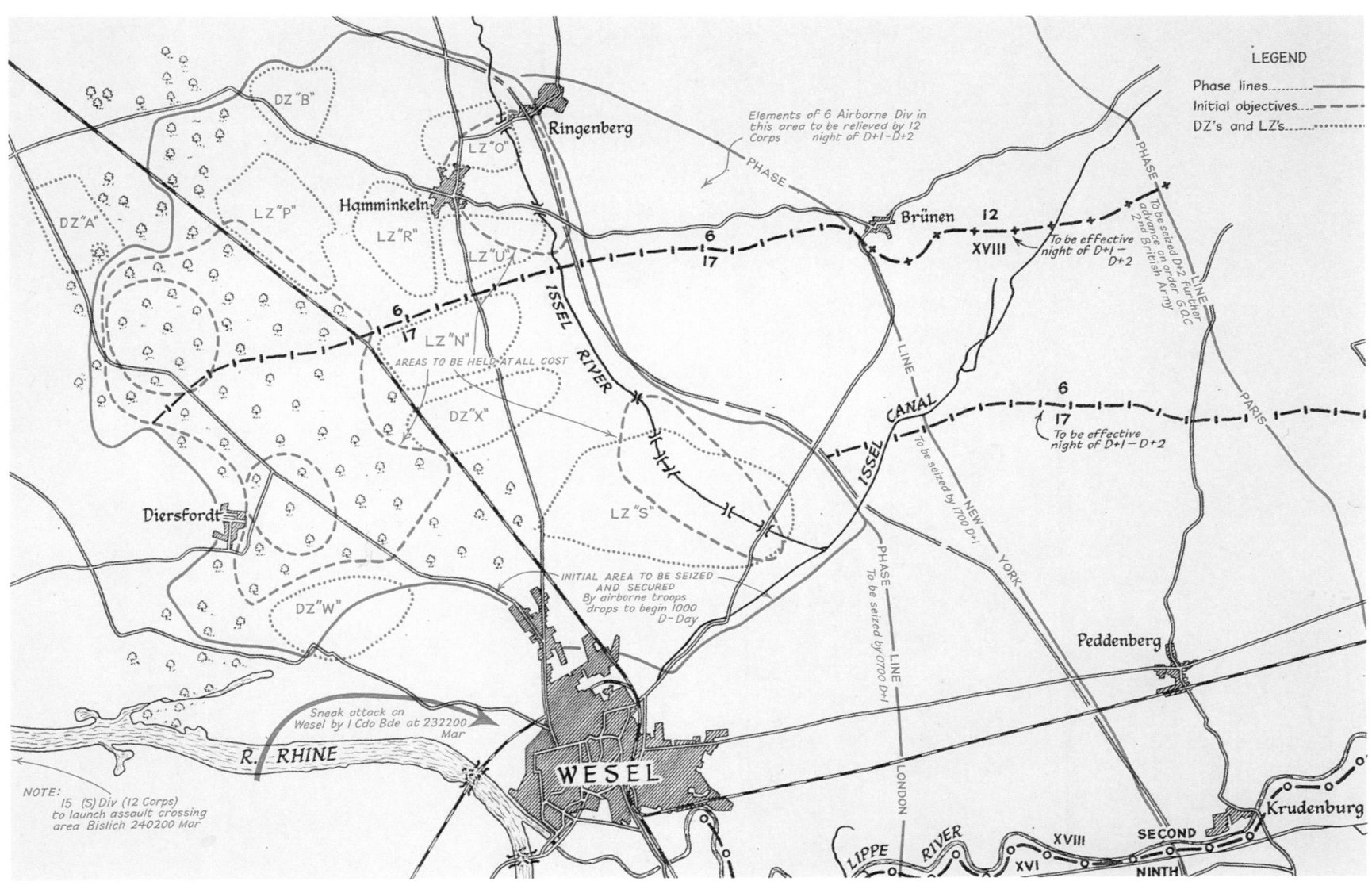

RIVER ROER, 10 JANUARY 1945

LEFT: A simple sketch of Axis troop dispositions to the south of the River Roer in western Germany, dated 10 January 1945. Note the concentrations of field (Fd) and medium (Med) artillery, wooded areas and the Siegfried Line, a three-mile deep series of fortifications along the German western frontier opposite the French Maginot Line. CAB 44/256

OPERATION 'VARSITY', MARCH 1945

ABOVE: Detailed map of the area around Wesel, showing phased objectives for U.S. XVIII Airborne Corps during Operation 'Varsity' (the airborne crossing of the Rhine). Paratroopers and gliders of the British 6th and U.S. 17th Airborne Divisions, under the command of Ridgeway's XVIII Airborne Corps, were dropped at the zones marked on the map on 24 March, as Commandos (see bottom left) assaulted across the river in on the right flank of the Second Army. CAB 44/260

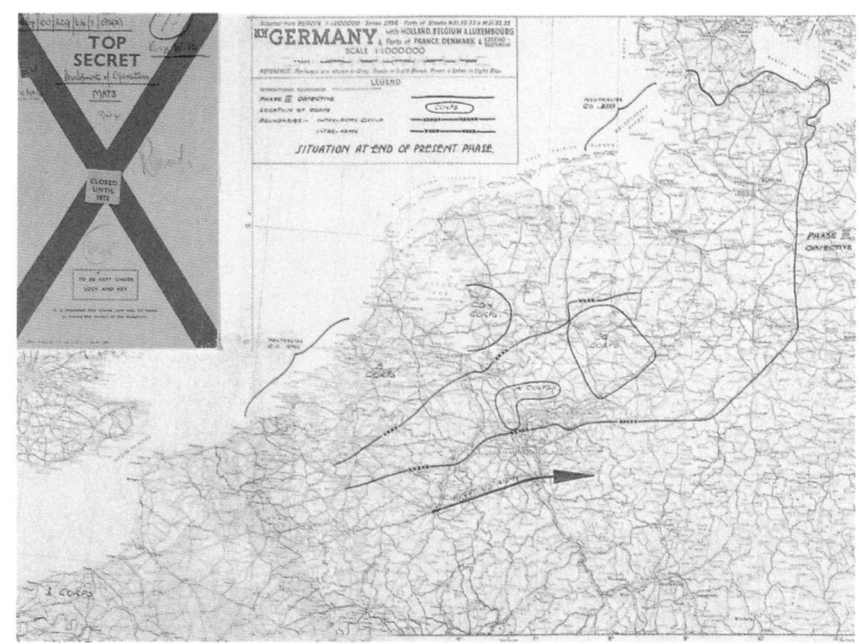
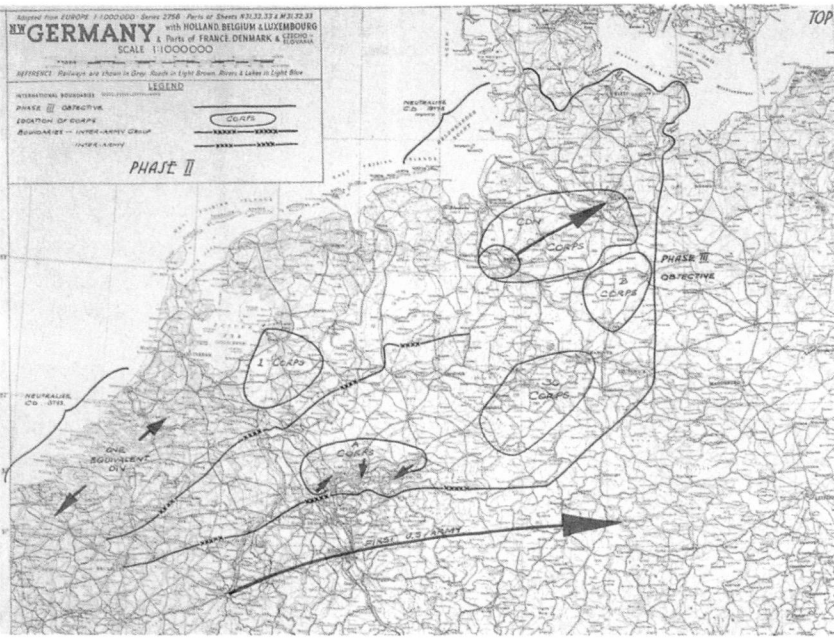
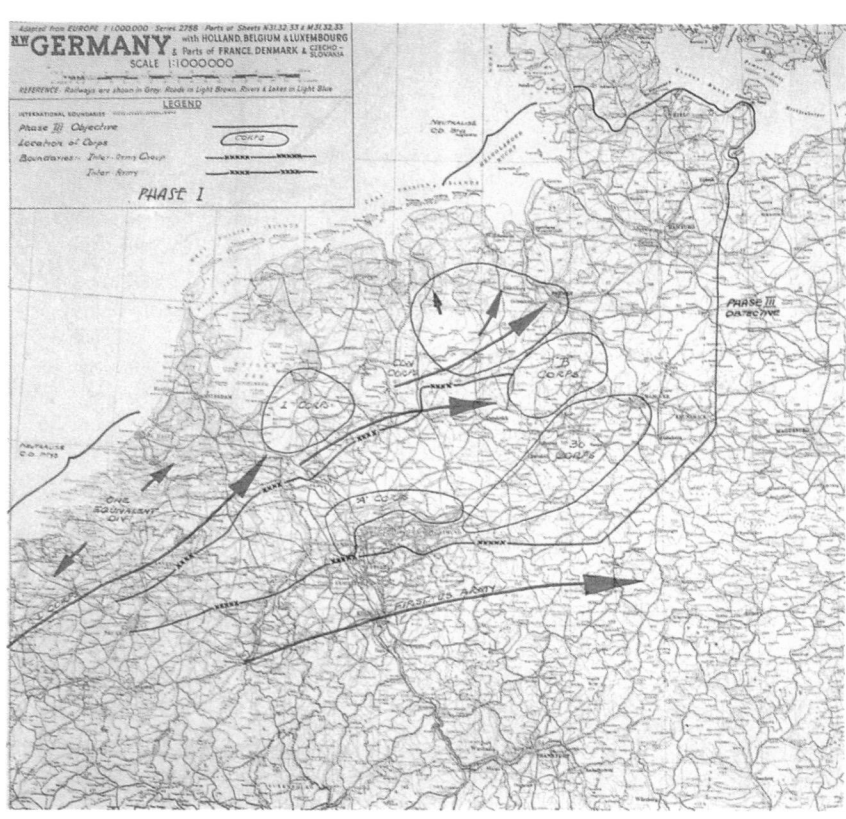
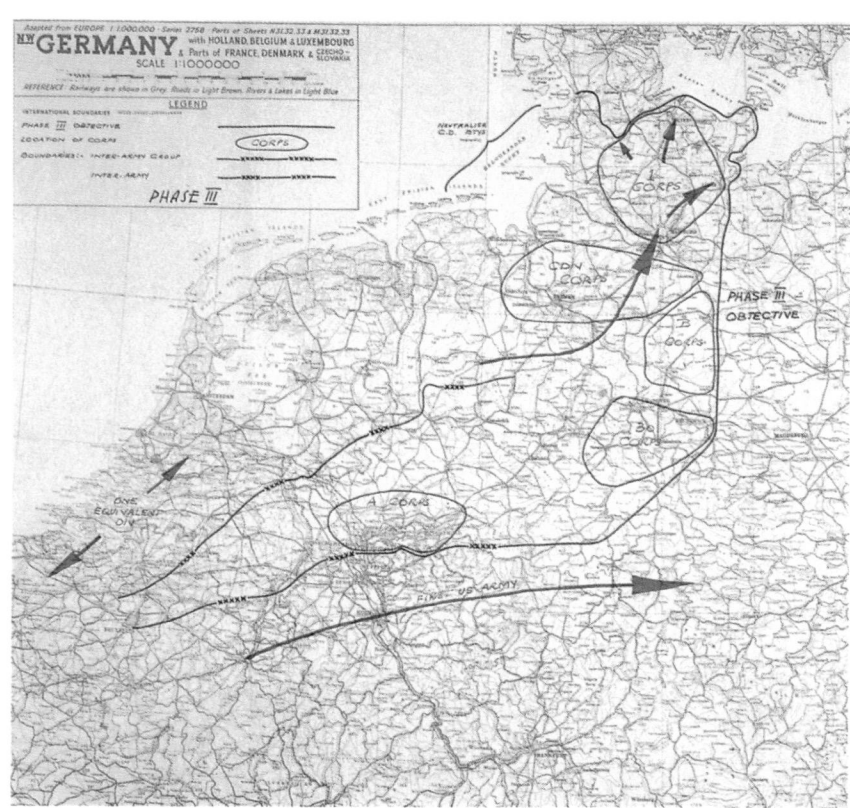

ALLIED ZONES OF OCCUPATION, NORTHWEST EUROPE, 1945

After the breakout from Normandy the Allied forces began their steady advance across Northern France and into the Low Countries, driving on to the Rhine. Beyond the Rhine, the last natural obstacle in their path, Germany lay almost undefended. These maps **(left)** show the planned three-phased occupation of northwest German territory by Anglo-Canadian army groups under Montgomery, after the crossing of the Rhine (Operation 'Plunder') which would begin at Remagen on 23 March, the British Second Army assaulting between Xanten and Rees and the U.S. Ninth Army south of Wesel. The Phase III objective, marked on all the maps as a thick black line running from the Baltic south to the Kassel, was agreed at the Yalta conference in February 1945. Note the annotation indicating the intentions to neutralise the coastal batteries and the route of Bradley's U.S. First Army to the south. The final map in the sequence **(right)** is produced under the codename 'Talisman', the 1944 plans for the occupation of Germany after the cessation of hostilities. The actual advance lines can be seen on the map on page 140. WO 205/120 (1–5)

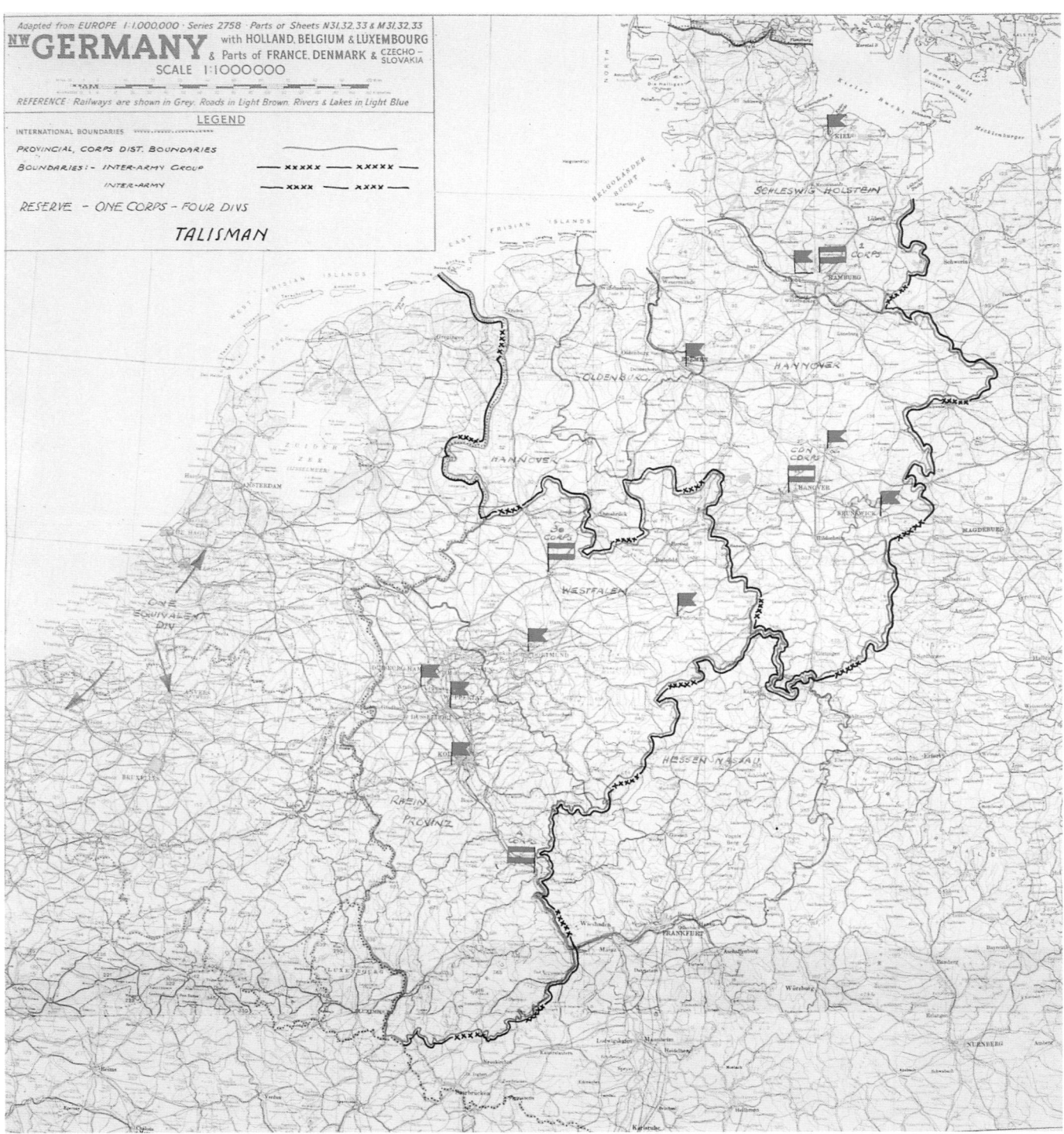

I.S.T.D. C/548

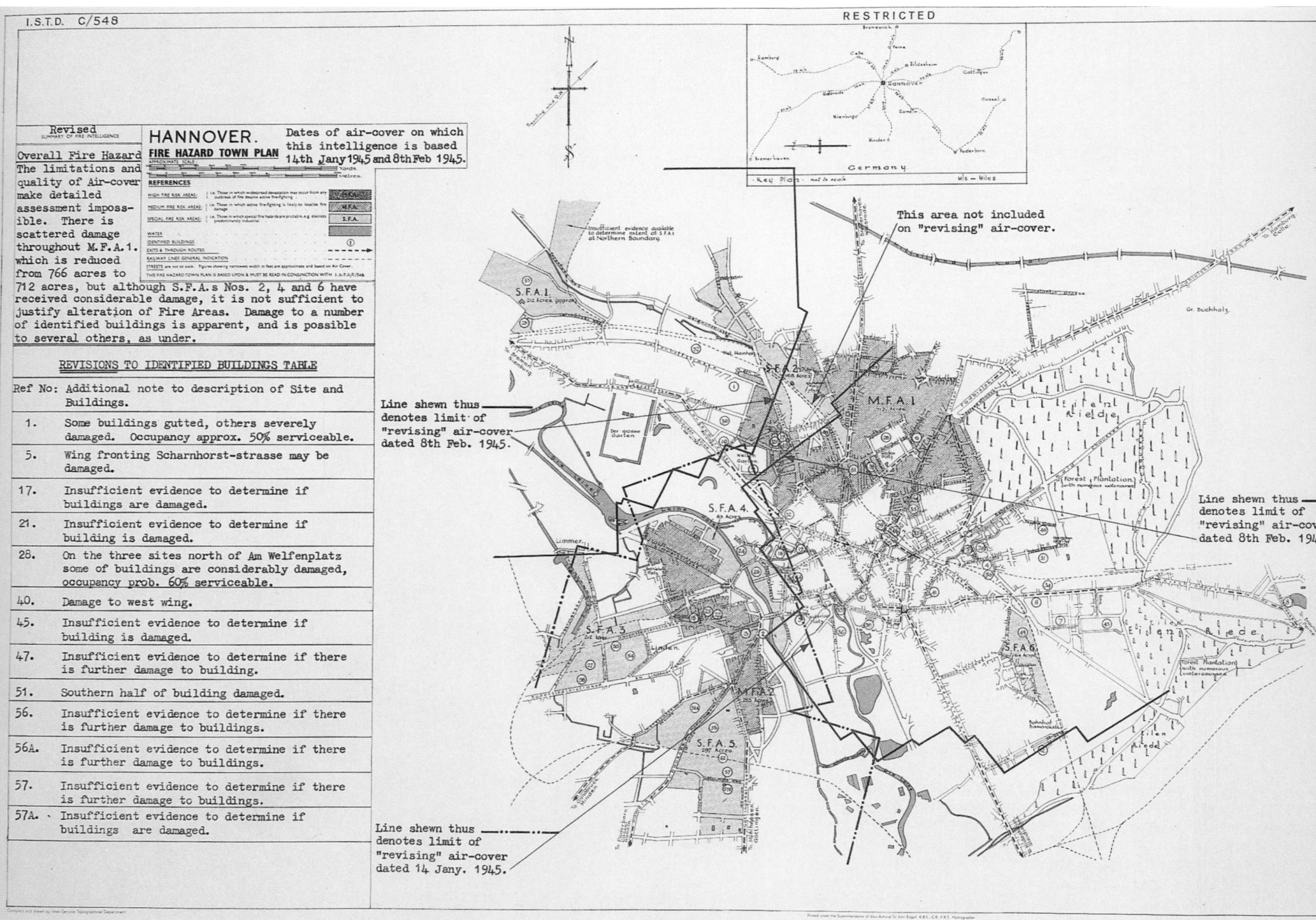

HANNOVER.
FIRE HAZARD TOWN PLAN

Dates of air-cover on which this intelligence is based 14th Jany 1945 and 8th Feb 1945.

Revised
SUMMARY OF FIRE INTELLIGENCE

Overall Fire Hazard
The limitations and quality of Air-cover make detailed assessment impossible. There is scattered damage throughout M.F.A.1. which is reduced from 766 acres to 712 acres, but although S.F.A.s Nos. 2, 4 and 6 have received considerable damage, it is not sufficient to justify alteration of Fire Areas. Damage to a number of identified buildings is apparent, and is possible to several others, as under.

REVISIONS TO IDENTIFIED BUILDINGS TABLE

Ref No:	Additional note to description of Site and Buildings.
1.	Some buildings gutted, others severely damaged. Occupancy approx. 50% serviceable.
5.	Wing fronting Scharnhorst-strasse may be damaged.
17.	Insufficient evidence to determine if buildings are damaged.
21.	Insufficient evidence to determine if building is damaged.
28.	On the three sites north of Am Welfenplatz some of buildings are considerably damaged, occupancy prob. 60% serviceable.
40.	Damage to west wing.
45.	Insufficient evidence to determine if building is damaged.
47.	Insufficient evidence to determine if there is further damage to building.
51.	Southern half of building damaged.
56.	Insufficient evidence to determine if there is further damage to buildings.
56A.	Insufficient evidence to determine if there is further damage to buildings.
57.	Insufficient evidence to determine if there is further damage to buildings.
57A.	Insufficient evidence to determine if buildings are damaged.

This area not included on "revising" air-cover.

Line shewn thus ——— denotes limit of "revising" air-cover dated 8th Feb. 1945.

Line shewn thus ——— denotes limit of "revising" air-cover dated 8th Feb. 194_

Line shewn thus ·—··—·· denotes limit of "revising" air-cover dated 14 Jany. 1945.

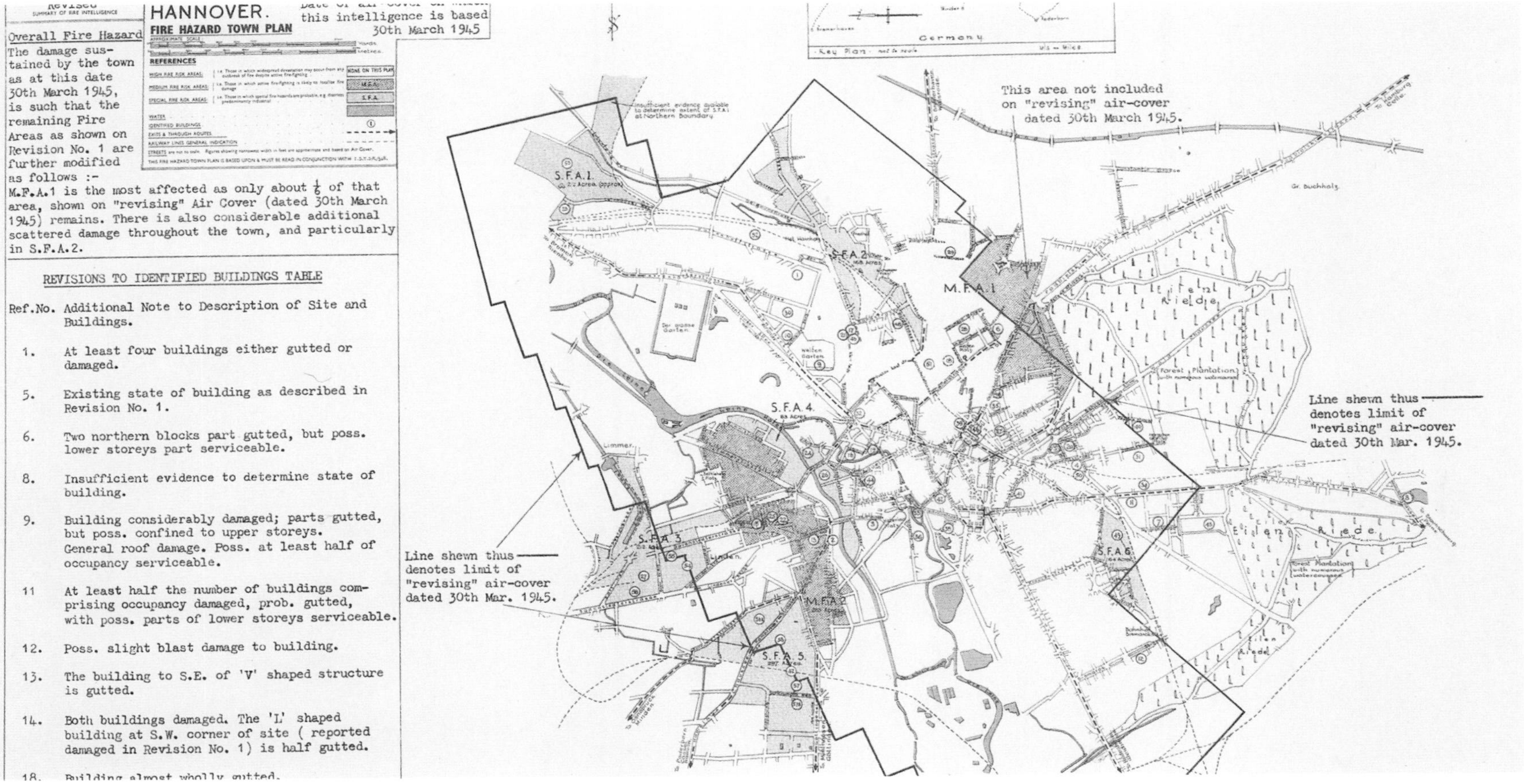

HANNOVER BOMBING DAMAGE ASSESSMENT, 1945

These maps detail the destruction wrought on Hannover in central Germany by Allied bombing raids between October 1944 and March 1945, based on intelligence from photo-reconaissance. In 1936 the area between Hannover, Magdeburg and Halle had been chosen by German industrialists as the most suitable area for the relocation of German industry, which formed part of the preparations for war, and it was here that the Hermann Goering Reichwerke had been built. As one of Germany's key industrial centres, Hannover was singled out before the war as a key target, and was subjected to concerted attack under the Strategic Bombing Offensive. However, after February 1942, the practice of 'area bombing', wherein whole areas rather than narrowly defined targets were destroyed from the air, brought destruction to the heart of German cities, and to their populations. One raid alone, on 19 October 1943, destroyed some 2.5 square miles of Hannover. MR 1974 (2) (3) (4)

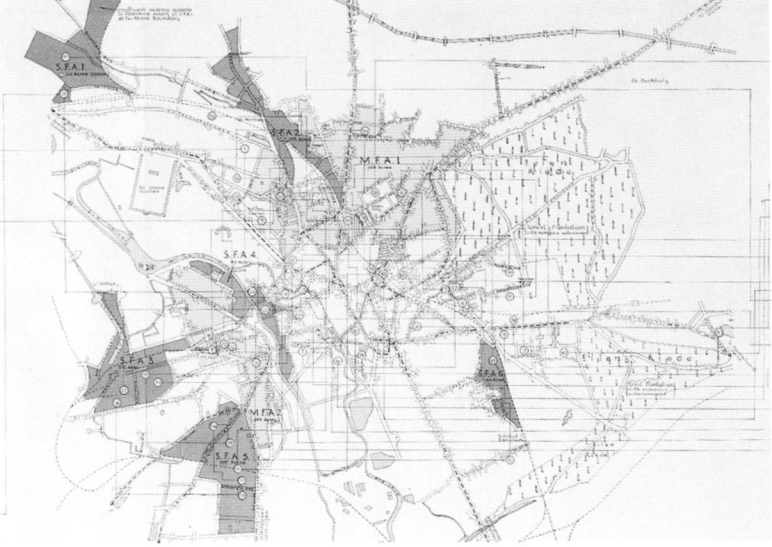

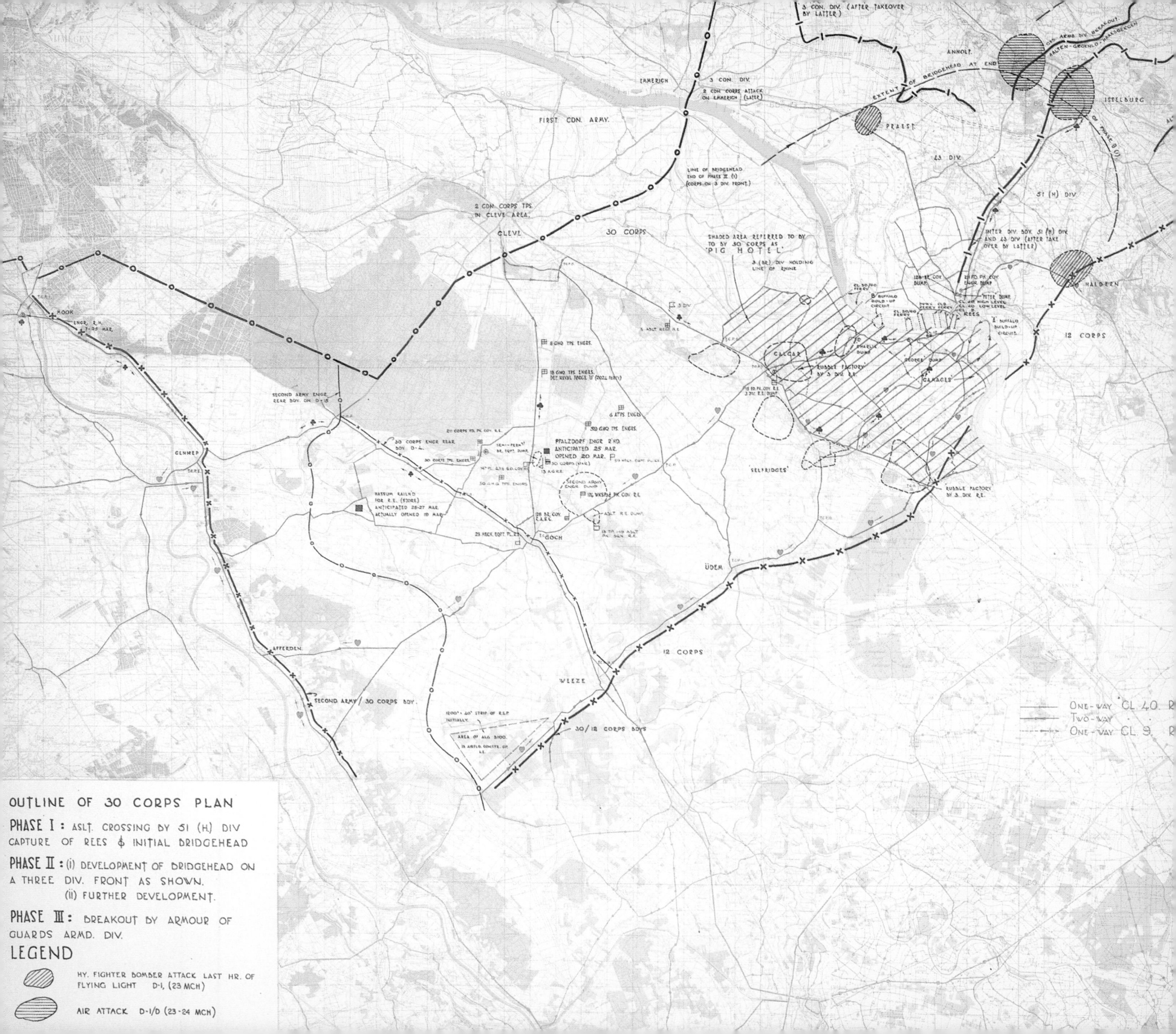

OUTLINE OF 30 CORPS PLAN

PHASE I : ASLT. CROSSING BY 51 (H) DIV
CAPTURE OF REES & INITIAL BRIDGEHEAD

PHASE II : (i) DEVELOPMENT OF BRIDGEHEAD ON
A THREE DIV. FRONT AS SHOWN.
(ii) FURTHER DEVELOPMENT.

PHASE III : BREAKOUT BY ARMOUR OF
GUARDS ARMD. DIV.

LEGEND

HY. FIGHTER BOMBER ATTACK LAST HR. OF
FLYING LIGHT   D-1, (23 MCH)

AIR ATTACK D-1/D (23-24 MCH)

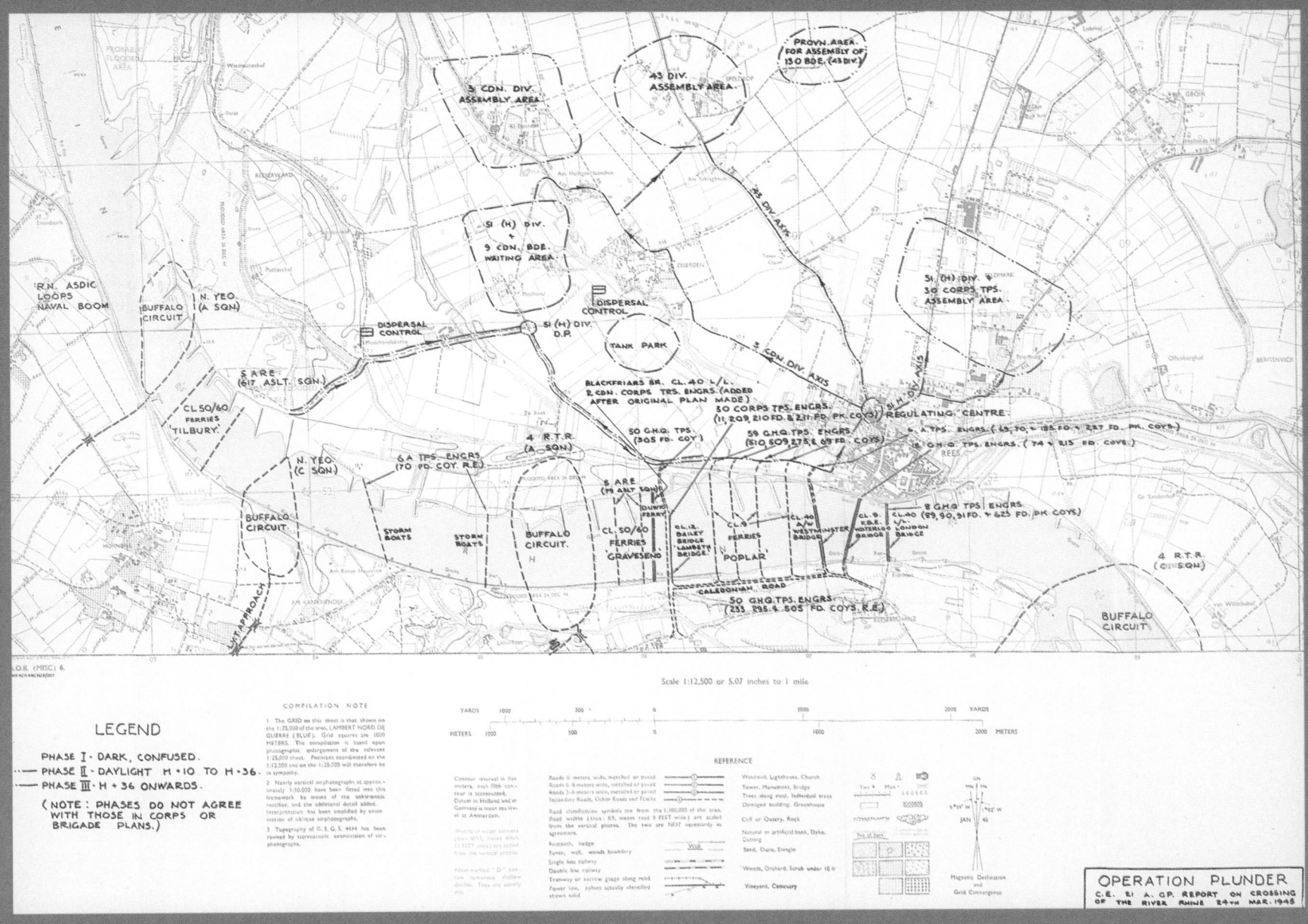

OPERATION 'PLUNDER', CROSSING THE RHINE, 23–24 MARCH 1945

LEFT AND ABOVE: Large and small-scale plans for the assault across the Rhine at Rees by XXX Corps of the British Second Army (Dempsey) on the night of 23/24 March 1945. The small scale map (a detail of the shaded area of the larger one) shows the planned assault and subsequent dispositions of 51 Division. Note how the division has chosen to name its pontoon bridges after famous London bridges. DEFE 2/512

THE RHINE, MARCH 1945

LEFT AND RIGHT: Maps showing the dispositions of troops along the Rhine on 24 March 1945, some 17 days after units of III Corps (of U.S. First Army) had secured a bridgehead over the river at Remagen (centre left), and the advances made in the weeks following the crossing of the river. As the Ardennes fighting ended in early spring 1945, Lieutenant-General Omar Bradley's 12th Army Group tried to swing east and jump the Rhine, in an effort to ensure the main focus of the advance remained with his command. The attempt failed when German engineers flooded the River Roer and Bradley had to wait until the British 21st Army Group in the north had unhinged the German flank. On 23 February Bradley crossed the Roer and rapidly drove to the Rhine, the most significant water obstacle remaining to military forces in Western Europe. On 7 March U.S. forces were rewarded with the capture of an intact bridge at Remagen. On 22 March the Twelfth Army launched a major assault over the river between Rhens and Worms, and by 24th it had completed clearance of the west bank of the Rhine. On that day the British Second Army and U.S. Ninth Army crossed the river at Wesel, then driving across the North German plain to the River Elbe. CAB 44/259

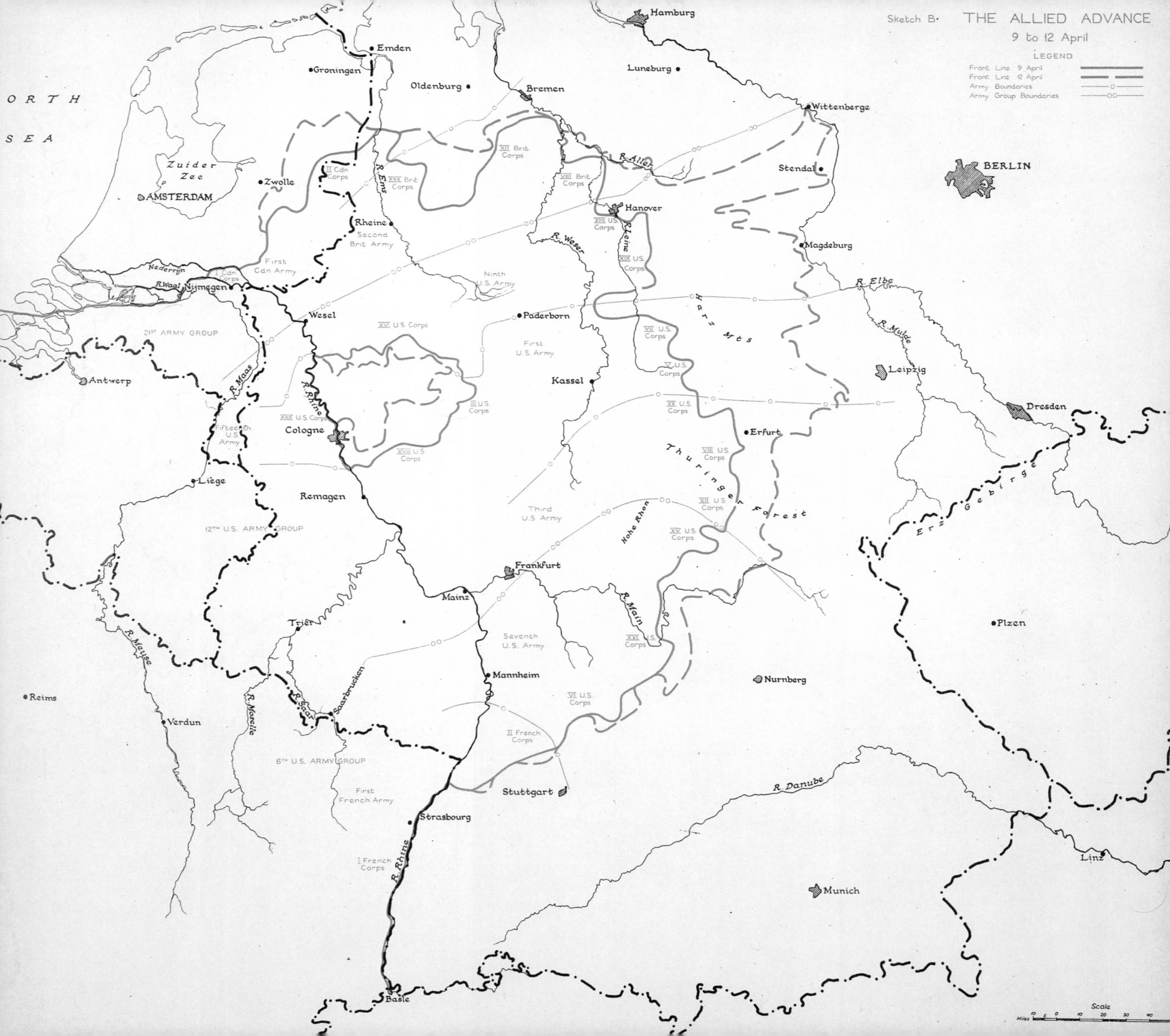

THE ALLIED ADVANCE
9 to 12 April

LEGEND

Front Line 9 April
Front Line 12 April
Army Boundaries
Army Group Boundaries

NORTH SEA

Zuider Zee

AMSTERDAM

Groningen

Emden

Oldenburg

Bremen

Luneburg

Hamburg

Wittenberge

Stendal

BERLIN

Magdeburg

Zwolle

Rheine

II Cdn Corps

XXX Brit Corps

XII Brit Corps

VIII Brit Corps

XIII US Corps

Hanover

XIX US Corps

R. Aller

R. Elbe

R. Mulde

Leipzig

Dresden

Nederryn

First Cdn Army

Second Brit Army

Ninth U.S. Army

Paderborn

VII U.S Corps

Harz Mts

R. Weser

R. Leine

R. Waal Nijmegen

I Cdn Corps

Wesel

XVI U.S. Corps

First U.S. Army

Kassel

V U.S. Corps

Erfurt

XX U.S. Corps

Antwerp

R. Maas

R. Rhine

XXII U.S Corps

Cologne

XVIII U.S Corps

III U.S Corps

Thuringer Forest

Erz Gebirge

21ST ARMY GROUP

Fifteenth U.S. Army

Liège

Remagen

12TH U.S. ARMY GROUP

Third U.S. Army

Hohe Rhon

VIII U.S Corps

XII U.S Corps

XV U.S Corps

Frankfurt

Plzen

Reims

Trier

Mainz

R. Main

XXI U.S Corps

R. Meuse

R. Moselle

R. Saar

Saarbrucken

Seventh U.S. Army

Mannheim

VI U.S. Corps

Nurnberg

Verdun

6TH U.S. ARMY GROUP

First French Army

II French Corps

Stuttgart

R. Danube

Linz

I French Corps

R. Rhine

Strasbourg

Munich

Basle

Scale
Miles

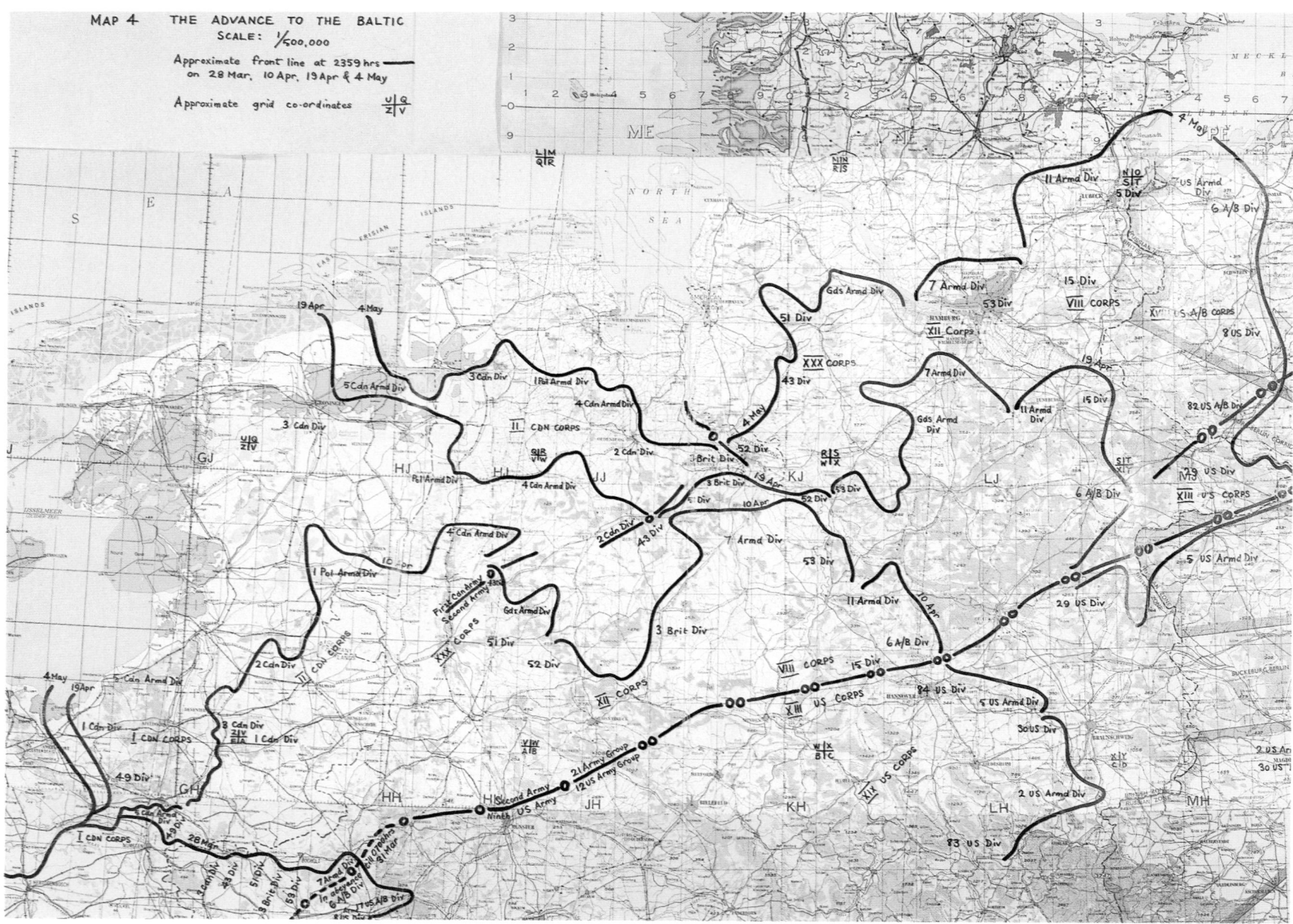

NORTH GERMANY, FEBRUARY–MARCH 1945

Map showing the advance of Montgomery's 21st Army Group across the North German plain to the Baltic coast in the final months of the war. Although the German defences were greatly reduced, and in many cases now reliant on young boys and old men, there was much tough fighting between the Rhine and the Elbe. On 1 April units of the First and Third Armies completed the encirclement of the Ruhr and on the 12th the Ninth Army reached the Elbe, where they halted to await the advance of the Red Army from the east. Army Group H under Blaskowitz was then trapped in the north. CAB 44/260

EUROPE
"THREE FRONTS"
SCALE 1:4,000,000 OR 63 MILES TO 1 INCH
MILES 25   0   25   50   75   100 MILES

O.R.6177

RED ARMY ADVANCES 1–8 MAY 1945 &
DISPOSITION OF RUSSIAN ARMY GROUPS ON CESSATION OF HOSTILITIES.

Front Line 1st May '45.
Captured 1st–8th May
Approximate Line of Contact between Eastern and Western Allies (ca. 1 June 45.)

EASTERN FRONT: GERMAN COLLAPSE, 1–8 MAY 1945

Red Army dispositions during the final week of hostilities on the Eastern Front, 1–8 May 1945. It shows the various armies and their commanders, and also the lines dividing U.S., German, French and the Soviet forces. It is interesting to note the enormous advances made by the Soviet forces during this period, as both camps scrambled to grab as much German territory as they could. The German forces and civilians, in turn, streamed west to ensure occupation by the western allies rather than the Soviets. U.S. and Russian troops met at Torgau and Nazi Germany was finally defeated. WO 208/1773

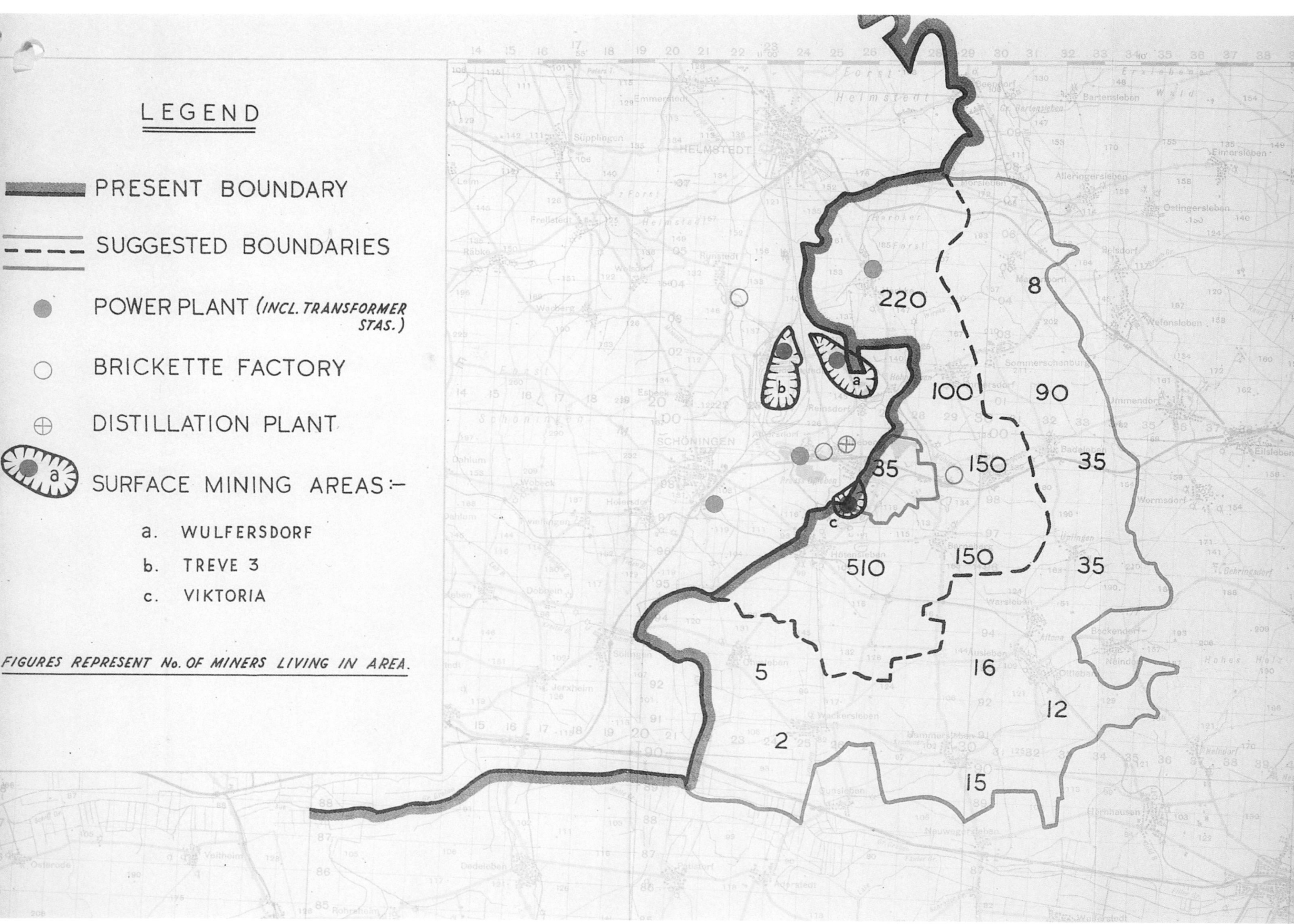

LEGEND

━━━ PRESENT BOUNDARY

- - - SUGGESTED BOUNDARIES

● POWER PLANT *(INCL. TRANSFORMER STAS.)*

○ BRICKETTE FACTORY

⊕ DISTILLATION PLANT

SURFACE MINING AREAS:—

    a. WULFERSDORF

    b. TREVE 3

    c. VIKTORIA

FIGURES REPRESENT No. OF MINERS LIVING IN AREA.

Map caption on the map itself:

TREBLINKA

Szkic sytuacyjny.

Białystok
Warszawa

Objaśnienia:

Tor kolejowy

Żywopłot przeplatany drutem kolczastym

Płot z drutu kolczastego

Parkan z desek

Las

×p.o. punkt obserwacyjny

+ + + Groby

WAR CRIMES: TREBLINKA

LEFT: After the end of the war the victors held trials at Nuremburg, to determine the guilt of those responsible for the horrors of Nazism. During these trials the world learned the full extent of the Holocaust. This is a smuggled map of the extermination camp at Treblinka in Poland, one of five such camps built by the Third Reich for the eradication of its declared enemies. Commanded by SS officer Fritz Strangel, who oversaw the deaths of some 700,000 individuals, Treblinka was liberated by the advancing Red Army in April 1945. The extent to which the Allied leadership was aware of true purpose of the camps is still a hotly debated issue. FO 371/42806

BRITISH–RUSSIAN ZONE BOUNDARIES, 1945

FAR LEFT: At the cessation of hostilities Germany was occupied by the Allies and divided into zones of administration. As originally drawn up on the map, these led to numerous small boundary problems such as here near Helmstedt where the boundary divided the miners from their mines and had to be altered. FO 1050/118

INDEX OF MAPS

Action against *Bismarck*, 27 May 1941 32
Agents in the Balkans, 1944 73
Alam Halfa, 16 July 1942 38
Allied zones of occupation,
      Northwest Europe, 1945 . . . 132–133
Athens, November 1943 76

Battle of Britain fighter defences, 1940 27
Battle of the Bulge. December 1944–
      February 1945 126–127
Belgrade, February 1944 77
Berlin, RAF target map, 1944 80–81
Blitzkrieg in the West,
      14–15 May 1940 24–25
Blitzkrieg in the West, April–
      May 1940 22–23
Boulogne defences,
      12 September 1944 112
Brest, August 1941 37
British–Russian Zone
      Boundaries, 1945 142
Bulgaria, February 1941 33

Calais defences, 12 September 1944 113
'Channel Dash', 12 February 1942 . . . 37
Convoy PQ18, 2 September 1942 44
Crimea, 1942 52

D-Day: 'Gold' and 'Juno' Beach defences,
      6 June 1944 90
D-Day: 'Omaha' Beach, 6 June 1944 . 88
D-Day: 'Sword' Beach, 1944 92
D-Day: Allied air operations,
      6 June 1944 86
D-Day: German coastal batteries,
      6 June 1944 84
D-Day: German defences on 'Omaha'
      Beach, 6 June 1944 94
D-Day: German defences on 'Utah'
      Beach, 6 June 1944 96
D-Day: German positions in France,
      1944 85

D-Day: Mulberry Harbours,
      6 June 1944 98
D-Day: Operation 'Neptune',
      6 June 1944 88
D-Day: U.S. Navy bombardment plan,
      6 June 1944 87
Deception prior to El Alamein,
      21–23 October 1942 48–49
Dieppe: Operation 'Jubilee',
      19 August 1942 39
Dunkirk, May–June 1940 25

El Alamein, 24–25 October 1942 . . 45–47

French Resistance, 1944 100

Eastern Front: German collapse,
      1–8 May 1945 141
German night air defences,
      December 1942 50–51
Gestapo HQ Paris, 1944 114
Guerrilla movements within
      Yugoslavia, April 1944 74–75

Hannover bombing damage assessment,
      1945 134–135

Italy: Monte Cassino, 11 May 1944 . . . 69
Italy: Operation 'Avalanche', Salerno,
      9 September 1943 66–67
Italy: Operation 'Shingle', Anzio,
      January 1944 70–71

Ljubljana, 1944 79

Malta, air defences, 1943 54
Marlag POW camp, Lübeck,
      January 1944 59
Möhne Dam, May 1943 58

Normandy: Falaise Pocket,
      7 August 1944 109–111

Normandy: Operation 'Goodwood',
      18 July 1944 104–106
Normandy: Operation 'Spring',
      31 July 1944 107
Normandy: Operation 'Totalise',
      August 1944 108
Normandy: U.S. First Army St. Lô before
      breakout, 1944 102
North Germany,
      February–March 1945 140

Operation 'Avalanche',
      9 September 1943 66–67
Operation 'Crusader', December 1941 34
Operation 'Goodwood',
      18 July 1944 104–106
Operation 'Husky', 10 June 1943 . . 61–65
Operation 'Jubilee', 19 August 1942 . . 39
Operation 'Neptune', 6 June 1944 88
Operation 'Market Garden',
      17 September 1944 115–123
Operation 'Plunder', March 1945 136–137
Operation '*Seelöwe*', July 1940 26
Operation 'Shingle', January 1944 . 70–71
Operation 'Spring', 31 July 1944 107
Operation 'Totalise', August 1944 108
Operation 'Varsity', March 1945 131
Operation 'Veritable',
      8 February 1945 128–129

Peenemünde, 1944 82–83

RAF escape map, 1944 125
River Rhine, March 1945 138–139
River Roer, 10 January 1945 130
Russia, 1 June 1943 60
Russia: Kalach,
      24 July–10 August 1942 40–41

Sicily: Operation 'Husky',
      10 June 1943 61–65

SOE arms' drops to Maquis, 1944 . . . 101
Sofia, January 1944 78
Southwest Russia and the Caucasus,
      14 August 1942–10 October
      1942 42–43
Southwest Russia and the Caucasus,
      19 November 1942–7 February
      1943 53
St. Nazaire, 27–28 March 1942 36
Stalag Luft III POW camp, 1944 124

Tirana, November 1943 79
Tobruk: Operation 'Crusader',
      December 1941 34–35
Tunisia, 18 February–15 March 1943 . 57
Tunisia, February 1943 55–56

U.S. 82nd Airborne Division, Nijmegen,
      September 1944 118–119
U-Boat War, August 1940 28
U-Boat War,
      August–September 1940 30–31
U-Boat War, September 1940 29
USAAF Eighth Air Force,
      5 August 1943 68

War Crimes: Treblinka 143

Yugoslavia, 1 November 1943 72